Issues in Christian Ethics

# Issues in
# Christian
# Ethics

## Paul D. Simmons
### Editor/Contributor

**BROADMAN PRESS**
**Nashville, Tennessee**

4261-22
ISBN: 0-8054-6122-1

Dewey Decimal Classification: 241
Subject heading: CHRISTIAN ETHICS

Library of Congress Catalog Card Number: 79-52982
Printed in the United States of America.

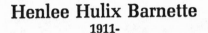

## Henlee Hulix Barnette
**1911-**
Author, teacher, prophet, friend, colleague
whose tireless efforts on behalf of truth
have won the admiration and love of many
whose lives he touched

# ACKNOWLEDGMENTS

Grateful acknowledgment for permission to quote material from other publications is extended to the following: Abingdon Press, *Politics, Poker and Piety: A Perspective on Cultural Religion in America* by Wallace E. Fisher; Augsberg Publishing House, *Bible and Ethics in the Christian Life* by B. Birch and L. Rasmussen; A & C Black, *The Quest of the Historical Jesus* by A. Schweitzer, translated by W. Montgomery; Broadman Press, *The Black Christian Experience* by Emmanuel McCall, *Introducing Christian Ethics* by Henlee Barnette, and *Should Doctors Play God?* edited by Claude Frazier; *The Christian Century*, "Living in the Political Brier Patch" by James M. Wall; *Christianity and Crisis*, "Eight Theses of Female Liberation" by H. Cox; *Clinical Pharmacology and Therapeutics* for material by F. M. Berger; *Collage*, "Theology and Ethics of Liberation" by B. Adams; *Daedalus* for material by Robert Sinsheimer; Doubleday & Company, *Black Religion and Black Radicalism* by G. Wilmore; Eerdmans Publishing Company, *The New Genetics and the Future of Man* edited by Michael Hamilton, *Politics of Hope* by André Biéler, *The Church and the Ecological Crisis* by Henlee Barnette, and *The Growing Church Lobby in Washington* by James L. Adams; Fortress Press, *The Passion for Life: A Messianic Lifestyle* by Jurgen Möltmann, translated by M. D. Meeks; George Allen and Unwin, *Out of My Life and Thought* by A. Schweitzer; Harper & Row, *Come, Let Us Play God* by Leroy Augenstein, *Treasure in Earthen Vessels* by James Gustafson, *Evolution in Action* by J. Huxley, *The Myth of Mental Illness* by T. Szasz, and *Ethics in a Christian Context* by P. Lehmann; Hawthorn, *Whatever Became of Sin?* by K. Menninger; Hinds and Noble, *A Manual of Ethics* by J. S. MacKenzie; Houghton-Mifflin, *The Subversive Science*, edited by P. Shepard and D. McKinley; *Interpretation*, "What Shall We Do with the Bible?" by G. Kaufman; Little, Brown and Co., *Man and His Future* edited by G. Wolstenholme; National Council of Churches, *Women Ministers in 1977* by C. H. Jacquet, Jr.; *New Times*, "Future Tribute" by F. M. Esfandiary; Oxford University Press, *Faith, Reason and Existence* by J. A. Hutchison; Pantheon Books, *Medical Nemesis: The Expropriation of Health* by I. Illich; Paternoster Press, *The New International Dictionary of the Christian Church* by J. D. Douglas; Prentice-Hall, *Ethics* by W. K. Frankena; *Review and Expositor*, "Protestants and Political Responsibility" by Henlee Barnette; Ronald Press, *Learning Theory and Personality Dynamics* by O. H. Mowrer; Scribners, *The Biblical View of Sex and Marriage* by O. Piper, *The Nature of Natural History* by Marston Bates; *Social Work Yearbook*, "Protestant Social Service" by E. Johnson and W. Villaume; Society for the Propagation of Christian Knowledge, *On the Authority of the Bible* by L. Hodgson; *Time, Inc.*, "What Next for U.S. Women?"; Tyndale, *Principles of Conduct* by J. C. Murray; Van Nostrand, *The Crises in Psychiatry and Religion*, "Some Constructive Features of the Concept of Sin" by O. H. Mowrer; Westminster Press, *The Secular Relevance of the Church* by Gayroud S. Wilmore, *The Situation Ethics Debate* by H. Cox, *The Church: New Directions in Theology Today* by C. Williams, *The Radical Imperative* by J. Bennett, and *The New Theology and Morality* by Henlee Barnette; Word Books, *Between a Rock and a Hard Place* by Mark Hatfield; and Yale University Press, *Fabricated Man* by Paul Ramsey.

## ERRATA

The American Association for the Advancement of Science, Washington, D. C., not Houghton-Mifflin, for permission to quote from Lynn White, Jr. "The Historical Roots of the Sociological Crisis," *Science*, Vol. 155, pp. 1203-1207. Zondervan Press, not Paternoster Press, for a quotation from *The New International Dictionary of the Christian Church*, 1974. Gayraud Wilmore, not Doubleday & Company, for quotations from *Black Religion and Black Radicalism*, 1972.

# CONTENTS

# Preface

Ethics is vital to the Christian life for it is central to the biblical perspective and at the heart of the gospel message. The call to faith is a call to do the will of God, both in becoming what we are intended to be and in doing what we ought to do. As a discipline of study, Christian ethics is concerned with the theological foundations of faith as well as the practical problems of daily life that confront the Christian. An understanding of both is necessary if those who follow Christ are truly to incarnate the will of God in mind and action.

These essays are written with the hope that Christians may be helped in dealing with the problems of faith. Faithful discipleship involves hearing and following the call of God whether it comes from the pages of Scripture, the insights of theology, or the needs of the neighbor. The task of Christian ethics is to facilitate hearing and doing the will of God.

The inspiration behind this book is Henlee Hulix Barnette, to whom it is dedicated. He is professor emeritus of Christian ethics at Southern Baptist Theological Seminary, Louisville, Kentucky, and professor of psychiatry and behavioral sciences at the University of Louisville Medical School. These essays were presented to him on the occasion of his retirement from Southern Seminary and his assuming the post at the University of Louisville Medical School. They are now being published as a tribute to Henlee Barnette and with the hope that they may contribute to scholarship in Christian ethics.

Throughout his twenty-six years of teaching at Southern Seminary, Barnette has been a serious student of Christian ethics as well as a persistent prophet of the church. His scholarly contribution to the field of ethics has been widely recognized. "Barnette is the most astute scholar Southern Baptists have had in the field of Christian Ethics," according to Frank Stagg. This is evident in his books and numerous articles. Always he has sought dimensions of faith that satisfied the demands of rigorous intellectual honesty as well as the concrete response required to confront pressing moral problems. He is neither a "pop moralist" nor an armchair philosopher. He sees ethics as an integrative discipline that draws from many sources in order intelligently to analyze and effectively to deal with practical problems. This gives his writings both depth and practicality. The task, for him, is "bifocal," which meant "looking to the Bible for the norms or principles of behavior and to other disciplines for factual data for intelligent action." [1]

Tennyson's insight that he was part of all that he had met could well be said of Barnette. Every component of his life story is reflected in his ethical perspectives. Born in a log cabin, he was an elementary school dropout, serving as water boy to a road gang by the age of twelve. At thirteen, he went to work in Cannon cotton mills working ten hours per day for eighteen cents an hour and a five and one-half day work week. His conversion at nineteen became a major turning point in his life. He was launched on an unrelenting pursuit of the kingdom of God under the leadership of the Holy Spirit. To better serve God, he completed school and entered Wake Forest College where his intellectual gifts were stimulated by professors like William Louis Poteat and Olin T. Binkley, with whom he also was to study in seminary. They pointed the way to religious commitment that combined intellectual integrity with heartfelt compassion. These became twin factors in his Christian understandings.

His first pastorate was in "the worst slum in town," called Frog Holler in Kannapolis, North Carolina. Then, while a student at Southern Seminary and under the inspiration and challenge of Clarence Jordan, Barnette became pastor of the Union Gospel Mission in one of the most depressed areas of Louisville. Jordan was then city missionary but Barnette became the "Bishop of the Haymarket." His parish included ten thousand unchurched people—among them pimps, prostitutes, gamblers, bums, and derelicts of various sorts. To them he became pastor, friend, counselor, and prophet.

Not suprisingly, the writings of Walter Rauschenbusch and Reinhold Niebuhr struck deep chords of responsiveness in the mind of Barnette the seminary scholar. Religion that had no word of hope and comfort for the oppressed or any word of discomfort and challenge for the oppressor could hardly claim to be the Word of God. He had seen and felt too much of the world's pain not to hear the cry of the disadvantaged. However, he was always convinced that no meaningful or lasting social change was possible that was not built upon genuine religious experience.

These themes persisted in his ethical thought. Convinced that social concern was rooted in biblical faith, he was equally convinced that the Christian moral life was impossible without the empowering work of the Holy Spirit. The stress on the relationship of ethics to the work of the Holy Spirit is a distinctive element in his thought among Christian ethicists.

Barnette's influence among Baptists and American Christians is immeasurble, of course. As a winsome and inimitable teacher, he has inspired numerous students to pursue prophetic ministries in church and denominational posts. Through Baptist state papers he has touched the minds of thousands in his own denomination. His books have had widespread use in churches and classrooms in colleges and seminaries. His *Introducing Christian Ethics* has been through seven printings and has been translated into eight foreign languages.

Furthermore, he has served with distinction in the American Society of Christian Ethics and the American Association for the Advancement of Science. He is credited with helping rebuild a badly diminished faculty at Southern Seminary in his role as acting dean (1957-1959). He assisted in the development of the United States–Soviet cultural exchange program during a visit with Soviet Premier Nikita Khrushchev in 1957. He marched with Martin Luther King, Jr., and helped to sponsor King's historic visit to Southern Seminary.

No stranger to controversy, Barnette's approach to social ethics has been marked both by courage and fairness. His teaching was influenced by a principle stated by Sir Roger de Coverly, that "there is much to be said on both sides of any subject." Once he discerned the will of God for him, however, no threat was sufficient to deter his pursuing the matter in every appropriate way. In a personal tribute to Barnette, George Buttrick noted that "you have refused to be leashed or to walk within the limits set by monied interests. It has been a brave witness." He was known as the "conscience of the seminary" and was characterized as a "compassionate Gadfly" in receiving the Distinguished Service Award from the Christian Life Commission in 1977. He has fearlessly and tirelessly fought the "four great plagues of mankind"—ignorance, intolerance, insensitivity, and irresponsibility.

His humble origins and unassuming attitudes belie the prominent place he occupies in the hearts of thousands who have been privileged to know and learn from him. He sometimes declared that he was a barbarian with a thin veneer of culture. But his colleagues knew better—he incarnated the essence of Christian ethics. He is truly a superb illustration of a man whose best argument for his ethical theory is his everyday life.

Needless to say, the temptation has been great to develop a volume of essays dealing exclusively with the life and thought of Henlee Barnette as an author, teacher, scholar, and friend. Collections of this type tend in the direction of hagiography, however, which would be inappropriate to his unassuming life-style and becoming modesty. A systematic, scholarly treatment is a more fitting forum for such a treatment and that will undoubtedly be forthcoming.

The format and topics selected in this volume were fashioned out of an awareness of the current issues in Christian ethics, the suggestions of colleagues in sister seminaries and Baptist colleges and areas of perceived need for material in the survey course in ethics. Interestingly, every topic dealt with was at some time treated by Barnette—either in a course or seminar, a book, or a series of lectures devoted to the subject. He offered courses on bioethics, liberation ethics, ecology, peacemaking, and politics. Ethical themes in the Bible constituted a major portion of his *Introducing . . .* , and he sought guidance from biblical principles for every issue he treated. All his students—graduate and undergraduate alike—were introduced to methodology in ethics and aided in developing their own.

The present volume is intended to provide an extension of Barnette's influence through those who have learned from him or have been colleagues in the tasks of Christian ministry. Not all the contributors have been his students. Some are lifelong colleagues and friends who have made major scholarly contributions to their respective fields, as Eric Rust and Wayne Oates. Others share his interest in ethical issues though their educational pilgrimage has not brought them directly under Barnette's tutelage, as Sarah Frances Anders and Bob Adams. All other contributors have been students of Barnette and have given this labor of love in his honor, and hopefully, to the glory of God.

As editor, I am deeply indebted to those who have worked so diligently in the preparation of the essays and to the final preparation of the manuscript. Tish Gardner and the typing pool at Southern Seminary have offered invaluable assistance in proofreading and typing the final copy. To all of these and more, I express heartfelt thanks.

> Paul D. Simmons
> Southern Baptist Theological Seminary
> Louisville, Kentucky

**Note**
1. Henlee H. Barnette, *Introducing Christian Ethics* (Nashville: Broadman Press, 1961), p. 4.

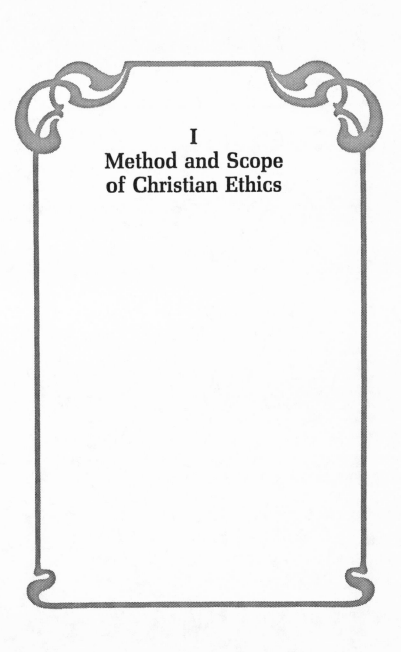

# I
# Method and Scope
# of Christian Ethics

# Introduction

Ethics deals with how people make decisions and act upon them. Why people make certain decisions and not others, and how they go about deciding between alternative courses of actions on moral issues, is what ethics is all about. Everyone has a way of moving from fundamental values to concrete action—from their framework of meaning and purpose to specific decisions. For Christians, this means moving from our understanding of God as revealed in Jesus Christ to the way we live out the Christian life. The task of ethics is to help us move faithfully from theology to discipleship.

The way one moves from the sources of meaning and purpose to specific action is called method. This may be done systematically—the result of consistent reasoning and analysis—or chaotic—immediate response without explicit rationale. One's way of doing ethics, however, can be analyzed and hopefully made more satisfactory and helpful. What is implicit can become explicit; uncritical attitudes can achieve a critical and analytical character.

Ethics tries to help people be aware of their theological and philosophical presuppositions, their attitudes toward rules or principles, their use of factual data, their concern for persons, the place of moral goals or objectives, and the way all these affect their life in community. The purpose behind the essays in Part I is to deal with some of the questions of foundations and method that are of importance to Christian ethics and to those who are interested in better understanding the life of faith.

The general direction and specific directives given Christian ethical thought by the Bible is the subject of the first essay by Paul Simmons, associate professor of Christian ethics at Southern Baptist

Seminary. Biblical ethics comprises a major component of Christian ethical thought though the particular way it is used varies from ethicist to ethicist. The authority of the Bible lies in its truth value, Simmons argues, since the Bible functions as the word of God for those whose actions are guided by it. Specific areas in which the Bible serves to influence the actions of Christians are cited in the concluding section.

Page Lee, professor of religion at Mars Hill College, explores the debate on methodology in the context of the "situation" versus "principles" debate. Lee, who wrote his doctoral dissertation on methodology in the writings of Paul Lehmann, first explores the scope of the debate and then indicates "base points" from which a systematic Christian ethic might proceed.

This discussion is pursued by Glen Stassen, associate professor of Christian ethics at Southern Baptist Seminary, who updates the debate on method. He identifies four major dimensions of ethical reasoning that constitute "critical variables" in determining the outcome of moral arguments. Formerly professor of religion at Berea College, Stassen has been engaged in studies in method for some time and has contributed articles to and edited issues of the *Journal of Religious Ethics* (see Spring, 1977), on this subject.

The concern of social ethics for community action is explored by G. Willis Bennett, professor of church and community at Southern Baptist Seminary. He contends that God is at work creating community and thus calls Christians to be involved in that work. Bennett, who also directs the Advanced Professional Studies Program at Southern and for a time taught with Barnette in the department of Christian ethics, also gives specific guidelines for the church's becoming involved in effective social ministry.

Wayne Oates, former professor of psychology of religion at Southern Baptist Seminary, deals with ethical dilemmas in pastoral care. Often referred to as the dean of pastoral care studies among American seminaries, Oates has written more than twenty books including *The Psychology of Religion* (Word, 1973) and continues his contribution to pastoral studies at the University of Louisville Medical

School. Psychiatry and medical care are creating as well as confronting moral dilemmas, Oates argues. The issues range from behavioral control to the careless and hasty classification of patients into categories that prevent effective therapy. These are moral dilemmas, says Oates, that require ethical analysis and correction.

# 1

## The Bible and Christian Ethics

Paul D. Simmons

The Bible is the Christian's primary source of guidance for dealing with moral issues. "Protestant ethics," declared Otto Piper, "must be based upon the Bible." [1] This seems to reflect a consensus in scholarly circles. Scripture is regarded as an indispensable guide to the faith and practice—the theology and ethics—of the church.

However, while wide agreement may be noted on the notion *that* the Bible is authoritative, it is equally obvious that there is wide disagreement as to *how* it is authoritative. Kelsey has pointed out that the term *authority* is conceived in very different ways by theologians and ethicists who use the Bible in their argumentation. There is, he says, no one "standard" or "normative" meaning of "authority." [2] However, the fact that the Bible is regarded as authoritative by such a diversity of theological approaches is just as, if not more, important than the lack of a normative definition of authority. The purpose of this study is to examine the question of biblical authority as it relates to the enterprise of Christian ethics.

### The Problem of Relating Bible to Ethics

In significant ways Christian ethics must be biblical, but Christian ethics is never the same as biblical ethics. Strictly speaking, biblical ethics is the enterprise of analyzing or describing the ethics of the Bible. For Stendahl, the task is to describe what is found in the Bible, which is not necessarily normative for contemporary thought. [3] Thus, Maston's book, *Biblical Ethics*, attempted to describe but avoid evaluating the material, [4] and Hempel analyzed moral attitudes in the Old Testament in terms of their sociological origins. [5] Similarly, a recent work by Jack Sanders studies New Testament ethics in terms of the impact of eschatological expectations.[6] None of these writers assumes that there is a one-to-one correlation between discovering the ethical content of the Bible and the answers to the questions raised by Christian ethics.

A partial reason for this is to be found in the very nature of the task of Christian ethics. As a theological discipline, the methodology of Christian ethics involves a study of several elements: the nature of man as a moral creature, the process of human decision-making, the sources of value, the standards of conduct and the goals or objectives of the Christian life. A significant part of its task will involve the use of biblical material, but it is not limited to the Bible as its only source.

Other problems are also encountered as one studies the Scripture in search for answers to moral questions. One is the incompleteness of the biblical wisdom. The Bible is simply not a dictionary of moral issues and answers. Many of the major issues of the present are not addressed in the Bible. Problems relating to technology and science, for instance, have come into focus centuries after the last page of the canon was written. Issues in biomedicine have altered definitions of *death* and *life*. Technology has made possible types of violence unknown in biblical times. Obviously, then, the Bible cannot supply *the answer* to every issue.

Another problem relates to the irrelevance of some of the prohibitions found in the Bible. Keck pointed out that even the strictest fundamentalist does not regard certain of the ceremonial laws as authoritative.[7] For instance, men were forbidden to shave and women to wear jewelry or style their hair (Lev. 19:27; 1 Cor. 11:2-16; 1 Tim. 2:9); clothes were not to contain mixed fibers (Deut. 2:11); farmers were forbidden to develop hybrids or crossbreed livestock (Lev. 19:19); and meals could not include pork, crabs, lobsters, or rabbits (Lev. 11). Such matters are now considered adiaphora—matters of moral indifference. They stand in the canon as items of interest to the historians or the student of comparative cultures. But they do not provide normative guidance for the contemporary Christian.

Still another problem relates to the variant perspectives in the

Bible itself. The attitude toward sexual relationships in Proverbs 7 seems quite different from that of the Song of Songs, for instance.[8] The perspective toward government found in Romans 13 is quite different than that of Revelation 13. The prudential attitude toward wealth found in Proverbs seems at variance with attitudes in the New Testament, especially in the Luke-Acts corpus (Matt. 25:31-46; Luke 16:19-31; Acts 2; 4). The task of Christian ethics is neither to accept nor reject either or both of these perspectives. Variety within the Bible reminds us that revelation is not static but dynamic. Each writer addressed God's word to his day. The ethicist's task is to discern the intention of God and render faithful obedience to His revelation through Scripture and the leadership of the spirit.

Another difficulty relating the authority of the Bible to ethics concerns the moral objections that might be raised against certain biblical practices themselves. From a Christian perspective, the killing of an entire family for the sin of one (Josh. 7), executing juvenile deliquents (Deut. 21:18-22), Jephthah's sacrifice of his daughter in celebration for a battle victory (Judg. 11), the total annihilation of the Amalekites ordered by Samuel (1 Sam. 15), and the angry destruction of children by the prophet Elisha (2 Kings 2:23-24) pose problems that must be dealt with in the light of God's revelation in Jesus Christ. At best, these would be judged sub-Christian or patently immoral at worst.

The historical nature of the biblical witness is focused in such matters. The inspired writers of Scripture spoke a Word from God for their day and their historical circumstances. This gave much of their writings a highly situational character as they dealt with the social attitudes and assumptions common to their community. Thus their moral attitudes reflect cultural standards and a type of "period theology." The notion of God as a "warrior" who waged war for his people against the enemy god and his people seemed to be dominant during the period of the judges. This makes Samuel's attitude understandable but not normative for Christian thought about war. Similarly, attitudes toward women often reflected a hierarchical structure in a society that knew little of democratic ideals or relation-

ships. Thus, the notions of the submissiveness of the wife (Eph.
5:22) and that women should keep silence in the church (1 Cor. 14:33-
36) reflect cultural patterns in biblical times not corresponding to
contemporary mores. These must be set in the larger context of
the biblical witness and interpreted theologically.

Problems such as these pointedly raise the question of biblical
authority. The problem is most acute, of course, where the Old Testament is concerned. Bultmann bluntly claimed that the Old Testament
is no longer to be regarded as revelation for Christians.[9] Such skepti-
cism about the authority of the Bible seems both unwarranted and
unnecessary. Nor does it represent the present state of the issue
in scholarly circles. The question now seems to be not *whether* but
*in what sense* is the Bible to be accepted as authority? [10]

### The Basis of Biblical Authority

The authority of the Bible may be considered both as a *formal*
and as a *functional* truth. Its authority relates both to its unique
place in the life of the church and to its use in the witness of Christian
scholars.

The formal authority of the Bible rests upon the fact that the church
"acknowledges (it) as a source of decisive influence in its life." [11]
The Bible is indispensable, unique, and irreplaceable. This is true
for several reasons. First of all, it is the only literary heritage that
links contemporary history to biblical history. As Kaufman pointed
out:

> The Bible contains the principal documentary remains from
> the history in and through which man's understanding of what
> we call God developed . . . the single indispensable source
> for recovering those developments is the . . . Bible. The docu-
> ments . . . were written . . . with no other end in view than
> to portray God's dealings with man and man's dealings with
> God.[12]

Thus, the Bible stands as a "given" in the life of the church, for it
is *the authority* for recovering *that* history. The New Testament has

special importance in this sense for it is the only literary evidence about the life and ministry of Jesus. It is the testimony of those closest to the living Christ and thus has authority in the sense of firsthand evidence.

Furthermore, the Bible is the only common point of reference for all Christian traditions—Orthodox, Catholic, and Protestant. While ecclesiological systems, theological dogma, and vested interest may divide the church, the Bible is a unifying factor.

The functional authority of Scripture is related to the fact that all ethicists use the Bible in supporting or arguing their position. The very fact that this is done involves at least three claims: (1) the biblical texts *ought* to be used; (2) the Scripture is normative; and (3) biblical claims establish the "Christianness" of ethical formulations.[13]

The authority of the Bible, therefore, rests upon both the intrinsic value of its documents and the purposes they serve in the life of the church. To hold that the Bible is authoritative for ethics is to acknowledge that the Bible can and ought to furnish norms for Christian conduct. It will provide useful guidance in rejecting certain moral values and in giving substance and power to others.

Biblical authority must also be related to its truth value. It is authoritative because it is still a link between the living Christ and the world.[14] The reader may be addressed by God as he confronts the witness of the Bible. God may communicate to man through the words of Scripture. A response by the reader may be elicited as the Scripture conveys reality in such a way that one "sees" and becomes committed to truth as so portrayed. The words of Scripture may so illuminate reality that the reader responds in faith and love to the God of Scripture. The fact that so many have confronted God in Jesus Christ in this way, under such diverse conditions and in various places, confirms the church's contention that the Bible is the only authority or witness of its kind that is necessary.

Authority, therefore, is related to a particular area or sphere of influence. As one statement puts it succinctly: "The Scriptures of the Old and New Testament were given by inspiration of God, and are the only sufficient, certain and authoritative rule of all saving knowledge, faith and obedience." The authority of the Bible is related to "saving knowledge, faith and obedience." For this, it is a faithful witness that leads one to God as the church knows him in Jesus Christ. This is the purpose of Scripture. Unless it in fact led unerringly to a knowledge of the will of God, it would not be regarded as Scripture or authoritative. Its truth is the truth of God, not the last word about the course of the world. Its truth is spiritual—focused in personal knowledge of Christ as Lord. It is not intended as the normative word for science but for theology and ethics.

This is basic to all understandings of authority since all claims *about* the Bible are meaningful unless the message of the Bible itself communicates the will of God. It is not so much "what does the Bible say," argues Hodgson, as "what is God using the Bible to say?" [15] The Bible has not been elevated to a position of prominence simply for veneration and adoration. It invites the reader to join the pilgrimage of faith recorded of those whose names and journeys constitute the human stories of the Bible.

## The Bible in Christian Ethics

In spite of the problems inherent in attempting to relate certain passages of the Bible to contemporary moral understandings, the Bible is indispensable to the task of Christian ethics. Ethics cannot claim to be Christian ethics unless the Bible is normative in some important way for the Christian life. The place of Scripture in the life of the church is secure. The debate centers in the manner in which the canonical materials are to be used in deciding various issues in theology and ethics. The fact that ethicists have in fact (1) regarded the Bible as authority, and (2) differed in their understanding of how the Bible is authoritative can be demonstrated by indicating a variety of ways in which the Bible is used in Christian ethics.

Edward L. Long, Jr., has pointed out that both legalists and contextualists appeal to the Bible, neither being able to settle the issues between them by citing Scripture.[16] He discerned three ways in which the Bible is understood as normative for ethics. The *prescriptive approach* attempts to discover the moral laws or rules of the Bible which become basic to Christian ethics. This is the notion that the Bible is a law book for moral guidance. What God has revealed in the Bible is propositional truths about himself and his will. The content of God's will for man is to be found in the biblical commandments and moral wisdom. As John C. Murray argued, "the revelation of the will of God for man, not . . . human standards of behavior . . . are enunciated in the Bible for the creation, direction, and regulation of thought, life, and behavior consonant with the will of God." [17]

A more moderate ethicist with this approach is Carl F. H. Henry.[18] He does admit that the Christian may have to use one injunction instead of another in certain circumstances and that there may be conflict between certain commands.

A second approach Long describes is *deliberative.* Here the effort is to discover the universally valid but general principles in the Bible. Often, these principles lie behind the specific commands. Whereas the specific command may be time and situation oriented, the general principle is always applicable. Albert Knudson, for instance, claimed that there are two principles all Christians should agree upon that are derived from Jesus' teaching: the principle of love and the principle of moral inwardness.[19] Liberal Christianity has championed this approach and is responsible for the widespread acceptance of such principles as that of the infinite value of every person.

A third approach is *relational,* focusing upon the response-in-faith the believer is to make to the living Christ. What ties the modern believer to those of biblical times is that both are related to the same God and both are equally responsible to relating actively to his presence. Contextualists such as Paul Lehmann [20] and T. W. Manson [21] stress this perspective. James Muilenberg's work on Old Testament ethics stressed the fact that all specific commands were related to and dependent upon a prior relationship that Israel had with God. Their obedience was a response to the address of God.[22] In each of these writers "what God demands" is a personal response, not rote obedience to principles or rules which may, in fact, obscure the divine will.

Here, then, are three approaches to Christian ethics, each distinctive in its own way. However, each may also claim to be biblical in its approach in that the Bible is regarded as authoritative and the materials of the Bible constitute significant norms for Christian ethics. Thus, while biblical authority is accepted, how the Bible is used differs significantly.

James M. Gustafson makes the same point by analyzing the significance of Christ for the moral life in various ethical analyses of the Christian life.[23] The uniqueness of Jesus in Christian revelation makes him and his teachings the norm for all Christian moral thought. How this is related to ethical thought, however, varies from one theologian to another.

One approach begins with the theological notion of Jesus as Creator and Redeemer. As such, Christ constitutes the ontological basis and final authority for all moral action. Not moral rules in the Bible but the immediate personal response of the individual becomes the important biblical perspective. A second approach portrays Christ as the Sanctifier and stresses the moral psychology of the Christian. Introspective piety and personal holiness become the biblical bases for Christian morality. Third, Christ has been portrayed as the Justifier who sets the person free from legalism to discover his human possibilities. A fourth model is that of Jesus as the Pattern or ideal for Christian morality. Obedience to Christ is conformity to his example of true faithfulness to the Father. Finally, some construe Jesus as the Teacher of a new set of rules or moral laws which the Christian is to follow. "What Jesus said" or taught is the new law for Christians to obey.

In each of these approaches, Jesus, as revealed in Scripture, is taken to be normative for ethics. At the same time, each construct is different, being determined as much by theological presuppositions informed by the Bible, as by what the Bible actually says. Scriptural passages could be used by each to contest the assertions of the other. Each approach could be criticized by considerations drawn from the other. Claims that one is more biblical than the others, however, seem unwarranted. Each is true to the witness of the Bible and accepts the Bible as authority.

### The Relevance of the Bible for Christian Ethics

The Bible, then, is always relevant to Christian ethics, even though a certain passage may not be decisive for particular judgments. The way the material of the Bible is construed varies from ethicist to ethicist and thus the way in which the Bible functions as authority also varies. Such divergent approaches are to be expected because of the very nature of biblical interpretation. Every ethicist uses a process of interpretation that filters biblical material through personal experiences, perceptions of Jesus Christ, and certain theological presuppositions. One is in constant dialogue with the text. "An analysis of Christian ethics," said Lehmann, "involves a kind of running conversation between the New Testament, on the one hand, and our situation, as heirs of the New Testament, on the other." [24]

Such an approach to Scripture will avoid two errors. One is to assume that the Bible contains all the answers to every human and social problem. Obviously, it does not since organ transplants, genetic experimentation, overpopulation, and chemical pollution of the environment are not dealt with in the Bible. The other error would be to assume that the Bible is irrelevant to shaping Christian moral thought. Scripture is no more dispensable to the ethical task than is reason and faith. Just as the Bible cannot be used as a catalog of ethical norms neither can it be ignored or rejected by an authentic Christian ethic.

The authority of the Bible in Christian ethics is focused precisely in the fact that it is the primary source for shaping the church's understanding of the nature of the Christian life. This is true in three primary ways: (1) shaping Christian identity, (2) the formation of Christian character, and (3) guidance for decision making.

### Shaping Christian Identity

The Bible sets forth the essential elements of Christian identity. What it means to be a Christian is set forth in such a way that the reader is challenged to follow or reject the will of God. The primary feature of that call is to live consciously in relationship to God as he is understood in Jesus Christ. This is the basic presupposition of all Christian ethics for it ties all dimensions of human life to self-conscious responsibility before God. No amount of imitative behavior or obedient action to the moral directives in Scripture is truly biblical until it is behavior elicited as a response in faith to God. The Scriptures are to be read in such a way that they might illuminate the believer's understanding of and evoke commitment to doing the will of God. The Christian is identified by this responsiveness to the activity and presence of God in his life.

The Christian is also identified as a part of the people of God. Whether understood as "Israel," or "the people of God," or "the new Israel," or "the church," this is a community identified by its awareness of a unique relationship between God and his followers. For Israel, this was a consciousness of election and covenant by which God had set them apart from other nations. For the church, the history of Israel is both fulfilled and transformed in Jesus Christ. The Bible reflects the history of this community's self-awareness both in its immature and limited origins in antiquity, its pilgrimage through centuries toward more perfect understandings and its redirection and fulfillment in Jesus Christ. Through all of this, a single history is reflected—the history of self-conscious awareness of relationship and responsibility to God.

This awareness has two profound meanings for Christian ethics. First of all, it sets all individual responsibility in the context of community responsibility. The person's identity is shaped by community self-understandings. The Bible itself is the *canon of the church*—of the Christian community. This is true both because the church has made the judgment that this body of writing authoritatively reveals the will of God and because the church takes its clue for its life and action from the Bible.[25] What the church is intended to be is normatively portrayed in Scripture.

The church becomes, therefore, the context for all Christian moral decision making. Whether conceived of broadly as the sphere of the redemptive activity of God in history or more narrowly as the local community of believers, the church molds individual moral identities and shapes the moral atmosphere in which social decisions are made. In that context, individuals and community deliberate contemporary understandings in the light of biblical revelation. For Lehmann, the task may be described in terms of the question and its answer: "What am I as a believer in Jesus Christ and as a member of his church to do?" [26] This makes the enterprise of Christian ethics truly dialogic in the church.

A second meaning for Christian ethics is that an absolute norm is established from which all moral questions are addressed. Christian identity is shaped by the understanding that the will of God in Jesus Christ is the only moral absolute. H. R. Niebuhr described this as the awareness that faith in God establishes the center of value for the people of God.[27] For him, both faith and loyalty involve an active commitment to live and wok for *this* God and no other. Elsewhere, he defines this loyalty Christologically. "Christ" is the focus of the believer's commitment. He is of supreme importance in the believer's self-understanding, knowledge of God, and of good and evil.[28] Loyalty to Christ relativizes and makes secondary all other loyalties or values. Those may be derived from politics or economics from totalitarianism to materialism, but all are values created by culture or what the Bible calls "the world." When "the will of God" conflicts with the values and loyalties of "the world," the Christian is one who "obeys God rather than men."

### The Formation of Christian Character

Christian identity and character are integrally related. They may be distinguished but cannot be separated. The stress on character serves to emphasize growth toward moral maturity by the disciplined cultivation of virtue. In this process, the Bible can play an essential role for it specifies both the need for growth and gives character-oriented goals toward which the Christian can grow.

Character, it should be noted, is to morality what being is to doing. This means both that one does what one is and that one becomes what one does. Action and being affect one another. Thus, the Bible links together faith and repentance, righteousness and works. For Jesus, participation in the kingdom of God requires repentance before one can either "see" or "enter into" the kingdom (John 3:3,5). Conversion both precedes and is correlative to one's commitment to follow the Christ. Thus, *kerygma* and *didache* are inseparably related since both focus on the person or the character of the one who becomes a follower of Jesus Christ.

Traits of character must be consciously cultivated if one is truly to do the will of God. Virtues associated with Christian character in the New Testament are not there simply to be known or admired, they are to become incarnate in the life of the person. The traits of character in the nature of God and revealed in Jesus Christ are also to become characteristics of the people of God. The indicative of what is known of God establishes the imperative for God's people. They are to reflect in character what they know of the character of God.

Biblical paraenesis gives specific guidance in this regard. The lists of virtues or "fruits of the spirit" in the New Testament indicate characteristics which are appropriate to and consistent with a commitment of life to Jesus Christ. While love is the all-encompassing trait of character (1 John 4:16*b*; Gal. 5:14), the requirements of love are many-faceted—forgiveness, truth-telling, patience, respect for others, kindness, self-control—the list could be expanded (see Gal. 5:22; 1 Cor. 13; Jas.). All such specific traits, however, are parts of the whole—the development of character. This is the goal and aim of Christian moral discipline (Matt. 5:48).

The Bible also contributes to character formation through its images, stories, and parables that are integrated into the patterns of one's thought. One's vision of the world is shaped by the images and models that dominate the imagination. Again, character is related to moral action for *"who we are* and are becoming as a result of the faith we hold determines in large part *what we see."* [29] One's values and commitments define the perspective from which the world and reality are viewed. In turn, one's life is absorbed and invested consistent with those perspectives—whether "in getting and spending" or in seeking "the kingdom of God and his righteousness" (Matt. 6:33).

Considerations relating to character also include dispositions and intentions. Dispositions may be defined as those persistent attitudes or moral orientations of the person. Intentions involve self-conscious or volitional activity in the direction of pursuing certain goals of life or a particular style of life. In either case, intentions provide a type of moral compass that gives direction to one's living or choosing.

The formation of conscience is also a major factor in the development of character. Moral identity is closely related to the identity of the self. Conscience is the product of moral teachings internalized by the person. These have been learned from persons important to one's personal growth—parents, teachers, peers, ministers, and others. Both personal example and moral admonitions have been important to the inculcation of values that shape one's conscience. Often moral instructions are drawn directly from the pages of the Bible. These shape the person's moral understanding of right and wrong—appropriate and inappropriate behavior and attitudes. Often the images and metaphors drawn from the Bible are even more important than the rules. The moral persuasiveness of the image of the good Samaritan is probably greater than that of any direct command in the Bible to assist persons in need. Such vivid images are applied with directness, variety, and meaning.

**Moral Decision Making**

The essential framework for Christian moral decision making is established by the self-identity and character of the person, of course. But where concrete problems are confronted and decisions must be made, the Bible offers concrete guidance and direction.

This does not mean that the Bible makes ethical decisions for us. That burden of responsibility is never removed from the moral actor. Nor does the Bible have a specific formula or method set forth for moving from the general moral imperatives in the Decalogue, for instance, to their specific application to concrete cases. Even where a biblical mandate is taken as directly applicable, the specific meaning of obeying the command still remains to be decided and

acted upon. "Love your neighbor as yourself" (Matt. 19:19, RSV)
must still be interpreted as to its specific direction where such issues
as world poverty, racism, and women's rights are concerned. The
command is direct and must be obeyed. The specific action, however,
must be decided upon and carried out.

Even though it would be false to construe the Bible as a book
of moral rules, it does contain a rich repository of moral wisdom.
Its moral insights are the gleanings from the experience and the
distilled wisdom of generations of the life of the people of God.
The contemporary Christian is both inheritor and bearer of that wisdom. It is composed of moral maxims or paraenetic sayings as in
Proverbs and James; of commandments, as in the Decalogue; and
of casuistical or specific problem-oriented applications, as Paul's
dealing with the question of eating meat offered to idols. To be
sure, some of these no longer offer obvious guidance but most of
the wisdom still provides relevant and viable moral direction. This
is true in several ways.

First, the Bible offers *specific moral directives* that are founda-
tional for all Christian moral thought.[30] Love for God and neighbor
(Matt. 22:37-39) is the biblical summary command for the will of
God. This imperative constitutes the *sine qua non* of all Christian
moral understandings. The Ten Commandments provide specific
guidance in how to act out one's love, both for God and neighbors.

The Christian's concern for justice is also prescribed by Scripture:
"What does the Lord require of you but to do justice, and to love
kindness, and to walk humbly with your God?" (Mic. 6:8, RSV).
The close relation both in terminology and emphasis in the Bible
between justice and righteousness illustrate the inseparability of
act from character. Those who are or have been made righteous
are those who do or seek justice.

The Bible also gives specific moral guidance for the Christian's
decisions about the poor and oppressed. Both the Law and the Prophets reminded Israel of her special responsibility to care for and protect the rights of the poor. Jesus identified with the poor and says
one's attitude toward the poor is a sign of attitudes toward himself

(Matt. 25:40) and determinative for life in the eternal kingdom (Luke 16:19-31). The early church established special procedures for dealing with the poor and organized itself in such a way that no one would go hungry (Acts 2:44 f.; 4:32-37).

Other types of specific commands establish the boundaries of morally permissible behavior.[31] These are the prohibitions of the Bible— from the "Thou shalt not's" of the Ten Commandments to the lists of vices in the epistle of Paul (1 Cor. 6:9 f.; Eph. 5:3-5; Col. 3:5-8). Hatred, violence, gossip, slander, lying, overindulgence, and various types of sexual behavior are prohibited as inconsistent with a Christian life-style.

A second way in which the Bible is concretely related to decision making is by giving theological focus for current moral issues. The Bible has relevant perspectives even when it gives no specific directives. The ethicist may creatively develop norms for novel issues by building upon theological perspectives in the Bible. Thus, Barnette develops an "ecological ethic" by emphasizing the theology of the land, the goodness of creation, and covenant.[32] Similarly, Lehmann develops an ethic that takes account of the revolutionary movements of the world—political, economical, and racial—by appealing to the story of the transfiguration.[33]

Biomedical issues such as fetal research and organ transplantation are others that require ethicists to develop norms by extrapolating from biblical motifs. In this case, the biblical notion of man is crucial as is the relation of man to God's continuing work of creation. The sanctity of human life is a principle that has important moral bearing on the question of human experimentation and abortion. This notion is based on the theology of creation and God's love for every person. All persons are bearers of the image of God and thus deserve respect and care in the human community.

The move from biblical perspectives to moral issues is never simple for the agenda is drawn from the contemporary world. The ethicist must dialogue with the full range of biblical materials and take account of positions that are not easily harmonized. Abortion, for instance, is nowhere explicitly dealt with in the Bible. However, both the notion of the sanctity of life and the *imago dei* are rooted in the Bible. The question arises as to whether these concepts are to be applied equally to both fetus and woman and thus conclude that they have *equal* moral worth? The story of miscarriage by accident in Exodus 21:22-25 seems to establish a different moral value for the fetus and the woman while still showing that the fetus has value since a monetary settlement was to be made.[34]

The issue of euthanasia also involves a balancing of the biblical notion of the sanctity of human life with the notion of quality of life. The fact that medical technology may "kill" or "keep alive" in such a variety of ways makes the biblical mandate "Thou shalt not kill" very difficult to apply to every case. Plainly a Christian theology of death influences the way an ethicist applies the Commandment to cases where machines are withdrawn from patients who are comatose with incurable illnesses.[35]

Thus, the Bible gives relevant guidance even where it does not give a specific moral solution. The Christian is given sufficient direction to enable a faithful response to God's will and purpose in the concrete circumstances one encounters. The importance of character and moral self-identity at that point cannot be overemphasized. Translating biblical perspectives into contemporary categories is not simply an intellectual enterprise, but one which engages and tests the faith commitments of the translator. Commitment and obedient faithfulness determine one's perception of the issue confronted, the creative use of biblical materials and the decision-action that is made.

## Conclusion

The Bible serves the enterprise of Christian ethics in a variety of ways. Its perspective provides normative guidance and solid clues to discerning the will of God. In this respect the Scripture is authoritative, providing an indispensable and unique witness. What is required by the contemporary follower of Christ is an imaginative and discriminating use of one's intelligent commitment to Christ as Lord in order to enter into dialogue with Scripture.

To be sure, some will continue to speak as if the Bible itself is the dictator of the way the disciple is to walk before the Lord. This legalistic approach to ethics will construe the Bible as a collection of rules, laws, or principles that spell out in exact detail the commands of God for every age. Others will stumble upon the problematic sections in the biblical story and regard it as a hindrance on the way. For them, the Bible will be disregarded and its authority rejected for what they regard as moral reasons. A more fruitful approach is to recognize the Bible as an illuminator of the way—as an authoritative witness that serves as "a lamp to my feet and a light to my path" (Ps. 119:105). The Bible helps the faithful follower see the way, discern the will of God, and render responsible obedience.

### Notes

1. Otto Piper, *The Biblical View of Sex and Marriage* (New York: Scribner's Sons, 1960), p. 13. See also Jams M. Gustafson, "The Use of Scripture in Christian Ethics," in *Theology and Christian Ethics* (Philadelphia: Pilgrim Press, 1974).

2. David H. Kelsey, *The Uses of Scripture in Recent Theology* (Philadelphia: Fortress Press, 1975), p. 2.

3. Krister Stendahl, "Biblical Theology: Contemporary," in *The Interpreter's Dictionary of the Bible*, I (Nashville: Abingdon Press, 1962), p. 418.

4. T. B. Maston, *Biblical Ethics* (Cleveland: World, 1967), p. vii.

5. J. Hempel, "Ethics in the Old Testament," in *The Interpreter's Dictionary of the Bible*, II, pp. 1153-1161.

6. Jack T. Sanders, *Ethics in the New Testament* (Philadelphia: Fortress Press, 1975).

7. Leander E. Keck, *Taking the Bible Seriously* (New York: Association, 1962), p. 168.

8. See Brevard S. Childs, *Biblical Theology in Crisis* (Philadelphia: Westminster, 1970), pp. 184-200 for a fuller treatment of this issue.

9. Rudolf Bultmann, "The Significance of the Old Testament for the Christian Faith," *The Old Testament and Christian Faith*, ed. B. W. Anderson (New York: Harper & Row, 1963), p. 31.

10. See the article by James Barr, "The Old Testament and the Crisis of Biblical Authority," in *Interpretation*, January, 1971, pp. 24-40.

11. Bruce C. Birch and Larry Rasmussen, *Bible and Ethics in the Christian Life* (Minneapolis: Augsburg, 1976), p. 144.

12. Gordon D. Kaufman, "What Shall We Do with the Bible?" *Interpretation*, XXV:1 (Jan., 1971), p. 100.

13. Kelsey, pp. 152-153.

14. Kaufman, p. 101.

15. Leonard Hodgson, et. al., *On the Authority of the Bible* (London: SPCK, 1960), p. 8.

16. Edward L. Long, Jr., "The Use of the Bible in Christian Ethics," *Interpretation*, XIX:2 (April, 1965), pp. 149-162. See also his *Survey of Christian Ethics* (New York: Oxford, 1967), Part I, "The Formulation of the Ethical Norm."

17. John C. Murray, *Principles of Conduct* (London: Tyndale, 1957), p. 14 (cited by Long).

18. Carl F. H. Henry, *Christian Personal Ethics* (Grand Rapids: Eerdmans, 1957).

19. Albert Knudson, *The Principles of Christian Ethics* (New York: Abingdon, 1943), p. 39.

20. See Paul Lehmann, *Ethics in a Christian Context* (New York: Harper & Row, 1963).

21. See T. W. Manson, *Ethics and the Gospel* (New York: Scribner's Sons, 1960). Also, "Is Manson Among the Situationalists?" in *Expository Times*, Vol. 81 (May, 1970).

22. James Muilenberg, *The Way of Israel: Biblical Faith and Ethics* (New York: Harper and Brothers, 1961), p. 15.

23. James M. Gustafson,*Christ and the Moral Life* (New York: Harper & Row, 1968). See also, A. M. Hunter, *A Pattern for Life*, rev. ed. (Philadelphia: Westminster, 1965), ch. IV, who indicates the fact that theological presuppositions determine the way one interprets the teaching of Jesus in the Sermon on the Mount.

24. Lehmann, p. 29.

25. See Childs, p. 131 and Birch and Rasmussen, p. 184.

26. Lehmann, p. 25.

27. H. R. Niebuhr, *Radical Monotheism and Western Civilization* (Lincoln: University of Nebraska, 1960), pp. 11-18.

28. H. R. Niebuhr, *Christ and Culture* (New York: Harper, 1951), p. 11.

29. Birch and Rasmussen, p. 88.

30. Long, *A Survey of Christian Ethics*, chs. 5, 6, and 7.

31. Ibid., p. 117.

32. Henlee Barnette, *The Church and the Ecological Crisis* (Grand Rapids:

Eerdmans, 1972). See also his, "Toward an Ecological Ethic," in *Review and Expositor* LXIX:1 (Winter, 1972), pp. 23-36.

33. Paul L. Lehmann, *The Transfiguration of Politics* (New York: Harper & Row, 1975), esp. Part II.

34. See Paul D. Simmons, "Dialogue on Abortion" in *A Matter of Life and Death*, Harry Hollis, ed. (Nashville: Broadman, 1977) where this is treated more fully.

35. See Paul D. Simmons, "Death with Dignity: Christians Confront Euthanasia," in *Perspectives in Religious Studies*, Summer 1977.

# 2

## Methodology in Christian Ethics

H. Page Lee

What John A. T. Robinson's *Honest to God* did for doctrines, and Harvey Cox's *Secular City* did for the mission of the church, Joseph Fletcher's *Situation Ethics* has done for Christian ethics. Each one has brought the issues to the public in an interesting and understandable way. But there is more. The story is told about a series of lectures by four theologians on Robinson's *Honest to God*. They concluded that Robinson did not have anything to offer because, one, he did not say anything new, and two, he did not say it as accurately as the experts would have liked. The master of ceremonies, in summing up the lectures, said to them: "Well, now, if what Robinson said has been old hat to you theologians for a generation, why hasn't the church heard it before?" [1] The same thing could be said to many of Fletcher's critics. He not only has put the question of the method of doing ethics on the lips of many people but he also has brought about a new concern for methodology among Christian ethicists.

The term *methodology* is used in the sense of the way in which ethics is done, the procedure of ethical reflection, the systematic treatment of a subject, the kind of thinking involved, and the rational structure of a system. Every systematic treatment of Christian ethics consciously or unconsciously employs some methodology. When the methodology is unconsciously chosen, whether it be eclecticism, pragmatism, or just plain whim, the result is confusion on the part of the ethicist and his hearers. The basic problem in Christian ethics is this confusion or lack of clarity, which is the direct result of a lack of concern for methodology. The purpose of this essay is to indicate the status of this problem and to suggest a solution in the form of the necessary tools for analyzing the methodology of any system of Christian ethics and for laying the groundwork for the development of a consistent one.

## Status of the Problem

Few Christian ethicists have concerned themselves with the question of methodology before setting forth their systems of ethics. Emil Brunner, Reinhold Niebuhr, Karl Barth, Dietrich Bonhoeffer, H. Richard Niebuhr, Paul Ramsey, Paul Lehmann, and James Sellers are among the few Christian ethicists who have raised the issue. Although no definitive work on methodology in Christian ethics has yet been done, James M. Gustafson and William K. Frankena have dealt explicitly with this problem in Christian ethics. Therefore, a brief summary of their approaches to the problem is presented at this point.

Gustafson has written one of the most cogent essays on methodology in Christian ethics.[2] According to him, the debate, which has been going on for the past decades in the field of Christian ethics, between the principle approach and the contextual approach has ceased to be a fruitful one. The term *contextualism* has been used to cover views that are significantly different, while adherents of the principle approach reveal different grounds for their approach and use principles in different ways. Gustafson argued that there are four possible starting points for Christian ethics and that regardless of which one of the four the ethicist begins with, he will move into the other three if he seeks to complete his Christian ethics. These four starting points are: theological affirmations, moral principles, an analysis of the social situation, and a conception of Christian existence.[3]

Gustafson pointed out that the debate has located the problem of Christian ethics at the point of the method of making ethical decisions, that is, How does a Christian make a moral decision? He gave credit to Henry David Aiken's essay, "Levels of Moral Discourse," for providing Christian ethics with a helpful tool. Aiken suggested four levels of moral discourse: "Expressive-evocative," "moral," "ethical," and "postethical." At the second or "moral" level the question is raised: What ought I to do? It is at this level that reasons are given for the choices that are made. At the third or "ethical" level questions are raised concerning the reasons which are given for making the choices or moral decisions. It is at this level that reasons are given for the immediate reasons for moral decisions. As the fourth or "postethical" level morality is brought into question, that is, Why should man be moral? It is at this level that the usage passes beyond reason to a commitment. Gustafson suggested that the debate between the principle approach and the contextual approach has emerged on the "moral" level of discourse. The principle approach has suggested that one ought to look to the objective principles of conduct in the Christian tradition which have been derived from nature and revelation. The contextual approach has suggested that one ought to immerse oneself in the situation in which one lives, and in which God is acting, and then in faith do what appears to be the right thing. The debate then moves to the "ethical" level where each side gives reasons to justify its approach. Both sides agree at the "postethical" level that a Christian should be moral.[4]

Gustafson demonstrated that all contexualists cannot be grouped together under the same category. For example, he showed that Kenneth Underwood's starting point is an analysis of the social situation; Karl Barth, Joseph Sittler, and Paul Lehmann start with theological affirmations; and H. Richard Niebuhr's starting point is a conception of Christian existence. Yet all are included in the contextualist category. Although each of these ethicists begins with one of the four starting points, each ethicist moves into considerations that involve the other three starting points. However, the starting point does set the pattern for the working out of a Christian ethic.[5]

Principle approach ethicists, Gustafson pointed out, use principles in different ways. For example, Reinhold Niebuhr and John C. Bennett would have moral principles give direction to the consequences and effects of moral action, while Paul Ramsey would have moral principles be used for the right means of conduct. This is not an absolute differentiation, since Ramsey is aware of ends and Niebuhr and Bennett are aware of means. Yet, their emphases are different. Therefore, they cannot be grouped together under the same category. Among these writers, principles also have different degrees of authority. For example, in Niebuhr love and justice are norms which receive a minimum of definition. In fact, Niebuhr could be considered on the contextual side of the debate because of his stress upon social analysis and his pragmatic judgments. For Ramsey, Christian moral principles have so much authority that they in effect prescribe rather than merely illuminate the right conduct of Christians.[6]

As Gustafson observed, Paul Ramsey begins with moral principles and moves to the other three starting points. He also noted how Paul Lehmann begins with a theological affirmation and moves to the other three starting points. Furthermore, he described how Kenneth Underwood begins with social analysis and moves to the other three starting points. Finally, he disclosed how H. Richard Niebuhr begins with an interpretation of moral existence and moves to the other three starting points. Thus the tendency among Christian ethicists is to focus on one base point, even declaring it to be the proper starting point, and then move consciously or unconsciously to the other three base points.[7]

Gustafson argued that the debate between the principle approach and the contextual approach has been misplaced partly because it has been carried on at the moral level of discourse and has not sufficiently moved into the other levels. If one argues against the contextual approach the arguments must be directed to the theological and ethical reasons given for the emphasis on context. The quarrel with Barth, Lehmann, and Sittler ought to be theological. Disagreement with H. Richard Niebuhr should be theological and on the grounds of moral anthropology. If one is at variance with the principle approach, the argument must include the question of source, use, and authority of principles. Gustafson cites a number of questions which must be raised by those who persist in the debate. The larger question, however, is whether there is *one* normative starting point for Christian ethics.[8]

In another series of essays on Christian ethics,[9] Gustafson said that the procedures of ethical reflection are deeply affected by the basic theological convictions of the Christian ethicist. The ethicist's view of the Bible, moral propositions, man as a creature who responds to God, and tradition all help to shape his ethical thought. Issues which divide the principle approach and the contextual approach to Christian ethics are both philosophical and theological. Moreover, contextualists earn their name for several reasons: their emphasis on social analysis; their stress on the freedom of God or God as Creator, Governor, and Redeemer; their stress on Christ as the living Lord; on their emphasis on man as one who lives in response to actions upon him, especially the action of God. He pointed out some of the bases for the principle approach and then indicated that the problem of methodology is a very live issue in Christian ethics today. With the recent publication of H. Richard Niebuhr's *The Responsible Self,* Gustafson predicted that the extreme positions of Paul Lehmann and Paul Ramsey will be subject to a critical revision, and that a methodological pluralism will probably be recognized as valid in Christian ethics.[10]

William K. Frankena has also dealt explicitly with the problem of methodology in Christian ethics. Writing from the perspective of a moral philosopher and within the context of a discussion of methodology in that discipline, he claims that there are three kinds of thinking which relate to morality: "descriptive," "normative," and "meta-ethical." [11] The first kind is carried on principally by the anthropologist, psychologist, and sociologist. This approach involves a descriptive empirical inquiry. A second sort of thinking involves questions concerning what is good or right, and it either implies or expresses oughtness. The third type of thinking asks logical and epistemological questions concerning the meaning and justification of ethical statements. This latter kind of thinking appears to be necessary in order to have a satisfactory normative theory.[12]

Frankena declared that there are three types of moral or ethical judgment: "moral obligation," "moral value," and "nonmoral value." In the second or "normative" kind of ethical thinking, an attempt

is made to arrive at a set of acceptable judgments of "moral obligation," "moral value," and of "nonmoral value." In the third or meta-
ethical kind of ethical thinking, an effort is made to set forth a theory
of the meaning and justification of judgments of "moral obligation,"
"moral value," and of "nonmoral value." [13]

Normative judgments of moral obligation are divided by Frankena
into two types of theories: deontological and teleological. There are
two kinds of deontological theories: "act-deontological" and "rule-
deontological." The first kind maintains that the judgments of moral
obligation are purely situational, while the second affirms that one
or more rules make up the standard of right and wrong. There are
also two kinds of teleological theories: "act-utilitarian" and "rule-
utilitarian." The first maintains that the obligatory act in each situation is the one which is likely to bring about the greatest balance
of good over evil. The second asserts that the rules which promote
the greatest good for everyone are the right ones. In addition to
the principle of utility, Frankena introduces the principle of justice
as a "mixed deontological theory," that is, a theory which includes
utility or benevolence and justice.[14]

At this point Frankena related Judaic-Christian *agapism* to his
discussion of methodology. He decried the fact that philosophical
ethics has generally neglected *agapism,* while Christian ethics has
been neither clear nor of one mind concerning its classification or
methodology. The ethics of love has been worked out in both teleological and deontological theories, but these theories have not been
pure *agapism.* In fact, the theologians who say that man ought to
love God and neighbor because God commands it are basically nona-
gapistic deontologists, because their ethics are based on the principle
that man ought to obey God. Frankena goes on to suggest that "pure
agapism" might be a third kind of normative theory in addition to
the teleological and deontological ones. Furthermore, he says that
pure agapism might take two forms: "act-agapism" and "rule-agapism."

The pure act-agapist would maintain that one, without appealing
to rules, should analyze the situation and then do the most loving

thing in it. This view is characteristic of some religious existentialists and has been called antinomianism or situationalism. The rule-agapist would maintain that one should determine which rules are most love-embodying and then follow the rules in every situation where possible. In both forms of pure agapism, Frankena declared that the primary injuction is to "feel a certain emotion (love) toward God and fellowman and to express it in one's actions or rules of actions." [15] He noted that the injunction to love provides no directive unless some resort is made either to the principle of utility or to revelation. Hence, he found it hard to see how all of one's duties could be derived from the instruction to love by itself, that is, how justice can be derived from love. In his opinion love must be supplemented by the principle of justice; therefore, he disavows a pure agapism.[16]

Frankena continued his discussion of methodology by treating normative theories of moral value and of nonmoral value. Finally he dealt with the questions and theories of metaethics. The central questions are those of the meaning and justification of ethical judgments. In this context he discussed the relationship of ethics to theology, concluding that if ethical principles can be justified by appeal to theological premises, it is not a logical justification.[17]

In an essay dealing explicitly with the problem of methodology in Christian ethics,[18] Frankena pointed out the absence of clarity of definition, statement, and argument in the literature of Christian ethics. In an effort to remedy this situation, he sought to apply his own methodology to Christian normative ethics. He attempted to do this by dealing with the debate between the principle approach and the contextual approach or the relation of principles and love in Christian ethics. He held that the Christian ethicist can state his position more clearly and more cogently if he uses Frankena's terms. Frankena set forth his terms in the following categories: "pure agapism," "pure non-agapistic," and "impure or mixed agapism." He divided "pure agapism" into three forms: "pure act-agapism," "modified act-agapism," and "pure rule-agapism." He divided the "pure non-agapistic" category into three forms: "pure rule-deontologism," "pure act-deontologism," and "modified act-deontologism." The mixing of the forms of "pure agapism" and "pure non-agapism" makes many combined forms which Frankena calls "mixed agapisms."

After multiplying and subdividing the several categories, he sought to apply them to various Christian ethicists. However, he expresses his frustration time and again at not being able to place everyone in his categories, such as, Reinhold Niebuhr and Paul Ramsey.[19] He left for others to decide whether this is on account of richness of mind or confusion on the part of the ethicists. Frankena ended his discussion by raising the question concerning which method is correct. He said that this is a question for metaethics and that the moral philosophers have not arrived at any agreement on this question; however, they have argued more clearly on this point than the Christian ethicists have. Frankena concluded with the challenge that Christian ethicists have no alternative but to become acquainted with moral philosophy and to express Christian ethics in the terms of moral philosophy, especially his terms.[20]

The essays by Gustafson and Frankena have made a contribution to the study of methodology in Christian ethics. Yet neither has provided the adequate tools for analyzing the methodology of a systematic Christian ethics or for laying the groundwork for the development of a consistent one. In the thought of both men there is an oversimplification of the problem of methodology. Gustafson, for example, betrays this fact when, in his discussion of starting points, he says that H. Richard Niebuhr must be approached from the standpoint of both theology and moral anthropology. He says this in one sentence, but one of the main thrusts of his essay is that Niebuhr begins with moral anthropology and then moves toward the other three starting points. Methodology involves more than starting points and levels of discourse; therefore, Gustafson's essay oversimplifies the problem of methodology. However, his essays are helpful and make a contribution to this problem. Likewise Frankena's approach oversimplified the problem of methodology. Even though he multiplied the categories *ad infinitum*, they are still not comprehensive enough to deal with Christian ethicists. However, his approach provides some light in the Christian's search for a more adequate methodology in ethics.

## A Solution to the Problem

If an analysis is to be made of the methodology of any system of Christian ethics and if the groundwork is to be laid for the development of a consistent one, then adequate tools must be used. The rest of this essay is a suggestion that the necessary tools of analysis are those which will involve the ethicist in a search for three variable factors: the given, the method, and the model. The shape of any discipline is determined by these three factors.[21] The *given* refers to that with which a systematic Christian ethic begins, the bedrock upon which the system is built, or the sources from which the system is developed. The *method* refers to the way in which the given is used. The *model* refers to the symbol or motif which is used in the systematization of the given.

1. A determination of the scope and content of the given is the first task in this analysis. In order to make this determination, four criteria are used: *sophia,* presuppositions, the basis for making ethical decisions, and the major ethical concerns. *Sophia* refers to the question of epistemology and the relation of faith to reason, that is, how does one know and what are the sources of his wisdom? Presuppositions refers to the theological and philosophical assumptions. The basis for making ethical decisions refers to the beginning point from which a systematic Christian ethic is developed. The major ethical concerns refers to the range and content of the ethical concerns and the relation of the church and the world, that is, about what is man concerned and what is the relation of Christ and culture?

Within each of these four criteria, one seeks to determine the relation between Christ and culture. In the fourth criterion, Christ and culture have the same reference that they have in H. Richard Niebuhr's *Christ and Culture.*[22] However, Christ and culture have an epistemological reference in the first three criteria.

In applying the first criterion, or *sophia,* to a systematic Christian ethic, one raises the question of the relation of Christ and culture or faith and reason. There are four possible types of relationship: "(1) reason is primary and excludes faith, (2) reason is primary and includes faith, (3) faith is primary and excludes reason, (4) faith is primary and includes reason." [23] For purposes of analysis and with no intention of implying a dichotomy between faith and reason, this approach seeks to determine the faith-sources and the reason-sources of the wisdom upon which the system is built. The faith-sources are: the Bible, the church and its tradition, and the Holy Spirit. The question of revelation is raised here, although it can also be raised in connection with the reason-sources, such as, with those in the Augustinian tradition who consider all knowledge to be revelation. If the Bible is considered a source of wisdom, the question concerning hermeneutical approach is raised. The reason-sources are all other disciplines, but especially philosophy, sociology, and psychology. Thus, a twofold analysis is made: one, the relation of faith and reason; two, the relation of Christian ethics and its faith and reason sources of wisdom.

In applying the second criterion or presuppositions which are derived from Christ and culture and their relationship. Again, this is for purposes of analysis, and it has no intention of implying a dichotomy between theology and philosophy. Major theological and central philosophical presuppositions in their order of priority are determined. Philosophical is used in the broad sense, at this point, of including all major presuppositions which are derived from culture.

In applying the third criterion or the basis for making ethical decisions to a systematic Christian ethic, the beginning point from which the system is developed is sought. Furthermore, an attempt is made to determine the relation of this beginning point to Christ and culture. Gustafson's four starting points would be utilized: theological affirmations, moral principles, an analysis of the social situation, and a conception of Christian existence. However, the beginning point could be made up of more than one of these starting points, being used in a bifocal or dialectial way. For purposes of analysis and with no intention of implying a dichotomy between faith and reason or Christ and culture a determination of the Christ-sources and the culture-sources of the beginning point from which the system is developed is sought. The Christ-sources are: theological affirmations and a conception of Christian existence. The culture-sources are: moral principles and an analysis of the social situation. It must be stressed that this distinction is only for the purpose of a part of this analysis, for a further intention is that of determining the relationship of the beginning point to both Christ and culture. At this point, a preliminary question about authority is raised, that is, From what authority is this beginning point derived as the basis for making ethical decisions? Although the first two criteria, *sophia* and presuppositions, are involved in the question of authority, this problem comes to a preliminary head in this third criterion. The final and more comprehensive question of authority is raised in connection with the second major factor in this analysis, the method, or the way in which the given is used.

In applying the fourth criterion, the major ethical concerns, to a systematic Christian ethic, this approach seeks to determine the range and the content of the ethical concerns and the relation of Christ and culture. The first three criteria in the given obviously have a reference to the beginning, ground, or source of the system, whereas this fourth criterion has reference to the object and intention of the system. It is this object and intention that helps to form the given from which the method and the model are developed. Therefore, the range and content of the major personal and social concerns are determined. Furthermore, it seeks to apply H. Richard Niebuhr's five types of relationship between Christ and culture to the system of Christian ethics. Finally, it seeks to discover the intention of the ethicist for the system, that is, Does he present it as an apologetic or in a positivistic way? For whom is the ethic intended?

The application of these four criteria to systematic Christian ethics is made in order to determine the scope and content of the given.

Account is taken of both that which is explicit and that which is implicit in the system. After determining the given upon which the system is built, this analysis seeks to determine the way in which the ethicist used the given in building his system.

2. A determination of the method, the way in which the given is used, is the second major task. This involves an investigation into the kind of ethical thinking that is used and an interpretation of the process of conformation.

In the first place, the system of ethics is related to the categories and types of ethical thinking which have been set forth by William K. Frankena. Specifically, an attempt is made to determine whether the system employs a descriptive, normative, or metaethical kind of ethical thinking. Furthermore, Frankena's multiplied and subdivided types of ethical theory are used, in spite of the fact that he could not place Paul Ramsey's ethics in one of the categories.[26]

What process of conformation is involved in the systematization of the given is the second step. This is the way in which the ethicist arranges and structures the given into a system. Because the process of conformation itself depends upon a method, this study uses three criteria in order to determine what this method is. The first criterion is consistency. Is there a confluence of all the criteria in the given into a consistent system? Does this system contradict any of the criteria in the given? This analysis seeks an answer to these questions.

Order of preference is the second criterion by which the process of conformation is determined. Are the four starting points, which determine the basis for making ethical decisions, kept in their order of preference? Does the system have a consistent beginning point throughout? Is the basis for making ethical decisions consistent throughout the system?

A third criterion, which goes beyond consistency and order of preference, is wholeness. This refers to the result of the process of conformation. Is the process of conformation carried out so that the system cannot be explained in terms of one of the criteria of the given? Can the system be explained only in terms of its whole, rather than in terms of its parts?

At this point in the analysis, the problem of authority is raised again. Although it comes to a preliminary head at the point of the basis for making ethical decisions, it is raised in a more comprehensive way in connection with this second major factor, the method. An attempt is made to determine the nature and source of the appeal to authority in the normative and metaethical kinds of ethical thinking. Furthermore, it attempts to interpret the source of authority in the process of conformation, especially at the point of the order of preference. An effort is made to determine whether or not the same basis for making ethical decisions and the same source of authority are kept throughout the system. Thus, the kind of ethical thinking and the process of conformation determine the way in which the given is used, or the method.

3. A determination of the model, the symbol which is used in the systematization of the given, is the third major task. Account is taken of both that which is explicit and that which is implicit in the system. First, an effort is made to discover the supportive models, if any, as well as the central model. In the second place, an attempt is made to interpret the function of the model, using McIntyre's five categories as criteria for interpreting the function of the model in the system of ethics.[24] These criteria are: medium of disclosure, ontological reference, descriptive, normative, and integrative. Does the model participate in the reality which it models so that it creates a disclosure situation in which God addresses himself to man and declares his will and purpose for man? Does the model bring about an ontological commitment? Is the model merely used in a descriptive way? Does the model become normative, or the criterion of truth for Christian ethics? Does the model become integrative for a variety of aspects of Christian ethics?

Thus, in an effort to determine the shape of a system of Christian ethics, an analysis is made of three variable factors: the given, the method, and the model. These factors are suggested as the necessary tools for analyzing the methodology of any system of Christian ethics and for laying the groundwork for the development of a consistent one.

## Notes

1. Quoted by Vernon L. Weiss, "Read Fletcher Aright," *The Situation Ethics Debate*, Harvey Cox, ed. (Philadelphia: Westmister, 1968), p. 247.

2. James M. Gustafson, "Context Versus Principles: A Misplaced Debate in Christian Ethics," *New Theology*, No. 3, Martin E. Marty and Dean G. Peerman, eds. (New York: The Macmillan Company, 1966), pp. 69-102.

3. Ibid., pp. 69-71, 89.

4. Ibid., pp. 71-72.

5. Ibid., 72-83.

6. Ibid., pp. 83-89.

7. Ibid., pp. 89-98.

8. Ibid., pp. 98-99.

9. James M. Gustafson, "Christian Ethics," *Religion*, Paul Ramsey, ed., The Princeton Studies, Richard Schlatter, ed. (Englewood Cliffs, New Jersey: Prentice-Hall, Inc., 1965), pp. 287-354.

10. Ibid., pp. 225-236.

11. William K. Frankena, *Ethics*, Foundations of Philosophy Series, Elizabeth and Monroe Beardsley, ed. (Englewood Cliffs, New Jersey: Prentice-Hall, Inc., 1963), pp. 42-45 *et passim*.

12. Ibid., pp. 1-5.

13. Ibid., pp. 6-10.

14. Ibid., pp. 11-42.

15. Ibid., p. 44.

16. Ibid., pp. 42-45.

17. Ibid., pp 47-98.

18. William K. Frankena, "Love and Principle in Christian Ethics," *Faith and Philosophy*, Alvin Plantinga, ed. (Grand Rapids: Eerdmans, 1964), pp. 203-225.

19. Ibid., pp. 214, 219-220.

20. Ibid., pp. 203-225.

21. See John McIntyre, *The Shape of Christology* (Philadelphia: Westminster, 1966), pp. 8-81. The methodological approach of this chapter, in the

methodology of Christian ethics, is influenced by some of McIntyre's central ideas. In summary fashion, he says: "The shape of any discipline is a function of three variables: the given upon which the discipline operates; the models which it employs for the systematization, exposition, analysis and interpretation of this given; and thirdly the method followed in operating the models" (p. 8).

22. H. R. Niebuhr, *Christ and Culture* (New York: Harper and Brothers, 1951).

23. John A. Hutchison, *Faith, Reason, and Existence* (New York: Oxford University Press, 1956), p. 97.

24. See McIntyre, pp. 54-81.

# 3

## Critical Variables in Christian Social Ethics

### Glen H. Stassen

Why do debates about method in Christian social ethics regularly change the subject from racial and economic injustice and peace and war to hypothetical questions for clever discussion by detached spectators? Why do they turn Christians with a conscience about real abuses into abstract rationalizers, defenders of the status quo, and armchair quibblers? One reason could be that debates about method usually see only one issue such as situationism *versus* principlism, or utilitarianism *versus* deontologism. Therefore, they leave unexamined those existential realities which actually guide our decisions. We need a comprehensive and inclusive method.

Recent studies of methodology in Christian social ethics have identified four major dimensions of ethical reasoning. These are: (1) a clear style of reasoning, (2) ground-of-meaning beliefs, (3) loyalties and interests, and (4) perceptions of data. The studies have also singled out pivotal presuppositions within these dimensions.[1]

These pivotal presuppositions may be called *variables*. Like independent variables in the social sciences, they are the factors that shape the outcome of moral arguments. They vary or differ in interesting ways. That is, people who engage in ethical discussion and decision make different assumptions about the content of these presuppositions, and this tends to explain the decisions they reach. Identifying the most important variables and describing their interrelationships might improve ethical discourse by providing certain points for self-examination and study. The need is to avoid the narrow vision that repeatedly stumbles into error and loses its way because it ignores major dimensions of ethical decision, ethical argument, and ethical character.[2] The purpose of this article is to describe the content of these variables, indicate some differing assumptions held by Christian ethicists on each variable, and point to some comparative studies that map the variations. The following schematic diagram may help track the discussion and indicate the interrelationships between the four dimensions.

**Schematic Diagram of Variables Underlying a Particular Ethical Judgment.**

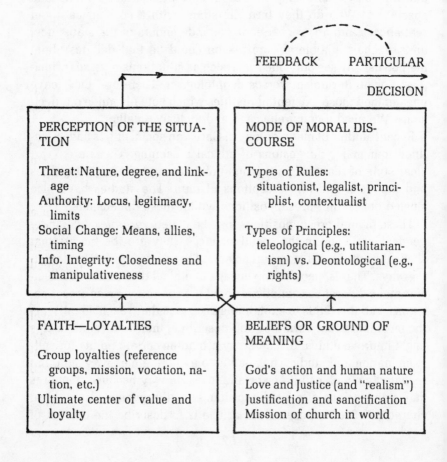

FEEDBACK        PARTICULAR

DECISION

PERCEPTION OF THE SITUATION

Threat: Nature, degree, and linkage
Authority: Locus, legitimacy, limits
Social Change: Means, allies, timing
Info. Integrity: Closedness and manipulativeness

MODE OF MORAL DISCOURSE

Types of Rules:
situationist, legalist, principlist, contextualist

Types of Principles:
teleological (e.g., utilitarianism) vs. Deontological (e.g., rights)

FAITH—LOYALTIES

Group loyalties (reference groups, mission, vocation, nation, etc.)
Ultimate center of value and loyalty

BELIEFS OR GROUND OF MEANING

God's action and human nature
Love and Justice (and "realism")
Justification and sanctification
Mission of church in world

## The Style of Moral Reasoning

The style of reasoning is one of the crucial dimensions in ethical discourse. This does not concern the *content* of ethics but the *logic* of how one puts the ingredients together. Different ethicists do this in different ways.

One important variable in the style of reasoning is what is meant by moral rules. In the infamous situation ethics debate, for instance, Joseph Fletcher defined *legalism* as the belief that rules are absolute, universal, and directive, telling us directly what to do rather than leaving room for imagination and creative improvisation. To this he opposed his own situationism, a style of reasoning which allows only "rules of thumb." Rules of thumb merely summarize what has worked best in a majority of cases in the past and do not in any sense obligate us. An example is "punt on fourth down"—usually effective but in no sense obligatory and clearly wrong in some situations. Thus, as Fletcher set up the situation ethics debate, the key variable is the understanding of rules.

However, most Christian ethicists have wanted another alternative besides the two definitions of rules Fletcher offers. Such an option might be found if the debate can be clarified somewhat. Notice first that ethical reasoning occurs on something like four levels.[3]

1. *The Particular Judgment Level.* Here one speaks directly of a particular case, expressing a judgment but giving no reasons. For example, Fletcher says a particular set of parents would have been right to have taken the life of their unusually severely handicapped mongoloid child, Philip.[4]

Fletcher is a situationist; he wants to free people from binding rules; therefore, his statement does not move on to the rules level but tends to stay on the particular judgment level. He emphasizes the particular situation (unfortunately without making clear how unrepresentative Philip was, compared with most mongoloids, who typically can have happy, communicative, and productive lives).

2. *The Moral Rules Level.* At this level a reason is given for one's moral judgment. The reason is not a general principle, like "the sa-

credness of human personality," but a specific directive telling what to do in particular cases like the rule, "Thou shalt not kill."

By contrast with situationists, legalists tend to operate exclusively at the rules level and to assume that rules are absolute. Some others who are not legalists nevertheless may use the Bible as if it were intended to be a rule book. In the rules style of reasoning,[5] a question about abortion, for instance, is to be answered by finding a biblical rule that says directly whether abortion is right or wrong. When one then discovers the Bible teaches no rule about abortion, the result is either perplexity or the adoption of a conventional rule.

3. *The Principles Level.* Rules are based on reasons or general principles. We may ask why a rule is obligatory or why a rule should be overridden in a particular case. The answer is that the rule is a specific application of a more general principle which does not give specific direction for what to do but gives a reason for rules that do. Furthermore, the principle is more deeply related to our basic ground-of-meaning beliefs. For example, William E. May has written a thoughtful reply to Joseph Fletcher's position on euthanasia. He argues the importance of the rule against killing and the importance of choosing right means, rather than merely effective means, in the pursuit of good ends. But he is not a legalist. The rule against killing is based on the deeper principle of the sacredness of human life, and there are exceptional cases where obedience to the principle requires an exception to the rule. Following Arthur Dyck, he uses the philosophical concept of the prima facie rule, which suggests that the rule is universally obligatory but that it may be overridden in some cases by a more obligatory rule or principle.

Ethicists who work primarily at the principles level are called "principlists." Barnette's principlism has enabled him to avoid legalism but at the same time to give more specific guidance than the situationists do. In his interpretation of the Ten Commandments, Barnette consistently seeks to identify the principle that is expressed in each commandment.[6] Similarly, in the last five chapters of *Introducing Christian Ethics,* he develops principles to guide decisions in specific problem areas such as marriage, race, and economic life. Or again, in "Elements of an Ecological Ethic,"[7] he develops a set of principles for guiding policies and actions on environmental issues. Barnette's principlism resembles John Bennett's middle axioms approach or Philip Wogaman's method of presumptions, except that he grounds his principles more directly and explicitly in biblical teachings.

At the principles level, there is a debate between teleological types of ethics, including utilitarianism, and deontological types. Frankena describes this debate and convincingly argues for a deontological position.[8]

4. Moving beyond the principles level, one may ask why the principles are binding or upon what they are grounded. This moves to the ground-of-meaning level or the *level of basic beliefs*. For example, in his response to Fletcher, May grounded the principle of life's sacredness on the nature of God and on human nature as the image of God:

> As Christians we believe that human beings are the images of God, his living ikons as it were. And just as the living God, the only God, is an Emmanuel, a God who, as Karl Barth has noted, exists "neither *next* to man nor *above* him, but *with* him, *by* him, and above all *for* him," so we, his ikons or created words, exist with and for one another.[9]

Christian ethicists who work primarily on the ground-of-meaning level are often called contextualists, such as Paul Lehmann, Joseph Sittler, or James Gustafson. The response ethics of H. Richard Niebuhr similarly emphasizes the faith-belief context rather than the rules or principles approaches. Similarly, Everding and Wilbanks point to beliefs about God and human nature as particularly pivotal: "The guidance that faith provides in (the) situation . . . is not given in the form of rules or (principles) but in biblical pictures or images of God and human responsibility." [10]

The strength of contextualism is that it hears the biblical message at a profound level and does not reduce it to a book of proverbs announcing rules and principles. It speaks profoundly to the human situation from the richness and depth of Christian faith, and avoids the closed and boxed-in rigidity of legalism.

Nevertheless, Bennett, Rawls, and Barnette are right in emphasizing the importance of rules and principles. Rules and principles make an ethic specific and concrete, rather than hidden in the depths of mysterious generality. They encourage a prophetic stance based upon a concreteness that "gets to the point," reaches a specific decision, declares it clearly, and is able to be understood and remembered by persons who need specific guidance. Therefore, it is not, as Everding and Wilbanks argue, that faith's guidance "is not given in the form of rules or (principles)." Instead, the importance of all four levels of moral reasoning, and of each level in proper relation to the others, should be emphasized. Rules are not absolute, they rest on principles; principles are not absolute, they rest on basic beliefs; both rules and principles can be overridden by a deeper level of reasoning. But within that contextual understanding, rules and principles are helpful, necessary, and obligatory.

## The Ground of Meaning

When we recognize that moral reasoning rests on basic beliefs, we begin to focus on the second major dimension, theological or ground-of-meaning beliefs. Our task is to identify the pivotal variables in this dimension, and to indicate their content.

Not only Christian ethics, but *any* ethics rests on basic *ground-of-meaning* assumptions. Therefore, we may proceed by a method of correlation, pointing first to the general question that any ethics needs to answer, and then to the terms with which Christians often discuss the question.

The first general question at the *ground-of-meaning* level is, Why ought I act morally? or Why should I consider your way of reasoning ethically convincing for me? This question inquires about the basic relationship between the context in which the "I" has its meaning or purpose and the world in which moral actions have their meaning (the world of creation). Therefore, the Christian answer comes in terms of *human nature,* human purpose, human selfhood, and in terms of *God's creation* of the world and *his rule* in it.

Albert Camus, who does not claim to be a Christian, deals with the question in *The Plague*. For him, the nature of the world is that it is menaced by "a death instinct at loose amongst us." The nature of selfhood is to face the reality of the plague and to do what one can to fight it. Dr. Rieux, in the novel, says it's as simple as $2 + 2 = 4$; the plague is here, there is something I can do to fight it; therefore, I fight it. It doesn't depend on whether there is any chance of success; I simply do what I can.

However, the negative view of creation and the lonely view of the fight are not enough for Camus. In many of his writings (as *The Rebel* and *The Plague*), there is a sense of the call from the infinite—from the infinitude of the sea, the sky, the desert horizon, and the warm sun of the Riviera. There is a sense of solidarity with the Infinite, calling to us through the infinitude of the universe, providing companionship and setting limits for us in our acts of affirmation and rebellion. And there is a sense of solidarity with other selves who are part of the same context of calling and struggle.

H. Richard Niebuhr in *The Responsible Self* and James Gustafson in *Christ and the Moral Life* [11] approach the question from the pole of selfhood, the responding and intending "I." In this approach, the danger is introspective dispositionalism. Karl Barth in *Church Dogmatics* III/4 [12] approaches the question from the pole of the doctrine of creation, and the danger here is doctrinalism. When the two approaches are taken as complementary, a profound depth is given to this question and its answer. One ought to act morally precisely because this is God's world and one is intended to be a moral being.

The second general question is, What is the most basic norm or ethical imperative, and how should I handle the question of compromise between that norm and the realities of the fallen world? Here Christians usually speak of God's love or the kingdom of God as the basic norm, and they often relate this to the world's power-realities through the compromise norm of justice. The question then is the content and meaning of *love and justice,* and how love and justice relate to one another and to *realism.* In Jesus' teachings, the Sermon on the Mount expresses the norm clearly; therefore, a revealing test for Christian ethicists is how fully and how seriously they take the Sermon and how much they seek to limit its applicability to some narrow realm or some other age.

Two helpful statements of the issues involved in the love-justice variable are Daniel Day Williams' *The Spirit and the Forms of Love* and Gene Outka's *Agape: An Ethical Analysis.*[13] Outka shows that some Christian ethicists speak of the norm of love as *sacrificial love*—totally unselfish, uncalculating, noncoercive, not expecting a response or depending on a response. Anders Nygren and Reinhold Niebuhr both speak this way (even though they have significant differences). In this perspective, love is sharply distinguished from justice, which is coercive, self-assertive, and calculating. But in a fallen world justice is necessary; in fact, justice becomes the central operative norm. Its content appears to be derived not from love but from historical discussions of the balance between liberty and equality.[14]

Ethicists such as Williams speak of the norm of love as *mutual love,* hoping for a response of shared community, communication, and cooperation. For him, justice is the principle of right relationship for community. Thus, love and justice are less opposed to one another than they are for those who hold to sacrificial love.

Outka himself proposes that the primary content of the norm of love should be *equal regard* for every neighbor as a person, for his own sake and not for benefits to oneself. Understood this way, *agape* favors a concept of justice that is equalitarian in the sense of seeking to meet each person's needs, which would imply some differences in treatment for people who have different needs. Justice for a blind person would include some additional provisions beyond what others have a right to; justice to a person held back by discriminatory structures would include some compensatory provisions. Barnette's norm closely resembles Outka's equal regard, but he grounds it more directly in God's nature as Creator, and in Scripture: "*Agape* is the basic normative principle of judgment and action. This agapeic love means to will the welfare of all living creatures and things. It is grounded in God, whose being is love (1 John 4:8); and it extends, as does God's love, to the whole creation." [15]

I prefer to speak of *agape* as *delivering love*, emphasizing its dynamic nature as delivering us from varieties of bondage, of idolatry, injustice, and hopelessness. It frees us, delivers us into community, and seeks to meet our needs. Thus, liberty, community, and equal meeting of needs are part of the norm of love. This incorporates the motif of the self's death and resurrection suggested by sacrificial love but with resurrection, deliverance into new life in community, and therefore mutual love, being equally emphasized. Delivering love emphasizes the importance of liberty rather than benevolent paternalism.[16] And its emphasis on deliverance from need implies something of the equal regard motif. It sees justice or righteousness as a biblical term whose core meaning derives from Yahweh's delivering love; therefore, love and justice have almost identical meanings. Both require community with covenant stipulations of laws and rights and with the possibility of occasional coercion as part of the delivering action.[17] Without space to spell out its meaning, however, the norm of delivering love can be only a suggestive metaphor.

Ethics requires the empowerment, motivation, or redemption of the self to will and do what is obligatory. The question is (1) what is the nature of that empowering motivation or redemption? and (2) how is it related to the content of obligation? For Christian ethics, Christ as Redeemer is a central model. However, how or in what sense does his redemptive work give a norm, a content of obligation, to the self who is being redeemed? The classical way of putting this question is to ask what is the relation between *justification* (forgiveness) and *sanctification* (discipleship).

An excellent, systematic and comparative treatment of this question is James Gustafson's *Christ and the Moral Life*. Gustafson examines a disparate assortment of Christian theologians and ethicists, asking how each understands the relation between the work of the Redeemer and the content of obligation. Five major themes emerge, each with divergent understandings of the Christian life. (1) The theme of *justification,* or forgiveness, if emphasized alone and with animosity toward the other themes, leads to a Christianity in which Christ is not the norm for life—at least not in any specific way. Instead, it emphasizes freedom from legalism, freedom to love spontaneously, freedom to be open to the situation and the future. This freedom occurs only so long as Christ does not become a norm for living, a new law, a new and more righteous basis for claiming to be doing the works of goodness as revealed by the Redeemer himself. Still powerful in the Christian, sin is fed its favorite nourishment by the belief that some of us are relatively law-abiding citizens of the kingdom who transgress less than others. Hence, Gustafson says that Bultmann

> clearly dismisses those efforts to formulate ideals, or principles, or theories, or even a conscientious weighing of possibilities and consequences which might give rational guidance to human action. . . . The work of Christ . . . is confined to the gift of grace, of forgiveness of sins. . . .[18]

Bultmann's ethics, therefore, "is not a social ethics, and cannot be such on its own theological and philosophical grounds."

(2) At the opposite pole is the emphasis on *sanctification.*

> For some the principal effect is a new *will,* rightly directed by Jesus Christ. For others the *disposition* is changed—or there is a new motivation or a new intention to seek the good of the neighbor. Extreme perfectionists would tend to include a new *mind* and more perfect *knowledge* as fruits of sanctification.[19]

The serious Christian hungers and thirsts for sanctification. But the danger arises when Christians believe they are full of sanctification or when they believe the cure for the cancer of racism is sanctified individuals without any need for legal and ecclesiastical provisions for correcting Christians who are sinful in ways they do not know or in ways they have fooled themselves into ignoring or in ways they do not care about.

The other three themes all emphasize the normativeness of Christ in different ways. (3) One may emphasize Jesus Christ as *teacher*— either of an attitude or disposition, a direction in action, a law, an ideal or a norm. (4) One may see Jesus himself as the *pattern* we are to follow. He is pattern as a moral example and ideal, as the model of obedience, suffering, and humility, as the one whose desires and flesh are crucified in his passion, or as the revelation of the action of God that can be recapitulated in one's moral life.[20] (5) Finally, one may emphasize Jesus as the *Lord* who is both Creator and Redeemer. The lordship of Christ means that he is Lord in reality and that Christians are called to obey him in the actual situation. Because he *is* Lord, Christians may live with joy and optimism; because he calls people to *serve* him as Lord, Christians may follow him in discipleship, obeying the Holy Spirit and accepting his teachings as norm for their lives.[21] This is the theme emphasized by Dietrich Bonhoeffer, and the theme that best fits the norm of delivering love, because deliverance involves power as well as love. In power and love the Redeemer liberates and calls persons into his community of caring for one another.

4. The final variable in the ground-of-meaning dimension is the answer to the necessary question, What do you assume is the channel or vehicle through which goodness becomes effective in the world, especially in the face of conflict, change, and hope? The answer for Christian ethicists usually comes as the understanding of *the mission of the church.* As Potter suggests, this is usually "derived from the perception of what God is doing in the world through his creation and providential rule, his special revelation in Jesus Christ, and his witness through the Holy Spirit." [22]

The major ways of defining the mission of the church have been analyzed in two helpful typologies—Ernst Troeltsch's *Social Teaching of the Christian Churches* and H. Richard Niebuhr's *Christ and Culture.*[23] The latter already has become something of a classic, but it has two problems that may mislead its readers. It distorts the Christ-against-culture position, suggesting that adherents of that position intend to do without all culture, when in fact their intention is to develop a culture which serves Christ rather than rivals him. And it neglects to suggest what ecclesiastical form each type of Christ and culture relationship requires. Consequently, Niebuhr's readers usually go away thinking they are transformationists but do not discover or develop a church that can support the required tension between Christ and culture. Hence they often slip into dualism or accommodationism.

For a radical Chrisitan, the church must take the shape of an alternative community. For an accommodationist, the vehicle is usually an individual or a church understood individualistically. The church of the synthesist is the established church of Christendom, and the dualist's church is a preaching station. A transformationist requires a *community* that is at once an alternative to the world and a *mission* penetrating the world.[24]

## Perception of the Situation

The third crucial dimension of moral decision-making concerns one's perception of the situation or the interpretation of data. There are many more ways of perceiving the situation of decision than we usually realize, and there are greater disparities between different perceptions than we usually imagine. An unthinking approach is simply to look at what appears to be going on or to read some research and then to accept the results uncritically. Usually one is unaware of how complicated perceiving is, how many different assumptions and values shape one's unconscious selecting, synthesizing, and interpreting.[25] Identifying some of the variables that shape perception might help to show how complicated this process actually is.

One powerful variable is the *threat* that a person perceives—its *nature, degree,* and *linkage* with other elements. For example, Barnette sees the ecological threat primarily as environmental pollution. Its degree is extensive; in fact, it is a crisis. And he sees it as linked to several causes. He warns against the fallacy of the single cause and points to the anthropocentrism of Western culture, to the dominance of technology, to consumerism, overconsumption, and overpopulation as interlocking causes. With the threat being extensively linked like this, the logical solution has to be more extensive, more profound, more radical than adding a technological fix or two. Others describe the cause as intimately linked with a particular economic system or with lust for power and greed for gain. For those who suggest such extensive linkage, the logical solution must range from a change in the economic system to fundamental repentance by masses of people.

How the threat is perceived powerfully shapes one's ethical perspective. And, in turn, threat perception is heavily influenced by ground-of-meaning assumptions about human nature. Threat perception, therefore, is a fundamentally important issue for ethics.

A second critical variable in perception concerns the nature of *authority* in society and its relation to the basic ground-of-meaning norm (love and justice). The authority of government might be thought of first, but other potentially authoritative members of the social system must be added such as the business establishment, the American Medical Association, or the scientific elite. Where one assumes authority in society is *located*, how *legitimate* it is, and what are its *limits* must be asked. The question of limits to authority is also the question of liberty and its rights. Clearly the authority variable is related to the question of the authority of Christ, to love and justice, and to "realistic compromise."

In Christian terms, the authority question is related to the question of the principalities and powers. On this issue, a perceptive typological study of contemporary American theological-political thought has just been written.[26] Four theological norms are derived from the Pauline texts on principalities and powers, which are used to evaluate leading contemporary positions. The norms are: (1) The tension between the already and the not yet in Christ's victory over the powers. This rejects liberal optimism, moral cynicism, and other-worldliness. (2) The lordship of Christ as not only subjective but at least partly objective and normative over the authorities. This rejects any dualism that puts the gospel in a place where its norms are not relevant to political or economic life. (3) The powers as fallen but not demonized. As fallen, they can nevertheless be fulfilling an ordering or preserving function and are called to the service of mankind, to participate in the redemptive activity of God. (4) The powers as potentially demonic when they become idolatrous or unjust. Since the powers are always somewhere on the thousand-step continuum between serving human need and serving demonic injustice and idolatry, there is always need for correcting them with Christ's values of love and justice.

The third variable is the view of *social change*, which is closely related to the view of the mission of the church. Here we ask what *means* of change are preferred, what *allies* are acceptable, and what *timing* is expected.[27] Martin Luther King, Jr. was especially concerned about these elements. His books specifically take up the questions of allies, means, and timing. Again, Barnette illustrates the importance of this variable in his book on the ecological crisis, devoting his fourth chapter to "Strategies for Survival," which is a discussion of ways and means for bringing about the desperately needed changes.

Finally, there is the *information integrity variable*. Some authors openly seek to appreciate viewpoints contrary to their own, and others are closed to dissonant perspectives. Some authors have a manipulative view of information, using it willfully to support their point; others are deeply respectful of objective information. Illustrating the importance of this variable, Barnette writes:

> Perhaps some ecologists have engaged in exaggerated rhetoric. But an "alert-stage" was essential for awakening people to the crisis. The findings of numeous scientists agree—on the basis of research, not vested interests—that there is a genuine environmental problem that threatens the quality of man's life on a worldwide scale . . . .

> Since there are scientists who claim that there is no ecological crisis, should we even be concerned? It should be noted in the first place that such studies have largely been undertaken

for persons or groups with vested interests in business, government, and the military.[28]

Besides the obvious relation of this variable to vested interests, it
also seems related to the theological justification-sanctification variable. For example, to be open to positions that conflict with one's
own, one needs to know on the one hand that one is accepted and
need not be rigidly defensive and to know on the other hand that
one is still a sinner biased by selfish interests and in need of correction from other viewpoints. To be objective rather than manipulative
in communicating information, one needs to have some hope that
truth (sanctification) is possible and can be appreciated and accepted; one must not be purely cynical about the possibilities of
honest communication between persons.

### Loyalties, Interests, and Trust

Barnette's mention of vested interests brings this discussion to
the fourth and final dimension of ethical argument, the *faith-loyalties
dimension*. The loyalties of the heart are what drive the mind's interpreting, and the eye sees only what the mind interprets. Where the
heart's interests are, there will the eye be also; that is why people
are so skilled at detecting the speck in the brother's eye, but so
resistant to perceiving the log in their own eye. They have an interest
in defending their own loyalties. More than one is aware, the log
of the self's narrow interests and unrepentant loyalties filters what
is seen and dominates what is decided. Therefore, ethics that notices
only rational style-of-reasoning questions and overlooks loyalties
and interests condemns itself to ignoring its own motivating forces.

Everding and Wilbanks emphasize the importance of the loyalties
dimension. They call it the *faith* dimension. "The Bible quickly and
persistently cuts through to the core question: 'Who is your God?'
'Whom will you serve?' Our answer to that question is the determining factor in decision making. And it is an answer that is given
more in our lives than in our words." [29]

Because faith-loyalties are so important, they deserve a separate category for themselves. Everding and Wilbanks include them in the ground-of-meaning or belief dimension, but these are two different dimensions, and each needs to be studied in its own right. The difference is between faith as personal trust and belief as doctrinal affirmation. Some who confuse these say we are saved by our faith but mean we are saved by our right doctrine. Then their theology becomes defensive and rigid, their doubt about a particular doctrine drives them to fear for their security, and they attack others who express doubts which they themselves are repressing. Others make the opposite error, reducing belief to personal trust, ignoring the importance of theological articulateness.

The importance of the distinction is clear when Everding and Wilbanks say Jesus and the Pharisees were both loyal to God, had their *faith* in God. However, the Pharisees believed in God as Law-giver, while Jesus believed in God as merciful and loving. A different ethic resulted. Another example: A person holds orthodox *beliefs* about God, but his life indicates that his ultimate *loyalty* is to his money, his automobiles, and his social standing. If only his doctrinal beliefs are analyzed and the faith-loyalties dimension is overlooked, the real disease will be missed.

In addition to the question of ultimate loyalty, there is also the question of *group loyalties*. Everding and Wilbanks describe the issue well in their sixth chapter, "Communal Context." People are powerfully influenced by loyalties to family, to friends, to the place where they work, to race and nation and interest-group ideology. Often these are unconscious loyalties, but they need analyzing, since 96 percent of the distortion in biblical interpretation and ethical decision comes from group loyalties and interests, and only 4 percent comes from minor differences in the wording and translation of the biblical text. Yet the attention and argumentation are often focused on the 4 percent, ignoring the 96 percent. We argue over the speck, ignoring the log. What is desperately needed is to focus on the work of repentance, the work of the Holy Spirit, the work of the church as loving admonisher and corrector. This, of course, relates the question of group loyalties to the mission of the church. If the church is only a one- or two-hour-per-week preaching station, not much correction in group loyalties is likely to occur. The church needs small group admonition and regular communal interaction, engaging those ethical issues and those loyalties where people really are. It needs to be an alternative community that engages loyalties, so they do not hinder but aid sensitive hearing of the needs of all who are in bondage.

## Method in Christian Ethics: A Prospective View

Once the essential ingredients in ethical argument and decision making are noticed, we gain a clearer view of the locations where careful work must be done. Skills in moral reasoning, in the biblical-theological ground of meaning, and in some kind of social theory need to be developed. All these strengthen understanding of the critical variables that have been identified. And in all three of these dimensions, we should be alert to the way faith-loyalties are disclosed that are heightening or obscuring important aspects of an issue.

Furthermore, interactions between the four dimensions should be examined. How critical variables influence each other, and how some variables are hidden in arguments, need to be noticed. We should also look for inconsistencies—and for forced consistencies, achieved by overinterpretation of the data or by screening out important value considerations.

The four-dimension diagram may be seen as depicting key dimensions of a responsible self, of personal character in decision and action. Complete character requires sensitive perception of situations, consistent moral rules and principles, basic beliefs about underlying meaning, and personal loyalties. Moreover, a responsible self stands behind its decisions, accepts accountability for their outcome, and uses the feedback to correct the rules, perceptions, beliefs, and loyalties that lead to bad decisions. In this correction process, the flow of the arrows is reversed and the feedback penetrates deep into the beliefs and loyalties, as well as into the superficial rules and perceptions. This process of correction may be aided if we have identified some of the key variables correctly, so that we can know which variables need correcting. The name for this process of character-correction is repentance.

## Notes

1. Ralph B. Potter, Jr., "The Structure of Certain American Christian Responses to the Nuclear Dilemma, 1958-1963," unpublished doctoral dissertation, Harvard University, 1965; *War and Moral Discourse* (Richmond: John Knox Press, 1969); Glen H. Stassen, "Individual Preferences vs. Role Constraints in Policy-making," *World Politics* (October, 1972), pp. 96-119; "Revising the Operational Code," presented at the annual meeting of the American Political Science Association, September, 1973; "An Operational Code for Studying the Ethical Values and Perception Patterns of Foreign Policy Decision-Makers," presented at the annual meeting of the American Academy of Religion, December 30, 1977; "A Social Theory Model for Religious Social Ethics," *Journal of Religious Ethics* (Spring, 1977), pp. 9-37.

2. The social theory of Karl Deutsch, Talcott Parsons, Alexander George, Ole Holsti, Robert Jervis, and John Steinbruner has aided our research in moral argument on various ethical issues.

3. The discussion of levels that follows is a revision and modification of the work by H. D. Aiken, *Reason and Conduct.* This work has two logical errors which subvert its helpfulness. Corrections incorporated here are explained in my essay in the *Journal of Religious Ethics* (Spring, 1977), pp. 11-14.

4. Bernard Bard and Joseph Fletcher, "The Right to Die," in Paul T. Jersild and Dale A. Johnson, *Moral Issues and Christian Response,* second edition (New York: Holt, Rhinehart, and Winston, 1976), pp. 390 ff.

5. See H. Edward Everding and Dana W. Wilbanks, *Decision-Making and the Bible* (Valley Forge: Judson Press, 1975).

6. Henlee Barnette, *Introducing Christian Ethics* (Nashville: Broadman, 1961). Barnette apparently coined the term *principlism.*

7. Henlee Barnette, "Elements of an Ecological Ethic," *The Church and the Ecological Crisis* (Grand Rapids: Eerdmans, 1972).

8. William K. Frankena, *Ethics* (Englewood Cliffs, New Jersey: Prentice-Hall, Inc., 1972). See also John Rawls, *A Theory of Justice* (Cambridge: Harvard University Press, 1971), who has greatly influenced my own deontological human rights emphasis.

9. William E. May, "Euthanasia, Benemortiasia, and the Dying," in Jersild and Johnson, *Moral Issues and Christian Response,* pp. 399 ff.

10. Everding and Wilbanks, p. 37.

11. H. R. Niebuhr, *The Responsible Self* (New York: Harper & Row, 1963); James Gustafson, *Christ and the Moral Life* (New York: Harper & Row, 1968).

12. Karl Barth, *Church Dogmatics,* III/4 (T. and T. Clark, 1961).

13. Daniel Day Williams, *The Spirit and the Forms of Love* (New York: Harper & Row, 1968); Gene Outka, *Agape: An Ethical Analysis* (New Haven: Yale University Press, 1972).

14. See Reinhold Niebuhr, "Liberty and Equality," in *Faith and Politics* (New York: Braziller, 1968); and chapter IX, volume two of *The Nature and Destiny of Man* (New York: Scribner's Sons, 1943).

15. Barnette, *The Church and the Ecological Crisis,* p. 36.

16. Richard Roach, "A New Sense of Faith," *Journal of Religious Ethics* (Spring, 1977), pp. 144 ff.

17. "All people need power, whether black or white. We regard as sheer hypocrisy or as blind and dangerous illusion the view that opposes love to power. Love should be a [the] controlling element in power, but what love opposes is precisely the misuse and abuse of power, not power itself. So long as white churchmen continue to moralize and misinterpret Christian love, so long will justice continue to be subverted in this land." National Committee of Negro Churchmen, "Black Power," in Jersild and Johnson, p. 146.

18. Gustafson, *Christ and the Moral Life,* pp. 118-119.

19. Ibid., p. 69.

20. Ibid., pp. 153-154.

21. Ibid., pp. 14, 32-34, and 44-45.

22. Potter, dissertation, pp. 422 and 303 ff.

23. Ernst Troeltsch, *Social Teaching of the Christian Churches* (New York: Harper and Brothers, 1960); H. R. Niebuhr, *Christ and Culture* (New York: Harper and Brothers, 1951).

24. See forthcoming book on the ethics of H. R. Niebuhr by John Howard Yoder and Glen Stassen.

25. See John Steinbruner, *The Cybernetic Theory of Decision* (Princeton: Princeton University Press, 1974); Robert Jervis, *The Logic of Images in International Relations* (Princeton: Princeton University Press, 1970).

26. Stephen Shoemaker, "Christ and the Principalities and Powers in Representative Twentieth Century American Theologians," unpublished Ph.D. dissertation, Southern Baptist Theological Seminary, Louisville, Kentucky, 1978.

27. See Dieter T. Hessel, *A Social Action Primer* (Philadelphia: Westminster, 1972) for a helpful discussion of these questions. See also Lyle Schaller,

*The Change Agent* (New York: Abingdon, 1972) and the perceptive typology by William Everett in *Journal of Religious Ethics* (Spring, 1977), pp. 91-114.

28. Barnette, *The Church and the Ecological Crisis*, p. 25.

29. Everding and Wilbanks, pp. 48-49.

# 4

## Christian Ethics and Community Action

### G. Willis Bennett

The community may be thought of as the context for Christian action and reflection. Community is to ethics what one's environment is to thought and action. Thus, it becomes the testing grounds for Christian commitments and the arena for engaging the forces that dehumanize and destroy those for whom the gospel of salvation is intended.

### A Theology Without Social Context

Unfortunately many Christians have not been willing to involve themselves in community affairs the way they might. Sometimes they have been quick to criticize when things go wrong. What they have failed to recognize is that they could be involved in the planning and formulation of much that affects community life. When Christians remain detached and uninvolved in the formulation when the opportunity exists, they forfeit a measurable degree of their right to be overly critical of the end product. By their sheer numbers in many communities, Christians could be far more influential in decision making if they would make the effort. They could contribute to designing the community along lines that more nearly reflects the human values their Christian faith tells them are important.[1] Why does this indifference and neglect persist? There are multiple reasons.

For one thing, the theology of some Christians does not encourage, or maybe even allow, involvement in efforts at social betterment. Some hold to a concept of faith that declares social improvement occurs by changing persons one by one.[2] If you want a better child, they say, you get it by changing individuals through personal conversion, and converted individuals will change the social order. This is only a partial truth. While it is not to be denied, lest one be accused of minimizing the importance of evangelism, it should be seen as an inadequate answer to many of the social ills that trouble society. Poor people living in depressed areas will not have their poverty removed by making professions of faith in Christ. Unemployed persons living in a city where no jobs exist will not have their economic problems solved by a revival meeting. Slums will not disappear, to be replaced by adequate housing, simply because the tenants "received the Lord." Crime does not leave the streets, highway deaths are not greatly reduced, war does not disappear from the earth because mass evangelistic efforts realized great success. If community life is ever to conform more nearly to the standards and ideals of Christ, it will require the conscious and concerted efforts of a sizable number of persons within the community who are committed to those ideals. Wrong theology can stifle; right theology can motivate.

Another obvious reason that many Christians fail to involve themselves in efforts toward community improvement may be traced to lack of knowledge and understanding as to how that involvement may be realized. Some persons wish to invest more of themselves and their influence but do not know where to take hold. They may even have responded with commitment to some appeal to "get involved" but were never told how and never found a way. Someone needs to pay the price required in leadership, for without it organized efforts are impossible of attainment.

Perhaps a third explanation exists as to the reason for social noninvolvement, and that is traced to misplaced priorities. Theology may not forbid it, and lack of understanding may not explain it, for the persons may have both the theology and the ability to become a creative change-agent. What he lacks is the ordering of his priorities in such a fashion as to allow for the time and effort required. He may be so preoccupied with doing other very good things that he never provides the time to work for community change. Gifted Christian people always can find more good causes than their waking hours will allow them to pursue. Encouragement must be given to such persons to devote a more adequate amount of designated effort toward the turning of faith into action within the social order.

Thoughtful and committed Christians do not always agree as to what kind of community action is required. During the recent past, especially throughout the 1960s, many national church bodies made bold pronouncements regarding race, war, amnesty, poverty, and other social issues. In many cases these bodies committed funding to groups designed to work for social justice or to otherwise improve the quality of human life. It has not been an uncommon experience for most of these national religious groups to discover that the action taken by selected few in national assembly was out of touch with the will of the grass-roots membership. Almost without exception, social action has diminished within organized religion within this decade. A return to more traditional approaches of ministry and witness has emerged. This has been true at the congregational level as well. In one survey almost one-half of the pastors questioned agreed with the statement, "My ideas about the church's purpose differ quite a bit with the ideas of my church members." [3] Younger pastors tended to find more disagreement than older ones, and a large portion of that disagreement revolved around the role they felt the pastor should assume regarding social action.

This disagreement between some pastors and their church memberships and between selected leadership at a national assembly and lay leaders back home should not come as any surprise. Converted Christians generally share the prejudices and blind spots of the groups within which they have been nurtured. Advanced education, majoring upon biblical thought, theology, and ethics can be expected to produce change in most ministers so as to bring them to a level of understanding on many social problems which is apt to be different from the position held by lay Christians. Change of attitude by most persons comes slowly unless confronted with a housetop experience like Peter's or other impelling challenges.

### Theology, Ethics, and the Community

How, then, shall the concerns normally associated with Christian ethics become translated into community action? Let us note, first of all, the recognition of the value of life in community and the theological rationale for wanting to preserve and improve it.

The community may be viewed as symbolic of people in the sense of their belonging. Surely God is there in the midst of them. In properly understanding the personhood of individuals one may begin with the personhood of God as Creator and Sustainer of all of life. Human existence is bestowed upon a person through an act of creation, and the Bible says he is made in the image of God. Whatever else this may mean, it implies clearly a likeness in character whereby one can relate to God and to others. Human life has not been brought into existence for life in isolation, but in community. The God who makes all persons ordains that life is to be lived in solidarity. When persons have come together, or have been drawn together, into the possibility of a common life in a given area, God recognized the possibility of his creation being fulfilled in solidarity.

It is not, however, the density of people in limited space that fulfills the purpose of God. Rather it is the recognition by those people that they belong to each other, that their lives are intertwined, that they love, hurt, serve, and bless each other every day. No one can insist on his right to the total disinterest and neglect of all others. The community symbolizes this common life, which can be conceived as a gift of God and guided by him if indeed persons are able to see themselves as related to God and to each other in their belongings.

The community also may be seen as symbolic of people in their efforts at self-preservation. Historically this may well have been the beginning of villages and cities—wandering clans and tribes of people coming together in one place and there building a type of fortress to provide refuge from whatever threatened. Initially, for example, the threat to the life of the city was from without, not within. This has been true of cities in every nation and in every age when cities were young and beginning. It was true of Jericho, and it was true of Plymouth, Massachusetts. How different we conceive of the threat to it shifted from being external to becoming internal. This becomes all the more reason for persons residing within to join their lives cooperatively in efforts at self-preservation and improvement of the quality of life. In cities established on new frontiers, the fort and the worship center sometimes stood side by side or were, indeed, merged into one facility. In a modern day city overwhelmed by its complexities, godly concerns surely are served when the community gives itself to the development of fire protection, health services, provisions for law and order, and other daily needs, just as surely as when it builds its sanctuaries.

Furthermore, the community needs to be viewed as symbolic of people seeking true humanity and fulfillment. Aristotle said, "Men come together in cities in order to live the good life." The organized community usually symbolizes human efforts at finding a better life. Persons drawn together into one geographic community usually have come there on a quest which is the basis of a rational choice deliberately made. This explains much of the mobility that exists in the world today. Persons leave one location and go to another in search of whatever they think will bring to them greater satisfaction.

Physical expansion in a particular community usually stems from an effort at securing a better life too. A new suburban area or a new high rise project is developed in an effort to provide homes and services for persons who have found themselves confined to areas already overcrowded.

Fresh interpretations need to be given to the nature of the good and godly life, and its pursuits clearly need to be seen as not determined altogether by materialistic and cultural norms. The wise person, however, frankly will recognize that human and social needs cannot be ignored if the good and godly life is to be realized. Indeed, this is one of the major concerns to be faced in many communities, both rural and urban. Deprived persons who are to be found among the poor and among minority groups know that their true humanity and fulfillment awaits opportunity of realization. In some cases it will never be realized fully until adequate employment, decent housing, counseling and health services, and equal treatment under the law become possibilities. It should be no surprise that the theologies of liberation have become strong in our day—black liberation, the liberation of women, economic liberation, and other emphases upon human rights.

Theologians ask, "What does it mean to be truly human?" [4] What is it one needs in order to realize true dignity and freedom to experience the life God wants one to have? The answer to these questions is to be found in the proper understanding of the nature of the Christian faith. God is at work in Christ reconciling the world unto himself, restoring his creation to true humanity, and setting persons into redemptive relationships. When the ongoing lives of persons are lived out in the community context, attention must be given to those forces and factors which dehumanize and which rob life of the meaning God intends it to have. Spirituality and religion need to find ways of giving ultimate meaning to daily life by transforming its activities in a manner that will enable the glory of God to be realized.

It seems difficult to believe that this can be accomplished to the fullest without fashioning an environment that will provide opportunities for men and women to rise to the height of their potentials. When one has been restricted by his or her environment from using those gifts bestowed by God, full potential has been stifled and frustration has occurred.

What is there in community life that lies outside the concern of God? Are his concerns so limited as to cause him to be indifferent to much that touches human life daily? No doubt most Christians will readily admit that every human concern is a concern of God. He who clothes the grass and takes note of the falling sparrow also cares for us in ways too minute to identify. If this is true, then a second question demands an answer. What is there in community life that lies outside the concern of the Christian seeking to be faithful to his intention to reflect Christ? If he is to be Christ's representative in the world, can he ignore the causes for such distress?

It is this kind of thoughtful reflection that seems to present compelling reasons for Christian involvement in trying to fashion a social order that will conform more nearly to what God would have it to be. This is not to commit Christians to the obligation of bringing in the kingdom for which they pray. It is, however, an effort at encouraging Christians to be willing agents who join with Christ in the doing of his will. Community action becomes a priority for those who think this way.

Christian faith does recognize that the initial stress for those who would follow Christ is upon *being* rather than *activity*. For Jesus, character always determines conduct. If the tree is good, the fruit will be good also. When the human will is identified with the will of God, right action results. The first question for the Christian is, What manner of person ought I to be? rather than, What acts ought I to perform? As long as the will to do evil is alive in the human heart, the individual cannot possess a thoroughly right disposition. But the redeemed person who has his will set in a new direction needs ultimately to reach beyond himself in the interest of others. The love the Christian experiences has both a Godward reference and a reference toward all persons with whom one has relationships. The Christian ethic, based on the assumption of personal regeneration, requires society for fulfillment. "The good man," John Mackenzie said at the turn of the century, "adapts himself to his environment, but tries at the same time to make his environment better. He does not simply try to keep himself 'unspotted of the world,' but also to clear the world of spot." [5] This insight is even more significant today.

## The Church in Community Action

How are Christians, and how is the church, to become involved in the process of community action? The answer to that question may well be determined by the nature of the desired action. For some Christians, community action is viewed as Christian ministry extending outside the sanctuary. It may consist of engaging in good and generous acts of mercy to persons in need. It may extend the ministry of the church, or of the individual Christian, into hospitals, jails, nursing homes, or other institutions. Or it many not be an institutional ministry but one that reaches human beings in need wherever they reside, work, or play. In recent years, more and more churches have responded to this concept of ministry and have involved themselves in significant ways. Many of them have caught the spirit of "servanthood" and see their new forms of ministry as being derivative from Christ and reflecting his concerns. The proclaimed Word has been merged with symbolic deeds in an effort to minister and to communicate in the name of Christ.

Colin Williams recognized the meaning of this truth and noted that the people of God must be trained "for servant life within the secular structures so that the world may be helped to find the way to its maturity in Christ." [6] Williams pointed out that because social structures have been changing, church ministry must change. The institutional life of the first century was limited when compared to today. Then the church maintained primarily an identification with the world of residence, while today the church has been developing an increasing variety of forms of presence in the public world. The public worlds of politics, industry, commerce, education, leisure, communication, and entertainment largely have been separated from the world of family and residence. New forms of church ministry need to recognize and identify with these public worlds.

This is not a new emphasis, even though for many churches it has become a conscious effort only in recent years. Twenty years ago the National Council of Churches sponsored the National Conference on Policy and Strategy in Social Welfare. From this conference came the following policy statement:

> Social welfare is an integral part of the ministry of the Church, not an optional part of its program . . . . For the Church the social welfare task in all its aspects is not an onerous duty which must reluctantly be undertaken, but a glad response to God in service of man . . . . It needs to be clear, however, that the social welfare mission of the church cannot be evaluated in terms of its success in making Christians out of those whose need is served. While the Church always desires to

open people's lives to the love and power of Christ, it serves human need because it *must* as the response of faith.[7]

In our day most major denominations have become committed to this concept of social welfare as "an integral part of the ministry of the church." Not all congregations have bought the concept, and therefore, many continue to engage in ministry which consists of little more than friendly visitation to those in distress. When limited to this, it falls far short of the type community ministry referred to above.

### Toward a Strategy for Action

A congregation desiring to engage in an effective community ministry to persons in need must begin with some type of survey which tries to document the factual situation. What is needed is to structure a profile of persons, families, and groupings of persons so as to have a valid understanding of the social and psychological characteristics of the people who will be the recipients of the ministry. What are these people like? What manner of life are they now leading? What are their aspirations and their fears? What are their needs not now being met by any organized group? How will they react to the efforts to engage in ministry to or with them? Armed with this kind of factual data, the church is then prepared to consider its next move.

An inventory of resources needs to be made. What resources does the church have which can be used to relieve human suffering, to awaken hope where only despair exists, to aid persons in physical need, to facilitate social adjustment, or to otherwise bring an answer to a troubling situation? Resources may be found from within the congregation or beyond. Sometimes allies exist whose resources may easily be tapped. It also may be true that sufficient community resources exist already and that there are organized channels already in existence to deal effectively with the need. In such case, referral should become the process used, for a church does not need to duplicate services already available.

Once needs and resources are identified, a course of action is devised and followed. It is evident that organized effort is required. Assignments of responsibility will need to be delegated and careful supervision will be useful. Ministry of the type being discussed may be limited to a particular action, or it may be continuous over an extended period. The nature of the ministry and persistence of the need will dictate which it is to be. Continuous ministry requires greater effort and patience, and periodic evaluation always proves helpful.

Let it be noted that the type of community action discussed as *ministry* is exceedingly valuable, and the ethics of love requires that Christians engage in it. We need an enlargement of such ministry. In this discourse, however, it is important that our attention turn to a second type of community action which more normally may be identified with Christian ethics. I speak of the type that generally is not viewed as ministry but as social action.

Christian ethical thought has enabled us to view the social order as not yet being what God would have it to be. At whatever point moral judgments can be made regarding social injustice, corruption, or inequity, opportunities for Christian social action may be identified. In the broader domain of the social order, one may speak of world concerns as related to issues of war and peace, hunger and the Third World, racial injustice wherever it is found, and situations viewed as a denial of human rights. These issues have aroused deep concern on the part of many sensitive Christians in recent years. Sometimes Christian activists have tried to find ways of expressing their alarm and concern so as to bring influence to bear upon decision makers. Actions have extended all the way from mild resolutions passed by church bodies to violent, militant action exercised by isolated individuals or small groups. There has been no concensus as to the issues or the methodology for dealing with these issues. As mentioned earlier in this essay, disagreement between persons is understandable and to be expected. It is unfortunate that disagreement cannot be tolerated in greater Christian graciousness where many of these issues are concerned. Christian social action, however, expects confrontation and learns to live with tension and conflict. Change does not occur easily and without feeling. Hopefully, Christians shall strive to make conflict creative and shall work for ultimate reconciliation.

At the community level, planned action may sometimes be taken which will be related to one of the broader issues mentioned above. During all of the struggles related to civil rights during the 1960s, for example, more action occurred at the community level than was ever experienced nationally. It was because of combined community actions all over the nation on buses, in restaurants, at schools, in organized marches, and numerous other ways, that national consciousness finally produced a climate where legislation and civil rights law enforcement became possible. Similar results could be documented as related to war and peace. National and international issues frequently can be viewed as a cause for action at a community level.

In addition to the broader social issues that may be national, there are issues sometimes identified as altogether local. For example, there may be a specific issue related to a housing code violation or an action at a particular school or an injustice resulting from police action. Whatever the situation, if it is rightly viewed as a violation of human rights, it may become a cause that should not be overlooked by sensitive Christians. As John Bennett has said, "Those of us who still have considerable freedom to speak and to act publicly have no excuse for adhering to a privatistic interpretation of Christianity." [8]

If community action related to social issues is to be effective, attention needs to be given to how such action is to be taken. Seldom can one person, one congregation, or one denomination act alone with very much success. This would cause us to point to the importance of establishing coalitions for action. Communication linkages are needed between churches both within and across denominational lines, and between churches and other organized groups. While an individual congregation may be able to be effective in social action efforts regarding specific and limited issues within the immediate community, there are other situations which demand a collective voice and effort. The official decision makers are not apt to heed the opinions expressed by a limited few when the larger majority of churches and religious leaders appear to approve the status quo or at least are not exercising any complaint regarding it.

Too many religious groups appear to go it alone in the community. They do not know what each other is doing. Little concentrated effort is made and numerous good causes are the losers for it. Communication linkages need to be extended to efforts to provide a greater use of the public media, including television, radio, newspapers, and billboard advertisements. Combined dollars and talents surely will make a much more significant impact upon the community at large.

Especially in the urban community is it important for organized religion to try to witness to social structures. Every urban community possesses a number of important social systems: education, health, welfare, recreation, economic, law enforcement, and others which may be subdivisions of the above. These organized efforts at improving the quality of life in a city are deserving of the support and interest of the church. Many of them are allies and may be used as chief sources for referral of troubled people in need of highly specialized services. Some public and private agencies look to churches for a supply of volunteers to serve on boards and committees or to provide direct service assistance. The church needs to view these opportunities as a part of its community stewardship. Whatever serves to make the city a better place to live, to make human life more human, surely must be seen as a godly venture.

If the church has cooperated in the ways mentioned above, it will be much easier to organize coalitions for social action when the occasion occurs. Churches frequently need to enlarge their religious coalitions to include secular organizations when the cause at hand is one all parties can endorse. Examples and illustrations exist where such groups have been exceedingly effective in appealing to a town board, county commissions, or to other leadership in high elective office.

Social action at a community level usually involves a process which follows a few basic steps. At the beginning there must be some means of enlarging the feeling of discontent with the situation as it is. This status quo does not change apart form a sizable number of persons feeling that a change is desirable. Religious leaders should be able to understand this feeling for it may be likened to a sense of conviction prior to a conversion experience. When the discontent grows, it becomes evident that change is almost sure to occur. It may become necessary to enlarge the discontent so as to create a demand for change. A second step involves whatever may be necessary to determine what changes are required and how they are to be brought about. This may include data collection and careful planning. A third step is the implementation of the change, and this must be followed by creating public support and acceptance. Final action probably will be the "freezing" of the changes so as to provide new stability. At the same time, particularly where Christian groups are involved, there needs to be the effort at reconciliation among those who have been caught up in any of the tensions or conflict.

The personal virtues stressed by Jesus and Paul which are to be identified with any Christian ethical system will serve well in all efforts at social action. I speak of what Paul called the "fruits of the Spirit," with particular stress upon love, justice, patience and forgiveness. Christian ethics speaks the language of "oughtness," and this is closely related to Paul's concept of justice. When he says in Philippians 4:8 to think on "whatsoever things are just," he is suggesting that one should think in terms of the loftiest conception of what is right. It is a Christian axiom that "to do justly" *is* "to love mercy." Justice as a Christian virtue never stood alone. For them one was to refrain from doing wrong or from acting unjustly. While retaliation was forbidden, a different kind of resistance was encouraged when one needed to answer to evil being done. When one resists evil with good, he is neither acting unjustly toward others nor passively submitting to injustice. Rather he is exercising a force which eventually will prove the strongest. This kind of resistance probably requires the free and full exercise of love. Love in the Christian sense requires that if one is to love others he is to recognize their rights, be considerate of their interests and needs, and actively care for their welfare. This will continue to be a goal toward which Christians should strive in all of their human relationships.

## The Minister as Model

This essay should not be brought to a close without some word being addressed directly to the work of ministers in this area of relating Christian ethics to community action. Certainly ministers need to provide models for action, always demonstrating in practice the deep ethical concerns to which they are committed. Such action at times may cause them to be misunderstood but will serve them well in giving validity to their words. Ministers need to have accurate understanding of Christian ethics as taught in the Scriptures and be prepared to preach these truths publicly and discuss them privately as opportunity allows. They need to relate themselves to both religious and secular groups committed to working for the enrichment of human life and the extension of opportunities to those denied them.

James Glasse cautions ministers about the importance of priorities and does so by saying that every minister must "pay the rent" (maintenance) so that he will then be free to serve (mission).[9] In calculating the rent, Glasse warns that the minister must maintain his whole ministry, and this involves personal, professional, and institutional needs. Personally he must not neglect his physical, mental, and spiritual health or that of his family. Professionally he must not neglect his continuing education and his skill development. Institutionally he must not neglect the unique requirements of his local church or agency or the larger group of which he and his church or agency are a part. Having taken care of the maintenance work—the "paying the rent"—he is then freed to give attention to other priorities.

One minister, because of his own unique commitments nad preferences, devoted a large proportion of his time and energy to community action to the neglect of pastoral care and the preparation of sermons. His parish ministry suffered as a consequence, and before long his congregation complained. Major conflict erupted and could be traced to conflict over role and priorities. After conversation with some of the deacons of the church, the minister saw what was happening and decided to start "paying the rent." Soon, with improved preaching resulting from more careful sermon preparation, and with improved relationships resulting from more attention to pastoral care, the minister was able to reduce the congregational complaints. Once in better grace with his people, he was then free to be a community leader who commanded respect and was not subjected to some of the criticisms which before may have been justified.

Priorities must be kept in order, but in any ranking of priorities, the minister must not neglect his commitment to Christian ethics and to appropriate involvement in community action. Some ministers have not used good judgment in exercising this priority and have fallen into serious difficulty with their congregations. When dismissed from their positions, or when they have resigned voluntarily because of the tensions and pressures, they have explained the action by denouncing the congregation as being too narrow, conservative, and closed on important ethical issues. While the denunciation may be rooted in truth, it may not tell the full story if the minister has acted less wisely than he ought and if priorities were out of balance. At best it is not easy to be a prophet in today's world!

There are signs of hope in our nation today. A fresh commitment to human rights has become a vocal point of emphasis in both national and international affairs. Liberation theology continues to find followers from among widely diverse groups. Evangelicals seem to have accepted a positive ethical stance as a responsible part of their witness. True religion and the American way of life are no longer viewed as synonymous. A revival of religion may again be emerging, this time with dependence upon the Holy Spirit in such manner as to not disregard the ethical message of the Scriptures. These signs, if indeed they exist in any valid way, should encourage us to take heart. Jesus Christ is Lord and human beings can still change! Both convictions bring reassurance and provide the hope that social structures also may one day more nearly conform to the ideals of Christ.

### Notes

1. See "The Church and the Dynamics of Social Change," *Review and Expositor,* (Summer, 1971).

2. See Howard E. Kershner, "What Should the Churches Do About Social Problems?" in *Your Church—Their Target,* Kenneth W. Ingwalson, ed. (Arlington, Virginia: Crestwood Books).

3. Paul Turner, "A Study of Attitudes of Selected Graduates of the Southern Baptist Theological Seminary Toward Ministry: 1950-1970," unpublished doctoral dissertation, Southern Baptist Theological Seminary, 1972, p. 144.

4. Paul Lehmann, *Ethics in a Christian Context* (New York: Scribner's Sons, 1963) argues that God's action in the world is aimed at "making and keeping human life human."

5. John S. MacKenzie, *A Manual of Ethics* (New York: Hinds and Noble, 1899), third edition, p. 369.

6. Colin Williams, *The Chuurch: New Directions in Theology Today,* Vol. IV (Philadelphia: Westminster, 1968), p. 102.

7. As quoted in Ernest Johnson and William J. Villaume, "Protestant Social Service," in *Social Work Year Book,* 1960, p. 441.

8. John Bennett, *The Radical Imperative* (Philadelphia: Westminster, 1975), p. 51.

9. James D. Glasse, *Putting It Together in the Parish* (Nashville: Abingdon, 1972), p. 55.

# 5

## Christian Ethics and Pastoral Care

Wayne E. Oates

The purpose of this chapter is to assess the place of moral responsibility in the maintenance of health and to assess the interrelationships of ethics and pastoral care as the contemporary pastor faces these issues. As more and more pastors are being called into specialized settings for doing the work of ministry, the need for a closer alliance between the teaching and learning of pastoral care and the teaching and learning of Christian ethics becomes more and more imperative. Hopefully, some of the observations in this chapter will contribute to that end.

### Moral Responsibility and the Maintenance of Health

No discussion of moral responsibility in relation to the problems of the maintenance of health can make a dichotomy between physical health and mental health. Such distinctions have a long history and reside in the way the modern hospital is set up. However, the modalities of treatment determine the placing of different patients in different areas of a hospital, not the basic nature of health itself. To the contrary, the psychiatric team is just as interested in the electrolyte system of the body, in the cardiovascular condition of the body, the impact of trauma, toxins, and the constituency of the blood as is the surgeon or specialist in internal medicine. Conversely, the purpose of interdisciplinary consultation concerning the welfare of the whole patient points away from the dichotomy of physical and mental disorders to the practice of comprehensive medicine for the whole person.[1] Similarly, we cannot effectively perceive ethical problems involving health by making dichotomies of the physical health and the mental health of a person. After all, a patient makes

decisions as to what he will do with his own body, whether it is
in relation to obesity, to emphysema, to abortion, to the acceptance
or rejection of chemotherapy for psychotic conditions or for inopera-
ble cancer. Life itself is the only physician that does not ask the
patient to decide whether he will take the treatment. In not deciding,
the course of life and the passage of time makes decisions whether
we do or not.

Another reason for rejecting the dichotomy of health problems
into physical and mental problems is that we have discovered since
1952 that mental disorders, so-called for historical and diagnostic
purposes, have their own biochemical and genetic bases. The genetic
bases have been identified in twin studies. The biochemical bases
have been demonstrated through the development of hypotheses
concerning the relation or disrelation of the neurotransmitters of
the body. Specific disorders are named. Schizophrenic disorders and
clinically definable psychoses are treated with phenothiazines. A
relatively wide number of antidepressants, such as the tricyclic
amines and the monoamine oxidase inhibitors, are used to treat
clinically definable depressions. "These increase the availability of
norepinephrine and serotonin at the appropriate synapses in the
brain by inhibiting reuptake of the biogenic amines by the presynap-
tic terminals in the case of the tricyclics, or by preventing the inacti-
vation of biogenic amines, as in the case of the monoamine oxidase
inhibitors." [2] These medications are used along with psychotherapy,
milieu therapy, and family-community therapy. They are not as effective when used in isolation from other treatment resources. The pride,
the greed, the envy, the anger, the sloth, the lust, and the gluttony
must be dealt with in the patient by considering him as a morally
responsible person at the same time. The most careful study of this
dimension of mental disorders—so-called—has been done by Donald
William Backus in his unpublished dissertation, "The Seven Deadly
Sins," at the University of Minnesota in 1969. Edgar Draper, M.D.,
has also made an important contribution in his study, "On the Diagnostic Value of Religious Ideation." [3] These studies are now being
used on an interdisciplinary basis in more than one psychiatric center

for the understanding and treatment of patients. They have been helpful even in staff discussions of whether a particular medication was appropriate. Seeing the patient holistically involves perceiving him as a value-cherishing person as well as a biochemical entity.

A third reason for rejecting a dualism of physical and mental disorders is in order to challenge within the medical settings superficial assumptions about the Christian faith on the basis of popular belief. The influence of Manichaean-like dualism on the thinking of psychiatric patients and medical personnel alike is great. Both are likely to assume that *the* stance of the Christian is to condemn the passions of the human being, the reality of the bodily needs and hungers, and the "rights" of the human body, as such. For the Christian ethicist to reject this outright as heresy after the order of early Gnostics and to assume forthrightly the totality of the human person comes as a surprise and breath of fresh air to the member of other professions. To convince the patient of the legitimacy of anger in the face of injustice, the legitimacy of sexuality in the face of loneliness, the reality of forgiveness in the face of irresponsible uses of the body is a continuing responsibility of the pastoral counselor. I rarely have to convince a patient of the reality of God and God's expectations of a just and holy life. I constantly am faced with persuading patients of the forgiveness of God.

The most important reason, therefore, for rejecting the dichotomy of human illness into physical and mental is the Christian understanding of the incarnation. Any person who does not believe that Jesus Christ is come in the flesh is not of God. To reject the incarnation as complete and thorough lays the groundwork for the rejection of the human body. To accept the incarnation of Jesus Christ as complete and thorough lays the groundwork for the consecration of and ethical devotion of the whole person to let the mind of Christ rule fully in his life. One of the major problems of acceptance of the self that persons in all walks of life face is that of accepting the limitations of their human bodies. In our pride and fantasy, we would rather be without such limits. Mental health, involving the whole person, then, is the disciplined commitment to use the human person to the fullest extent and to live within the limits of our humanity.

## Psychology, Pastoral Counseling, and Moral Integrity

One of the major points of intersection between Christian ethics and pastoral counseling is the importance of moral integrity to the emotional health and well-being of persons. Remarkably enough, this is an intensively busy intersection for strategists and clinicians in the field of psychotherapy behavioral modification. Much controversy and cooperation appears in the realm of the essentially moral issues involved in treatment of emotionally disturbed persons. In order to see this pattern of emphasis in perspective, a review of the different authorities' points of view is needed here. Although this emphasis has a long history, the more recent proponents tend to repeat some of the themes of an earlier time.

O. Hobart Mowrer, a clinical psychologist at the University of Illinois, has been one of the most articulate proponents of the moral context for counseling and psychotherapy. In 1950 he said that much of the Freudian analytic efforts with neurotic persons was "to get persons to 'see the difference' between . . . childhood, when gratification of certain impulses was hazardous, and adulthood when the individual's status is much different." [4] These efforts were aimed at getting the person to *believe* differently about themselves and their own behavior in the world. Mowrer further proposed: "The alternative point of view here proposed is that anxiety comes, not from the acts which the individual would commit but does not, from the acts which he has committed but wishes he had not." [5] Contrary to Freud, Mowrer proposed a "guilt theory" of neurosis rather than an "impulse theory."

Mowrer's quiet voice in 1950 was not heard by many in the field of counseling and psychotherapy. He himself had been in personal analysis. He was seeking to formulate the relationship between "insight therapies," such as psychoanalysis and theories of learning. He came to the conclusion that the moral bases of neurosis were in defective learning and behavior formations. At that time Mowrer was an avowed agnostic. Later, however, in the 1960s he wrote a book entitled *Crisis in Psychiatry and Religion.* He dramatically flayed psychoanalysts for implying that the psychoneurotic has no moral responsibility. He chided those of us in the field of pastoral counseling for abdicating our own commitment to a distinctly moral and ethical view of life in deference to psychiatric "disease" theories that divested the person of personal moral responsibility. I would respond to this by saying that he had not read the literature thoroughly in the field. If he had he would have found that some of us were saying the same thing as much as fifteen years earlier. He, nevertheless, felt that to focus neurotic behavior accurately one might as well "beard the lion and use the strongest term of all, sin. Sickness generates pessimism and confusion by assigning moral responsibility to the domain of psychopathology. Sin, for all of its harshness, carries an implication of promise and hope, a vision of new potentialities." [6]

About the same time, Thomas Szasz, a psychiatrist himself, began to delimit psychiatric disorders to those in which there is a demonstrable physical basis. He decried the tendency of his profession to be driven by the social expediency of the medical profession to identify defective patterns of behavior as *diseases.* He insisted that this was to remythologize older moralities as disease entities when in reality they are irresponsible forms of behavior for which the person should be held responsible as a person rather than to be given a "psychiatric out." Thus psychiatry becomes a form of social control rather than a discipline of medicine as he thinks it should be. Szasz says that the entire mental health movement is a gigantic pseudomedical ritual that has made a religion of mental health. Psychiatrists began to "call illness anything and everything in which they could detect any sign of malfunctioning, based on no matter what norm." [7] More recently he has insisted that psychiatry has now become a willing tool of the bureaucratic process of the state through the psychiatrization of behavior through laws and budgets of the government.[8] In his book on schizophrenia, he scores his own profession for the lack of specificity in the use of the category. He insists that this syndrome is approached more like it were a religious symbol than a disease.[9]

Even another psychiatrist has reexamined the concept of mental illness and personal responsibility. His name is William Glasser. He frankly set forth six principles as a form of treatment he named reality therapy. First, he rejects the concept of mental illness because it communicates to the person that he is not responsible for his own acts. Second, he works in the present of the patient as himself and not as some surrogate for a father, a mother, a sibling, or other person in the patient's life. Fourth, he does not look for unconscious "why's" of the person, which only allow the person to have excuses for behavior based on unconscious motivation. Fifth, he emphasizes morality and perceives the patient as a morally responsible, value-perceiving person. Sixth, he teaches patients better ways to fulfill their needs as opposed to conventional therapists who perceive teaching not to be their responsibility. The main thrust of Glasser's approach is to offset the iatrogenic disorders that arise out of conventional psychotherapy, such as intellectualization of superficial insights, projection of blame upon one's past, one's parents, one's unconscious, and so forth.

A final author who has taken the challenges of modern psychiatry seriously is Karl Menninger, in his book *Whatever Became of Sin?* Menninger traces the history of how deviant behavior was first interpreted theologically and psychiatrically. The norm of deviance is the least common denominator of culture, whatever one can get by with at the time and place. Menninger reevaluates the concept of sin as useful because it identifies something to be eliminated or avoided. Sin also calls for decision and further action. It implies answerability to someone to whom our behavior matters. He says that seeing behavior as sin can provide a hopeful view of a more righteous life. "The present world miasma are partly the result of our self-induced conviction that sin has ceased to be, only the neurotics need to be treated and the criminals punished. The rest may stand around and read the newspapers. Or look at television . . . If the concept of personal responsibility and answerability for ourselves and for others were to return to common acceptance, hope would return to the world with it!" [10]

A critical reconstruction of these points of view from within the field of psychiatry is somewhat as follows. At the outset, one sensed a considerable amount of professional competition between psychologists and psychiatrists in the somewhat wholesale attacks of Mowrer. Nevertheless, the psychologists made their point well enough that it was affirmed from within the field of psychiatry. Szasz and Glasser are psychiatrists and criticize the profession from within. However, as a minister and pastoral counselor, one does not "join up" in such interspecialty and intraspecialty rivalries if he is clearly identified and functioning as a pastoral counselor. Pastoral counseling does not need to apologize for itself or to run to either psychology or psychiatry for legitimization. It stands on its own.

In standing autonomously as a pastoral counselor, one can say that even in the work of Szasz, Mowrer, and Glasser, all of whom insist upon reviewing behavior from a responsibility and moral point of view, one does not find any clear answer to the questions of the source of authority for moral behavior or the definition of what the high, higher, and highest good really is. It is necessay to go to persons like Lawrence Kohlberg for any serious handling of these issues by a behavioral scientist.[11] Mowrer and others tend to rely upon operant conditioning models of consequential morality in terms of *paying* for wrong doing. They rightly reintroduce the whole idea of restitution and penance into moral instruction. Yet, they are not exempt from the bondage of the law of which Paul speaks; neither do they take into consideration the "expensive grace" of the ethical commandment of Jesus that we love one another as he has loved us. Jesus did not do away with the law; he personalized and incarnated the law into the spirit of his love. That is what pastoral counseling as done by a Christian ethicist is all about: an effective demonstration of the ethical seriousness of Jesus Christ in an intense and durable human relationship of counselor to counselee.

Finally, the discipline of Christian ethics cannot be based upon the least common denominator of what society considers as good.

The discipline calls for heavy examination of the thesaurus of Christian history in dealing with difficult ethical problems. This history reaches back and embraces the content and interpretation of the Old and New Testaments. For example, the "token economy" treatment of state hospital patients by rewarding them for appropriate behavior and denying them for inappropriate behavior was done on a mass cultural scale in both Judaism and Catholicism when they were the ruling power in the culture. Harmful side effects, or iatrogenic disorders, arose from this form of treatment just as they do from psychiatric treatment today. Nathaniel Hawthorne's *Scarlet Letter* reveals how Protestant New England's reward-and-punishment system produced similar iatrogenic effects. When any system of ethics is given the force of law, then the next move is to transform offenders of the law into criminals and to use some kind of force upon them. Compassion ensues and in a secular society that has been "medicalized," the next step is to consider the behavior as "sick." That is the situation today against which Mowrer, Glasser, and Szasz are protesting. As Ivan Illich says, "Medicine, like all crusades, creates a new group of outsiders each time it makes a new diagnosis stick. Morality is as implicit in sickness as it is in crime." [12]

Christian social concern is always tested for integrity at the point of its understanding and outreach to these "outsiders." Therefore, it is imperative that pastoral counselors maintain a clear sense of our own identity and prophetic responsibility by not simply blending chameleon-like into the medicalization of society. Religious ethicists have a reputation, thanks to Freud, for creating compulsive obsessional mental disorders. Medical doctors never cease to remind us of this. Yet, they cannot see our real flaw, that we love political power just as much as they love their power and are joint contributors with them to the *character* disorders of which they speak in their diagnostic and statistical manuals. They themselves have created a large group of outsiders to whom we must address our sense of mission as pastoral counselors. The incarnation of the Spirit of God in unconditional attempts at communication and the establishment of a Christian community is only beginning to be tapped as a source of strength for persons labelled "schizophrenic," "depressed," "character disorders," and so forth.

## Illness and Accepting Personal Responsibility

Several ethical issues emerge critically in relation to the patient's sense and acceptance of personal responsibility for his own life in any form of illness. The issue emerges every day when a person calls in "sick." This could mean anything. The person may have decided that he does not want to work that day in protest against real or felt injustices suffered on the job. He may feel a "bout of the flu coming on" and decide to rest in bed for a day rather than work so that he will not miss several days of work. Or another possibility is that he needs extra money, is due a "sick day" a month, and takes that day to do additional work elsewhere to add to his income. The possibility that he may be suffering a hangover from a drinking party the night before enters a new gray area of illness and personal responsibility.

A second issue arises within a hospital meeting. A patient will occasionally say that he would rather be in the hospital facility than at home. This patient will be in no hurry to be dismissed. When faced with the ordeal of returning to old stresses, he may "break out" with a new or an old set of symptoms. One of the most poignant examples of this I have seen was a middle-aged man who came to our unit early in the morning and asked to be readmitted. When asked what the trouble was, he said that he wanted to get back into the hospital because all of his friends were there. He did not like being away from his friends. There are a considerable number of patients whose *only* sense of home, community, and church is experienced in a mental hospital. The person who reads Isabelle Anderson's *Gentle Asylum: Life at a Mental Hospital* will get the interior view of the patient's adoption of the hospital as a home.[13] The ethical issues this poses for the excluding nature of the Christian community where only sameness counts and difference discounts are legion.

Yet from a medical ethics point of view, ethical issues arise which are vigorously debated in university faculties of psychiatry and in the literature. Let me enumerate a few of these in the form of questions:

1. To what extent does the psychotherapist provide the patient with a psychiatric "out" from responsibility? Would this person otherwise be in prison, for example? Is the hospital being used as a form of social control of illegal behavior instead of treatment for clinically definable disease? Does the psychotherapist himself get angled into the corner by authoritarian referrals from courts and law enforcement officials which make the person "serve his term" by getting psychotherapy? To what extent is such involuntary treatment effective and is the psychotherapist being used? Is this an encouragement of moral irresponsibility?

2. On the heels of the above questions, let us ask about the absence of any idea of restitution and/or penance in psychotherapy. Assuming that a young or old person has come to the psychotherapist under duress, would not a way of holding him responsible be to explore ways in which he can make amends for real wrong that has been done? Alcoholics Anonymous has included this in their "Twelve Steps" in their commitment to make amends for wrongs done to persons, except where to do so would cause more harm.

3. What are the ethical problems involved in space utilization in a private psychiatric hospital or in a public one, as well? In a private hospital, the pushing demand to keep beds filled to capacity for budgetary purposes makes the temptation to extend the treatment of a patient or to be lackadaisical about the time a patient is *allowed* for treatment necessarily one that has to be weighed against the ethical issues involved in pushing patients too hard to get well too fast. The recent flurry of excitement created by the book *The Solid Gold Stethoscope* raises many of these questions about treatment processes. Plush hospitals supported by insurance coverage are too often being referred to as "Blue Cross-Blue Shield Hiltons." In public hospitals, a more acute problem of the shortage of bed space arises. For example, in an eighteen-bed emergency and rapid treatment

hospital, how does the physician allot beds that are too few? Shall he use a bed for a man who is threatening to kill his girl friend or shall he use the same bed to hospitalize a patient who has decompensated into a psychotic episode shortly after open heart surgery? The ethics of "triage," or sorting out patients as more acutely in need from the less acute need, is a grim responsibility of the night call resident who makes such decisions while the rest of the community of care tries to get some sleep.

4. To what extent can or should a psychiatric facility be used to take over the failure of control of acting out adolescents? Does making an identifiable patient of the adolescent not increase his proneness to remaining an irresponsible adolescent? Behavior modification methods of treatment are the "in" thing with such adolescents. However, the behavior-modification therapists are more often psychologists than psychiatrists. Are hospitals used as a behavior modification center, with the hidden curriculum that the patients are not really sick and the formal treatment scheme being that they are in a hospital and therefore eligible for insurance coverage at the same rates a person with a coronary occlusion in intensive care? If other professionals than physicians, such as pastoral counselors, clinical psychologists, and social workers, are going to use nonmedical means to treat behavioral problems, then is it not an ethical responsibility to develop a nonmedical institution for such treatment and not rely upon the "medical model" for insurance coverage in a hospital setting? If insurance coverage is not used, then taxes from the state are used to support such institutions.

### Neurosis, Sin, and "the Law"

The treatment of psychiatric patients reveals an ethical problem confronting the religious establishments of the community. A steady flow of appeals from other staff members to clinically trained pastors involves the referral of patients who have such ideas as follow: "I have committed the unpardonable sin." "I have sinned away the days of grace and there is no hope for me." "I am at odds with everybody in my family because they say I neglect them in order to do the work of the Lord at my church."

The critical ethical challenge points toward the quality of preaching to which these people listen as a steady diet, whether from the pulpits of their churches or from radio and TV religious programs. The "Moonies" of the Sun Moon cult are not the only persons who are "brainwashed" with authoritarian messages that fall back into bondage to the law from which Christ died to set us free. One psychiatric resident whom I supervise has asked for additional time in the study of the New Testament. Last week she had read carefully the book of Galatians. She asked: "When Paul talks about the 'law' in his day, does this not also refer to the misuse of the rituals and practices of churches today in which people have lost their freedom in the Spirit through falling back into the slavery of the law?" I think so. Behavior control and thought control are one piece of cloth. Brainwashing and forced indoctrination are the same regardless of external trappings. A lockstep conformity to the "program" of this, that, or the other unbendable set of legalisms is, on balance, the same issue with which the psychotherapist and gospel are dealing. It is at hand: the loss of freedom through compulsive obsessional obedience. Lawrence Kohlberg and others have pointed out that this is the most infantile and primitive level on which ethical issues are solved.

## Ethics and Psychology in Pastoral Care

The practice of pastoral care has a data base that can be defined in terms of what the caring pastor has to do in his caring. About 65 percent of pastoral care situations are focussed upon the family and its cohesion and conflicts. The family provides the context in which much aberrant behavior takes place, many crises both traumatic and developmental occur, and a considerable number of times of celebration happen. Psychopathology is interwoven in the pastoral care of families and is inseparable from it. Therefore, I would suggest that the four bases of data for the practice of pastoral care are as follow: 1) biblical interpretations of the good life, 2) ecclesiastical teachings on ethical issues, 3) therapeutic psychology and psychiatric information, and 4) contemporary religious groups and their prevailing currents of influence.

Pastoral care is at heart the practice of moral theology. I would prefer to use the term *ethical theology,* because the word *moral* has popular connotations of either sexual or trivial implications. To be ethical means to be able to hang together as a whole person with integrity in the face of stressful decision making. The pastor has the responsibility of doing this himself. Can the pastor, with integrity as a whole person, take his stand as a faithful interpreter of the ethical standards of his church and/or denomination? The ethical stands of the churches themselves prompt many persons to seek pastoral counseling. Prominent among such stands is the teachings of churches about divorce and remarriage. The critical issue about the remarriage of divorcees is not the particular stand of a person as much as it is the psychological and spiritual coherence of the pastor and the church in the stand that they do take. For example, a graduate student in Christian ethics and I saw a couple together who have a handicapped child. The husband in the couple had been previously married. He says that they went to church regularly after they met each other and before they were to be married. However, when they asked the pastor to perform their marriage ceremony, he said that his own convictions would not permit him to do so. The regulations of the church would not permit it, and he was in agreement with the church. We asked how the couple felt about this. Much to our surprise, they said that they appreciated his honesty and his standing for what he believed was right. They said they appreciated him, too, because he did not just brush them off. He took an hour and a half to converse with them about their plans and hopes. He has stayed in touch with them ever since, even though they went to a justice of the peace for a civil ceremony. They said: "He would not perform our wedding ceremony, but he showed us he cared and he prayed for God's blessing upon us. He has been concerned about our life ever since." I must say, however, that this is an unusual story.

When the pastor begins to deal with such problems as divorce

and remarriage, he is both psychologically and spiritually related
to persons either with or without integrity. The man of the couple
above said: "I would have lost respect for him if he had said: 'I
can't marry you here in the church, but if you will come over to
my house I will do so.'"

The practice of moral theology has a long and venerable history.
The Catholic theologians have dealt with the problems of marriage
canonically and have accepted the responsibility of thinking and
searching through the reasons for the stands they have taken. Sometimes this is called casuistry, or the science of dealing with cases
of conscience. The pastoral theologian seeks to bring the whole counsel of God to bear upon particular cases of need. Pastoral care today
has too often been enamored of its psychotherapeutic sources of
data to take seriously the expectation that people with "cases of
conscience" have that we as pastors deal forthrightly and with integrity with them in particular. They expect of us rightly as William
Blake said in his *Jerusalem:*

> He who would do good to another must do it in minute particu-
> lars
> General Good is the plea of the scoundrel, hypocrite, and flat-
> terer,
> For Art and Science cannot exist but in minutely organized
> particulars
> And not in the generalized demonstrations of Rational Power.[14]

In dealing with particulars of cases, the task of the pastoral counselor is to take the ideals of the teachings of the New Testament with
a fierce kind of seriousness and at the same time to examine with
equal care the details of a particular person's life. Many Christians
do not want this kind of particular attention. They would prefer
that the pastor leave such matters alone. However, the commitment
of the pastoral counselor is to build prayerfully a relationship of
trust to the person that will enable that person to feel the grace
and freedom from threat as he makes his plight and possibility
known. As such, then, we learn how to deal ethically with persons

as individuals in the context of conscience, forces of community, and church.

Therefore, the particular data of the behavioral sciences are of primary concern as a part of the data base of the pastoral counselor. Enough literature has been developed by pastoral care as a field of knowledge to qualify the pastoral counselor as a behavioral scientist in his own right and not as a pseudo-copy of a psychologist, a psychiatrist, or a social worker. These data are little known and little read by these other professions, just as pastors are remarkably uninformed in large numbers about the data of the other behavioral scientists. In my own book *Pastoral Counseling*,[15] I have suggested that the uniqueness of the pastoral counselor is that he has expertise in the field of ethics and is an ethicist. This does not mean that he is a walking conscience for everyone, although many people consider themselves so wooden and without mind as to try to make Jimminy Crickets out of their pastors. Rather, the pastoral counselor works patiently at enabling the counselee to gather data and to reflect upon it before forming an impulse decision in haste. The pastoral counselor functions on the new covenant. As Jeremiah records, the Lord said: "I will put my law within them, and I will write it upon their hearts; and I will be their God, and they shall be my people" (Jer. 31:33, RSV). This respect for both the privacy of the individual and the power of God from within germinates wisdom and commitment. Germination and imposition are antithetical, the one is brought about by the Spirit and the other operates on the basis of law. One gives life. The other kills.

The integrity of the pastor as a caring person is the final issue of consummate importance both psychologically and ethically. Not to have sold one's soul for a single meal, as did Esau, or to have sold one's soul for position and place in the ecclesiastical establishment or the political establishment of the state provides the beginnings of that integrity. Yet, it is just this kind of person that people with "cases of conscience" are looking for. They will intuitively know when they see such a pastor whether he speaks words that have been given to him by other human beings to say or whether they should look for another who is indeed attuned to God first, last, and always. This makes the task of being a pastor a "case of conscience" in and of itself. The letter to the Hebrews (5:1-3) summarizes that case of conscience well:

> For every high priest chosen from among men is appointed to act on behalf of men in relation to God, to offer gifts and sacrifices for sins. He can deal gently with the ignorant and the wayward, since he himself is beset with sin. Because he is bound to offer sacrifice for his own sins as well as for those of the people.

**Notes**

1. See John Schwab, *Handbook of Psychiatric Consultation* (New York: Appleton, Century and Crofts, 1968).

2. Frank M. Berger, "Present Status of Clinical Psychopharmacology," in *Clinical Pharmacology and Therapeutics*, Vol. 19, No. 6 (Saint Louis: C. V. Mosby, Co., June, 1976), p. 726.

3. Edgar Draper, "On the Diagnostic Value of Religious Ideation," *Archives of General Psychiatry*, Vol. 13 (September, 1965), pp. 202-207.

4. O. Hobart Mowrer, *Learning Theory and Personality Dynamics* (New York: Ronald Press, 1950), pp. 338-339.

5. Ibid., p. 537.

6. O. Hobart Mowrer, "Some Constructive Features of the Concept of Sin," *The Crisis in Psychiatry and Religion* (New York: Van Nostrand,) pp. 40 ff.

7. Thomas Szasz, *The Myth of Mental Illness* (New York: Harper & Row, 1974), pp. 45-46.

8. Thomas Szasz, *Ceremonial Chemistry* (New York: Anchor-Doubleday, 1975), p. 52.

9. Thomas Szasz, *Schizophrenia: The Sacred Symbol of Psychiatry* (New York: Basic Books, 1976), p. xiv.

10. Karl Menninger, *Whatever Became of Sin?* (New York: Hawthorn, 1973), p. 188.

11. Lawrence Kohlberg, "Moral Stages and Moralization," *Moral Development and Behavior* (New York: Holt, Rhinehart and Winston, 1976), pp. 21 ff.

12. Ivan Illich, *Medical Nemesis: The Expropriation of Health* (New York: Pantheon Books, 1976), p. 46.

13. Isabelle Anderson, *Gentle Asylum: Life at a Mental Hospital* (New York: Seabury Press, 1976).

14. William Blake, *Jerusalem.* See Bennett Cerf, et al. (eds.), *The Complete Poetry and Selected Prose of John Donne and the Complete Poetry of William Blake.* (New York: Modern Library, 1941), p. 961.

15. Wayne Oates, *An Introduction to Pastoral Counseling* (Nashville: Broadman, 1959).

# II
# Current Issues
# in Christian Ethics

# Introduction

The most persistent problem confronting the church since its inception has been that of its relationship to society. Social issues confront people with challenges for their faith and opportunities for creatively and redemptively applying the gospel message. But they are also the issues that test the church's ability to translate theology into concrete response. Society itself becomes the testing grounds for the fruitfulness of faith. Too often, the church has responded by retreating into its own circles, refusing to speak to social problems, or else has aggressively attacked the world as the enemy of faith and addressed social problems with simplistic moralisms.

A more faithful approach is to translate the fullness of the gospel into terms which are healing and redemptive to society itself. Thus, the church will actively embrace the world as the arena of God's redemptive activity. It can be an effective instrument for God's salvation of the world.

To be sure, the issues confronting Christians are too numerous to mention. They range from those that threaten the survival of humanity itself to those that affect the quality of life in personal, family, and social dimensions. The issues treated in this section deal with four major areas of concern: family life, including the women's movement; bioethics; liberation movements; and issues related to politics. In all these areas, the church's commitment to seek justice and righteousness in the social order is a vital ingredient in its mission to the world.

Future directions for the family have been the subject of debate and speculation among family specialists for some time. The impact of the sexual revolution and rapid social change on the family have raised concern over its prospects for survival. Harry N. Hollis, Jr., associate director of the Christian Life Commission of the Southern Baptist Convention, examines this debate in the first chapter of this section. Hollis, who is author of *Thank God for Sex* (Broadman, 1975), helpfully steers between a despairing pessimism and an unrealistic optimism. The family will survive, he believes, but with considerable modification from traditional forms and functions.

Sarah Frances Anders, professor of sociology at Louisiana College, examines moral issues in the women's liberation movement. After assessing the "coming of age" of the women's movement, she explores its impact upon church and society. Author of *Woman Alone* (Broadman, 1976) and a contributor to *Christian Freedom for Women* (Broadman, 1975), she contends that the church has been a major hindrance to women's rights but has been the theological and biblical base from which to become a major force in the liberation of women from oppressive and unjust social forces.

The essay on bioethics explores the relationship of moral values to scientific technology and their impact upon the future of humanity. Paul Simmons, author of *Growing up with Sex* (Broadman, 1973) and contributor to *A Matter of Life and Death* (Broadman, 1977), first introduces bioethics as a discipline of study before assessing the various responses made to the "dangerous knowledge" of scientific technologies. These, he points out, are usually based upon one or more religious or theological assumptions about God's relationship to the created world. He concludes by offering moral guidelines for scientific research.

On a closely related subject, Eric C. Rust, senior professor of Christian philosophy at Southern Baptist Theological Seminary, deals with a Christian understanding of nature. The author of *Nature: Garden or Desert?* (Word, 1971) and *Science and Faith* (Oxford, 1967), Rust here sets forth a theological interpretation of man's relationship to the evolutionary process and calls for an ethic of ecological responsibility toward nature.

Themes in liberation ethics and theology are the concern of Bob Adams, who teaches Christian ethics at Southwestern Baptist Theo-

logical Seminary. Adams first became involved with liberation movements and theological concerns as a missionary in Brazil. He points
out that liberation theology had its inceptions in Central America
with the struggle for economic and political justice. Even so, says
the former professor at New Orleans Baptist Theological Seminary,
the theme of liberation has also become important to theologians
among blacks and women. He concludes by raising critical questions
for liberationists that should serve as points of discussion and debate.

Emmanuel McCall explores the role of the black church in the
struggle for justice in the United States. Director of the department
of cooperative ministries with National Baptists, McCall argues that
the black church has given birth to the leaders who have been most
effective in bringing about meaningful social change. The author
of *The Black Christian Experience* (Broadman, 1972) and adjunct
professor of black church studies at Southern Baptist Theological
Seminary, McCall argues—contrary to popular belief—that the basis
for the black church's concern for justice is in the character of its
theology. The social activism of the sixties is now to be found in
certain parachurch movements such as SCLC and PUSH, he says.

The need for the church's involvement in the political arena is
the focus of the chapter by C. Welton Gaddy, pastor of the Broadway
Baptist Church, Fort Worth, Texas. The frequently misunderstood
notion of religious freedom and separation of church and state are
helpfully explored by Gaddy, former director of Christian citizenship
development for the Christian Life Commission of the Southern
Baptist Convention and author of *Profile of a Christian Citizen*
(Broadman, 1974). His concern is that separation of church and state
be guarded but that it not be used to rationalize noninvolvement
in politics. He also points to specific ways in which the church can
create citizenship responsibility on the part of its members.

This theme is extended to the problem of war by Earl Joiner,
professor of religion at Stetson University. The prominence of war
within history does not mean that the church has failed in its search
for peace, he argues. Rather, it shows the complexity of the problem,

the church's own ambivalence toward violence, and the need for more intelligent and planned participation in politics. After surveying historic attitudes toward Christian participation in war, Joiner, himself a veteran of the European campaign in World War II, argues that more attention should be given to foreign policy. This is the area in which the ground is laid for conflict or for peace among nations.

# 6

## The Future of the Family

Harry N. Hollis, Jr.

The family is the most intimate and significant of all human relationships. It is a cell unit of society and a matrix of personality.

—Henlee H. Barnette[1]

The family, Michael Novak has suggested, *is* the future.[2] If he means by this that the future of civilization and the future of the family are closely intertwined, Novak is certainly correct. It is clear that the family's future is an issue of crucial concern to everyone. This chapter will examine the prospects for the family and offer some Christian guidance for families to use in facing the future.

### Contemporary Attitudes Toward the Family's Future

There are as many attitudes toward the family's future as there are people; but for the sake of analysis, three broad attitudes will be mentioned.

#### "Family Is Dead" Pessimism

Some pessimists say that family life, as we know it, is doomed. Ferdinand Lundberg declares, for example, that the family is "near the point of complete extinction."[3] Psychoanalyst William Wolf announces that the "family is dead except for the first year or two of child raising. This will be its only function."[4]

Although he is not a pessimist himself about the future of family life, Wallace Denton of Purdue University points out that most of the basic functions of the traditional family have been taken over by other institutions.[5] *Production* of goods has been assumed by factories and shops. *Protection* has been taken over by police, welfare agencies, insurance companies, and courts. *Education* has become the responsibility of the schools. *Recreation* has been assumed by commercial establishments. *Religious instruction* has, to a large degree, become the sphere of the church. *Reproduction* is still safely a function of the family, but there is a danger that scientific developments leading to the perfection of mechanical wombs might even place this function in the laboratory. The *socialization of the child* is probably one function that will remain a firm assignment of the family of the future, but day-care centers and other institutions may even usurp this task. A final function is *providing emotional security* which may be one of the family's most important functions in the future, but therapy groups and outside friendships have assumed some of this responsibility. Thus, those people who are pessimistic about the family's future claim that they have some solid ground for warning of the demise of the family as we know it.

**Golden Age Optimism**

In antithesis to this "family is dead" pessimism, some family observers maintain that the family is getting ready to enter its golden age. The forces of social fragmentation will drive people deeper into their families, according to Professor Irwin Greenberg, who believes that the institution of the family will become our "portable roots." [6] This optimism has been echoed by the influential sociologist, Talcott Parsons, who sees present family changes as mere "sparks off the anvil of adjustment." The important task of the socialization of the small child and the meeting of the family's deep needs of emotional security make the family more important than ever before, according to Parsons.[7]

**Family Realism**

The truth about the family's immediate future probably lies somewhere between the gloom of the pessimists and the glory of the optimists. The family will have its ups and downs. The family will not automatically enter a golden age—but neither is it doomed. Those who have written obituaries for the family have done so prematurely.

From the biblical perspective, the family is rooted in the will of God. The view that God "setteth the solitary in families (Ps. 68:6) is a foundation for believing that the future of the family is secure.

But, given the impact of sin on institutions and on individuals, blind optimism about the family's future is a luxury one cannot afford. What is needed is a realism based on a biblical understanding of the family.

Such realism begins in the belief that marriage is a divine relationship given by God so that a man and a woman can become one without losing their individuality. Marriage brings fulfillment and joy as its purposes set forth in the Scriptures are pursued: companionship (Gen. 2:18-22), procreation and rearing of children (Gen. 1:28), and constructive sexual fulfillment (Gen. 2:24). The future of the family is closely related to the foundations of marriage: (1) the principle of monogamy, (2) the principle of permanency, (3) the principle of fidelity, and (4) the principle of *agape* love which is the ultimate ground of marriage.[8]

Churches have a great opportunity to minister to families in our society. Indeed, more and more churches are developing family ministries which are not only strengthening families but also enriching the total life of the church. The future of the family can be undergirded by the church, and the future of the church can be vastly enhanced by healthy family life.

### Forces Affecting Families

The future of the family depends then, on a realistic examination of its foundations and purposes. Account must also be taken of those powerful forces at work on the family, shaping its forms, affecting its content, and to some degree determining its direction. Several things can be said by way of predicting the future course of the family and indicating certain influential factors already at work.

First, *family life in the future will be affected by a variety of marital patterns.*[9] Experimentation with various patterns of marriage is a present reality and will continue to influence the family of the future. Here are some of the patterns which families will have to face.

*Unmarried patterns.* An increasing number of persons will decide not to marry at all. Included in this group will be the *single celibate* who decides for various reasons not to marry. Some will not marry because the opportunity will not present itself. Others will be celibate for vocational reasons. Jesus serves as a model for these vocational celibates. The *single noncelibate* will choose to stay single and have sexual intercourse with one or many partners. Unfortunately, unmarried cohabitation, or *quasi-marriage*, a presently popular pattern, will continue to prove attractive to many people in the future.

*Monogamy.* Does the future have any place for monogamy? Absolutely, but there is little doubt that this pattern of marriage is under attack. *Traditional monogamy* is the pattern in which one man and one woman are married to each other for life and have sexual intercourse only with each other. This pattern reflects the ideal set forth in the New Testament; and it is certainly, at present, a minority pattern. Enrichment of marriage and the practice of contagious monogamy can bring this pattern into more widespread acceptance in the future.

In their book *New Dynamics in Sexual Love*, Robert and Mary Joyce describe *celibate marriage*. This is certainly a rare marriage pattern practiced from time to time in history, most recently by the Shakers in this country. The Joyces anticipate a "virginal universe" in the afterlife by practicing a marriage now with love but with no sexual intercourse.[10]

*Varieties in Marriage.* There are many departures from monogamy today, and these will have an increasing influence in the future. There is nominal *monogamy without sexual fidelity*, a pattern which has been called everything from "flexible monogamy" by Robert Francoeur to "structural adultery" by Robert Rimmer. Then there are *serial marriages*, the practice of marrying, divorcing, and remarrying perhaps several times, which is a modified form of polygamy.

The three-stage marriage is another form of serial marriage discussed by Alvin Toffler in his extremely popular book *Future Shock*.[11] Toffler predicts that in the future people will be characterized not by their marital status, but by their marital career. The first stage of this career will be a trial marriage, or several trial marriages, in which couples will live together without having children. The second stage of the marriage career is one in which a couple will chose to have or adopt children. This childbearing stage will last until the children are ready to leave home to work or to go to college. Then will come the third stage of marriage—the couple will either stay married to each other or marry someone else. This third stage will probably represent the longest stretch of uninterrupted matrimony and will last until one of the mates dies. These three-step marriages may be rather widespread in the future. As a matter of fact, they are already being practiced to some degree now.

*Contract marriages* represent another departure from monogamy. Just as an automobile operator's license has to be renewed every few years or it expires, so will the marriage contract have to be renewed if this approach is made legal. The couple will be given a license for several years, and the marriage will automatically be dissolved if it is not renewed.

*Homosexual marriages* are already widely practiced in this country. There is no indication that these marriages will diminish in the future. Indeed, many homosexual persons are now openly agitating for the legalization of such marriages.

*Polygamy.* Will polygamy make a comeback in the future? There is some evidence that it is being practiced now. *Triangle marriages* usually involve two women and one man, although occasionally this ratio is reversed. Robert Rimmer and others hold that triangle marriages are practiced widely on an informal basis in this country. *Group marriages* are also an informal kind of marriage being practiced today. This pattern will likely continue in the future. Some are advocating a kind of *golden-years polygamy* in an attempt to deal with the fact that there are more females than males among aged members of society. Will "Geritol power" lead to a continuing practice of golden-years polygamy in the future? It is possible, but doubtful.

How can Christians respond to the impact on the family caused by a variety of marital patterns in the future? The church is called to respond by upholding the New Testament ideal of marriage as a loving monogamy in the midst of changing marital patterns. The truth of the matter is that much monogamy has been filled not with love but with mutual manipulation and exploitation. It takes the kind of love that Christ had for the church to fill monogamy with joy and intimacy.

Christians are called, therefore, to practice a contagious monogamy in their families. They are called to share the good news that marriage can provide the intimacy and fulfillment that people so desperately seek.

Not all people will marry or stay married. Some are called by God for celibacy and some for marriage. In whatever pattern we find ourselves, we are called to practice self-giving love. Salvation is based not on being married or unmarried but on one's relationship to God in Jesus Christ.

Second, *family life in the future, in America at least, will be affected by a decrease in the number of children.* "Stop at two" is a popular button being worn by a number of young people these days. Some say they will stop at one child or even choose to have none! The bumper sticker, "The stork is not the bird of paradise," reflects the growing belief that an excessive quantity of babies does not guarantee happiness. Some groups call for compulsory birth control. Whatever the means, voluntary or otherwise, it is certain that the size of families of the future will be small. Leonard Benson predicts, in his book entitled *The Family Bond,* that an increasing number of poor people will practice birth control in the future, and this will have staggering social implications for family life at all levels of society.[12] This will mean that there will be fewer lower economic class children who can thus be better provided for by their parents. These children will be able to compete in education and economics with children of the middle economic class. The result will be a meritocracy, a society where children will compete across class lines so that people will be able to reach the level of economic achievement which their gifts and accomplishments merit.[13]

How should Christians respond to this decrease in the number of children? The primary purpose of marriage is not procreation but companionship. The church should advocate parenthood as a special calling and the responsible stewardship of childbearing. Further, Christians can seek to develop a sense of oneness with others in the global village so that the problems of the human family can be faced together. Birth control is one way of bringing quality to all relationships. The nations of the world must have a will to live in interdependence for "global cooperation" [is] essential to survival." [14]

Christians can respond with support for and advocacy of an economic system that enables more people to have an opportunity to get a better education and acquire more of the material goods essential to life. When this happens, the impact on the family is bound to be a positive one.

Third, *family life in the future will be affected by changes in male and female roles.* There is little doubt that liberation movements will continue in the future. Hopefully, unhealthy aspects of these movements will be eradicated, but there is no chance that important changes brought about by liberation will be undone. These changes will continue to have a profound impact on the family. More and more women will pursue careers outside the home and give less time to mothering. Professional parents with degrees in child development will specialize in rearing children whose parents leave home to work.

Men will change in the future also. They will give more attention to parenting, to tenderness, to expression of feelings. Stereotypes about "manly" actions will be shattered as more men spend time working in the home at tasks once considered to be the woman's responsibility.

Christians can respond to the changes in male/female roles by teaching that persons are called by God to be what one has been created to be—human beings of the male or female variety. Those changes which are taking place that humanize people can be celebrated and supported. The church can give active guidance and support to these efforts to remove unhealthy stereotypes about male and female in society and seek to rid itself of prejudice within ecclesiastical structures. In Christ each is freed to become a complete human being; for, "Christ's liberating grace is making it more possible for male and female to participate on an equal basis in the actualization of the new age of love and justice." [15]

Fourth, *family life in the future will be affected by the biological revolution*. Achievements in space, as awesome as they are, will prove to be far less spectacular than the changes brought about in family behavior and relationships as a result of scientific and technological developments. Sexual behavior in the family will be radically affected. One-hundred-percent effective contraceptives will enable people to separate sex entirely from reproduction. Artificial wombs may be developed. Frozen sperm banks will be used by more and more people. Test-tube fertilization will probably be routine in the future. The practice of embryo and ovary transplants will increase. The process of aging may be slowed down. The enhancement of intelligence and memory editing will take place. The modification of genes through genetic engineering will hold both wonderful and awful possibilities. Cloning—the process by which an entire organism is reproduced from one cell—may become a reality.[16]

The future development of human beings has been discussed by Professor Jean Rostrand who predicts that future humans may be strange bipeds combining the properties of self-reproduction without males like the greenfly; of fertilizing the female at a long distance like the nauiloid mollusk; of changing sex like the xiphosures; of growing from cuttings like the earthworm; of replacing its missing parts like the newt; of developing outside its mother's body like the kangaroo; and of hibernating like the hedgehog.[17]

Even if a portion of these biological predictions come true, family life in the future will be drastically affected. Christians can respond to such a revolution by accepting science's search for truth, while insisting upon the responsible use of what is discovered. All knowledge should be used in ways that enhance the dignity and personhood of women and men. Any attempts to manipulate humans by turning them into mere mechanical things should be resisted.

As families face complex decisions growing out of the biological revolution, they can use as a guide the biblical concept of the will of God as love: "Where the Bible does not speak directly to issues raised by biomedical technologies such as the transplant of organs, recombinant DNA (gene splicing to create new organisms), and genetic manipulations, one must seek ethical norms in harmony with love." [18]

In truth, the biological revolution offers great opportunities for enhancing family life. Better health care, safer contraceptive techniques, and the elimination of many hereditary diseases can add quality to life in general and family life in particular. Life-enhancing developments can be encouraged while those developments which would make family life subhuman should be resisted.

Fifth, *family life in the future will be affected by changing sexual attitudes and behavior.* Pluralism in sexual attitudes and behavior seems likely to continue in the future. Our society will certainly not adopt the sexual promiscuity of Aldous Huxley's *Brave New World,* where no personal commitment with sexual partners is allowed. But many will remain in a "sexual wilderness." It is probable also that society will be more tolerant of deviance from the standard of heterosexual relationships in marriage. Premarital intercourse will likely increase. The double standard will disappear as women demand the same so-called "freedom" to be sexually intimate outside of marriage that men have long had. Homosexuality will be more readily accepted. Pornography will always be around, but people may be less fascinated by its revelations as unhealthy sexual attitudes are discarded by many. Sex education will eliminate many of the unwholesome attitudes that make the exploitation of sex in television, movies, and books so popular.

The family will be strongly affected by these changing sexual attitudes and behaviors. The removal of sexual myths will enable husbands and wives to have more profound sexual intimacy. At the same time, greater anonymity and mobility in society will make possibilities for infidelity infinitely greater. Children will get better information about sexuality from parents and teachers. They will also face increased pressures for sexual experimentation. The often negative teachings about sexuality on television will work against sexual responsibility.

Christians can respond to this new sexual pluralism by sharing the good news that the Bible teaches that sex is God's good gift for the enrichment of human life. Furthermore, the necessity for the proper control of sex, so essential for genuine sexual fulfillment, should be affirmed. Sexual expression should be as God intended it, not because sex is evil but because sex is good and should enhance human growth and fulfillment.

Christians can work energetically to see that the church teaches and enables parents to teach positive sexual values. The crisis in sexual morality should be grasped as opportunity and challenge by the church for it "has the greatest opportunity of any institution to strengthen moral quality in sexual relations. It possesses the resources, personnel, and a Christian philosophy of sexuality." [19] The family profits most when sexual responsibility is taught and practiced and the family suffers the most when sexual irresponsibility flourishes. If families of the future are to be healthy, sexual integrity is essential.

Sixth, *family life in the future will be affected by changing religious beliefs and practices.* Religious pluralism in our society will strongly influence the family life of the future. Likely there will be periods of strong religious revival and decline from time to time. But all evidence points to a variety of religious beliefs and groups in the future. Children will bring home their friends of other faiths and increasingly family members will find themselves talking to people who profess no religion at all.

A significant rise in the amount of leisure may cause a decline in church attendance. In the future, more people will work four days a week and this will give fifty-two long weekends a year. Some predict that a three-day work week may be a reality by the end of this century. This will bring about radical changes in worship patterns. Families will go away on weekends, leaving places where they work and worship. Pastors will likely counsel people by means of picture phones. Worship services will be videotaped and played by the family at a time when they can all be together. During the week small groups will meet in the church for sharing and service in the community.

Such changes in the future undoubtedly will diminish the religious fervor of some families. Some church-related institutions will suffer as religious zeal declines, but the picture is far from dismal. Christ, who saw families through the changes of the Renaissance and the Industrial Revolution and who walked with humans blundering their way into the nuclear age, is great enough to uphold those facing the uncertainties of the future. There is a bright side. The new leisure will give families more time to laugh and pray together and to minister to human needs in the community. New technology will help provide food to feed the hungry and mass media to communicate more rapidly the good news to those who are spiritually starved. Genuine New Testament Christianity can enter a golden age if the guidance of God's Spirit is sought in the life of families. Both in the present and for the future, "Christianity has good news for all families. Problems in relationships are not taken lightly but seriously by Christian teaching. In Jesus Christ all barriers, no matter how large, can be removed. All fractured relationships can be restored." [20]

The church, according to Barnette, can assist families as they face the future in the following ways:

(1) stress the biblical view of marriage and family;

(2) provide studies for youth on the preparation for marriage and family life;

(3) establish a counseling program for those who are having martial problems and for divorcees and those who plan for remarriage;

(4) urge members to visit divorced people to provide emotional support, spiritual strength, practical guidance, and help with children;

(5) conduct family life conferences in churches to provide biblical exploration of all problems related to family;

(6) encourage the establishment of marriage enrichment programs so that all marriages can be strengthened and troubled marriages can be helped;

(7) study the Scriptures on divorce and remarriage, forgiveness and reconciliation; and

(8) provide a Divorce Anonymous group for people where there can be candid discussion of the problems and where support to each other can be given.[21]

## The Family's Future and Christian Hope

A realistic appraisal of the family in the future requires that we recognize that it will face tremendous pressures. But the family will survive. Its future is bright because it is protected by the great promises of God. Christians are called to work with God in the world to make families reflect what God intends them to reflect—self-giving love. To be sure, the family must not become an end in itself, for this would be an idolatry of the family. Rather, family life can be lifted to its place of rightful importance as the God beyond our families who lifts persons to himself and who enables persons to have quality in all relationships in the family is recognized.

**Notes**

1. Henlee H. Barnette, *Introducing Christian Ethics* (Nashville: Broadman Press, 1961), p. 111.

2. Michael Novak, "The Family *Is* the Future," *Reader's Digest*, (March, 1978), p. 110.

3. Ferdinand Lundberg, quoted by Alvin Toffler in *Future Shock* (New York: Bantman Books, 1970), p. 238.

4. William Wolf, quoted by Toffler, p. 238.

5. Wallace Denton, *Family Problems and What to Do About Them* (Philadelphia: Westminster Press, 1971), pp. 12-13.

6. Irwin M. Greenberg, quoted by Toffler, p. 239.

7. Denton, op. cit., p. 13.

8. See Barnette for a discussion of this understanding of the family in *Introducing Christian Ethics*, pp. 111-127.

9. For additional discussion of forces facing the family see Harry N. Hollis, Jr., *Thank God for Sex: A Christian Model for Sexual Understanding and*

*Behavior* (Nashville: Broadman Press, 1975), pp. 156 ff.; and Harry N. Hollis, Jr., compiler/contributor, *Christian Freedom for Women and Other Human Beings* (Nashville: Broadman Press, 1975), pp. 172 ff.

10. This pattern is mentioned in an article by Robert Francoeur, "Technology and the Future of Human Sexuality" in *To Create a Different Future,* Kenneth Vaux, ed. (New York: Friendship Press, 1977), p. 91.

11. Toffler, pp. 254-255.

12. Leonard Benson, *The Family Bond* (New York: Random House, 1971), p. 373.

13. Ibid.

14. Henlee H. Barnette, "Ethical Issues: 1971," a resource paper prepared for the Christian Life Commission of the Southern Baptist Convention, pp. 19-20.

15. Helen Barnette and Henlee Barnette, "Co-archy: Partnership and Equality in Man-Woman Relationships," The Edward A. McDowell, Jr. Lectureship at Furman University, May 3-4, 1977, p. 7.

16. For a discussion of some possible biological developments see Gordon Rattray Taylor, *The Biological Time Bomb* (New York: The World Publishing Company, 1968), pp. 204-205.

17. Cited by Taylor, p. 55.

18. Henlee Barnette, "Biomedical Ethics: A 'Now Christian concern'," Baptist Press release, February 10, 1977, p. 1.

19. Henlee Barnette, *The New Theology and Morality* (Philadelphia: Westminster Press, 1967), pp. 69-70.

20. Barnette, "Ethical Issues," p. 20.

21. Ibid., pp. 19-20.

# 7

## Moral Issues in Women's Liberation

Sarah Frances Anders

God's cosmic purpose is the liberation and maturation of all human beings, and indeed of all creation, to full participation in an ecstatic universe of love and joy. The current movements of liberation—of colonialized peoples, Blacks, peasants, women, and even of nature from its thralldom to man's greed— are the groanings and reaching-outs of this universal process. As such, people of faith rightly sing about these stirrings, struggle within them, and discern in their anger and aspiration the sure signals of a coming new era.[1]

The most recent movement for the rights of women nears the end of its second decade. The seriousness of its desire for moral and social change accounts, in large part, for its survival in spite of many diverse internal factions and considerable external ridicule or denigration. The prevailing current image of the "federated" parts of the movement is not "women's lib," but "feminism." As such, it is a deliberate surge for equality and equity to be taken seriously by church and society.

Thus, as some have declared, the National Women's Conference 1977 in Houston was something of a "rite of passage," where more than fourteen thousand women delegates of many persuasions discovered common grounds of moral unity. The greatest moral victory perhaps was for those who emerged with a new sense of identity, "I don't have to be a radical to be a feminist." *Time* magazine declared that during one weekend and one day, "American women had reached some kind of watershed in their history, and in that of the nation." [2]

131

At Houston moral and legal plurality, if not unanimity, developed twenty-five resolutions that called for presidential action. This, from a kaleidoscope of women, including such subgroups as three thousand strongly conservative, profamily delegates, over forty-five hundred non-Caucasian minority women, and at least four hundred anti-abortion, anti-ERA women. These resolutions concerned fourteen major issues, from which the media particularly labeled three as the "hot" ones: the Equal Rights Amendment, abortion, and lesbian rights.

This is not just another article about the history of the oppression of women in our civilization and nation nor of the role of the church in aiding and perpetrating discrimination against the sex of the "second creation." Rather it is intended as a "white paper" on the salient moral issues as viewed by the feminists *and* the church, certainly not two discrete bodies.

The church cannot deny the spiritual roots of the movement. Therefore, it must concern itself with the four major arenas of ethical concern in the movement: woman's personal identity, her roles in the home, her vocational life, her worship, and spiritual service. Along with concern about woman's moral and spiritual rights, the church must also take serious note of the predictable and already-present disruptions that the movement may be contributing to or enhancing.

## Personal Identity Issues

### Quality Humanness

The feminists are calling for first-rate personhood for women. The Christian feminists are maintaining that men, women, and children will have quality humanness separately only when they possess it collectively. The church must not play the game of one-upmanship in its theology of creation: the real issue in woman's right to full selfhood is not in the order or simultaneous nature of the creation of the sexes but in the joint claim to the "image" or model of the Divine for their own being and becoming. *Both* male and female are heirs to the nature and nurture of God. However unique they

may be between and within their sex groups, the overriding common-
ality is their divine role model.

**Status Rights**

A second moral issue in the women's movement is the right to
*individual status.* Granted, to be human is to be social and to be
ascribed some derivative statuses by virtue of one's relationships;
but thinking women are now observing that to be truly fulfilled as
wives, mothers, daughters, or friends, they must first be permitted
to attain personal and independent status. If there is duality of status,
then women, like men, must understand and cultivate their gifts
and natures before they can be fulfilled in a dyadic experience.

Critics have mistakenly accused all feminists of forsaking meaningful relationships, even opposing men, marriage, and motherhood,
of being radical, and nonsocial. The question is not personal status
*versus* derivative status. If there is a theology of personhood, it surely
must require equality for all people in attaining fulfillment both as
*self* and as *other* to someone else's self. Can the church and society
grant a woman the right to be a self and have some status apart
from her relationship to men and children?

**Sexuality**

Eventually one comes to a very basic issue in the movement—
the feminine principle in sexuality. Conservative women have stated
that proponents of the ERA want to reconstruct America into a gender free nation with no differences between men and women. Yet
in dialogue two of the oldest movers in the feminist crusade, Betty
Friedan and Simone de Beauvoir, found common ground in their
belief that neither unisex nor lesbianism are the trademarks of the
movement; indeed, these ideological concepts could immobilize it.
The movement to them is not a warfare against men nor a crusade
to become supermen. Likewise, motherhood and sex are *not* the
enemies women fight.[3]

Many criticize the movement for its apparent inconsistencies on
the issue of sexuality. On the one hand, it urges women to glory
in the exclusiveness of their bodies and to experience life distinctly
through femaleness. On the other, it measures success in terms of

male achievement patterns: "anything you can do, I can do—or better." This sometimes may be true and noteworthy, but it infers a rejection of feminine sexuality in an attempt to be supermales. The urgent need is for a positive modus operandi for attaining full humanness through femaleness.

Moreover, the church must not allow the attempts of lesbian groups at fusing their movement with the feminists to confuse the major ethical concerns. Just as there are qualitative differences between God and human, there surely are between man and woman. The moral issue is whether status assignments will be based on gender or on individual differences. Someday we may be secure enough to assert that maleness and femaleness are not absolutely discrete; we already know that masculinity and femininity are not. Most of us are hybrids possessing some of each of what society calls feminine and masculine traits. Hence, the moral problem and illogic of attaching superiority/inferiority to stereotyped sex roles become painfully obvious.

Acknowledging that there are unique female experiences, it is imperative to move on and acknowledge that there is a void of role models for women to see the full range of their beings. This is what Carol Christ has referred to as "the experience of nothingness," as she analyzes the archetypal and prophetic role of Martha in Doris Lessing's *The Four-Gated City*. Martha Quest in her spiritual journey to find her unique identity has no appropriate array of role models to aid her. So she drifts through the ordinary experiences of marriage, motherhood, sexual love, and the out-of-the-ordinary alternatives of Leftist politics and quasi-psychology only to find them all unsatisfactory for her. Yet the search to find the right image for herself seems ever hopeless.[4] Ms. Christ sees this as a social and theological commentary on the experiences of some contemporary women.

## Assertiveness

Another moral issue involved in the whole identity crisis of contemporary woman is the question of the *right to assertiveness*. John Scanzoni has written about this perceptively when he states that "Christian women seem to be able to be assertive toward other

women and toward children but not toward men." He defines assertiveness as determining what one must do because it is right in
God's sight and is just and fair to self and others—and then to act
on these convictions. It is neither offensive nor defensive in nature.
The total process is trying to help others profit by your assertiveness,
not trying to hurt or dominate them.[5] There are numerous biblical
and historical examples of assertive women: Deborah; Lydia; Dorcas;
Mary, who anointed Jesus' feet; Florence Nightingale; Jane Addams
of Hull House; Catherine Booth of the Salvation Army. Not only
must society provide the climate for such assertiveness, women must
rise to their moral obligation to know God's rightness, to process
their gifts, and to act courageously for the good of all in family,
church, and society.

## A Rightful Place in the Home

Perhaps there is no need for a reminder that the myth, "A woman's
place has always been in the home," is just that—a myth or, at
best, a half-truth. For a score or more of centuries, between the
pastoral economy and the Industrial Revolution I, all family members—men, women, and children—worked and consumed as a team
in and around the homesite. Historical honesty requires us to remember that all three left the household scene during the early phase
of the factory system. It was only a generation or so later that our
nineteenth-century forebears determined that home was the place
for women and children (not even school for them!).

### Truth in Labeling

We do not need to make "honest" women out of women in non-
domestic roles as much as we must make society honest in the use
of *housewife* and *mother* as the exclusive labels for the women
whose chief roles are connected with the home and family. Technology probably allows the average wife and mother to be no more
"married to the house" than the career wife who still tends to house-
keeping duties in her at-home hours. Certainly, schools and other
child-oriented groups remove children of working and nonworking
mothers the same number of hours from home and family supervi-

sion. The home-based woman may differ only in the amount of time
she can devote to personal, church, and community concerns.

## Choice and Sanction in Primary Role

The ethical concern becomes then: which life-style does a woman
prefer and which will church and society "bless"? Is any one life-
style inherently more feminine, more creative, more appropriate, better for society? Can the church claim scriptural priority for the woman
who chooses marriage, fertility, and home-roles above Lydia who
sold purple and Priscilla who partnered in a couple business in the
New Testament era or vice versa? If so, should it not investigate
the priority that fatherhood and male home responsibilities would
hold over corporation, professional, or even church positions?

One of the most interesting movements developing over the country is the Martha Movement, which affirms the value of homemaking
and the equality of personhood possible to those women who feel
most suited for and called to it as the primary vocation of their
lives. It seeks to encourage pride and skill in the choice for domestic-
ity in the event that the notion has indeed spread abroad in the
land that happiness no longer is possible in the domestic role or
strictly within the family unit.[6]

## Equal Benefits

The women's movement, in its strongest elements, has not made
the homemaker a forgotten woman, though some would claim it
has seemed to foster the woman of the business and professional
world as the more liberated model of feminism. The movers and
shakers among the feminists are making demands for legislation
to provide Social Security and other benefits for the homemaker.
Family economists are quick to point out that the average homemaker
may be producing services over a twice forty-hour week, even though
many of her activities are not confined to the household. Even at
minimum wage level, she would be worth work benefits deriving
from at least $14,000 worth of labor and skills.

## Choice in Parenting

So much controversy has developed over the issue of abortion
as related to the women's movement, that the much broader issue

of right to choose the parent role has been ignored virtually. At the heart of either contraception, childbearing and parenting, or abortion is the feminists' assertion that woman has claim over her body and any prospect of new life within it. It ignores the Christian feminists' stand that both marriage and parenthood (or childlessness) constitute dual decision making and commitment. Therefore, concern over one's life, health, and death as well as the creation of a new life and person are not independent, but other-related matters for deliberation, choice, and responsibility.

The broader perspective demands neither dominance nor exclusiveness in decision making, but equity and justice. No longer can there be a battle between patriarchal control over wife or child-making and complete, autonomous control over one's body or life. For the Christian, feminist or not, it is as ethically reprehensible for a husband/father to work himself into a fatal heart failure on the claim of concern for the welfare of his household (over the protest of his family) as it is for a woman to prevent or destroy life within her body without consideration for the husband's convictions, just because Mother Nature has designated her the first carrier and nurturer. The moment one enters a dyadic relationship, with God or man, one ethically forfeits the right to absolute sole decision-making rights over matters of mutual concern in favor of equitable, if not equalitarian input into couple solutions.

More specifically, responsibility does not stop when both husband and wife have decided to prevent parenthood and which method *one* of them will employ. Whether one has a vasectomy or one takes a pill, both continue to share responsibility for the decision and the act. Whatever the circumstances of decision making about aborting a new life, jointly produced, both mates share ethical responsibility before, during, and following the act.

## Parenting

The women's movement has raised questions about parental responsibilities that can not be brushed aside lightly: Why must it be the woman who gives up work before and after birth for the primary care of children? Why should the father not be called at work when a child is sick at school or the maid does not show up? Why not count all of child care expense as a legitimate tax deduction for a solo working parent, male or female? Should there be absolutely discrete behaviors for mothering and fathering? Can a parent preserve sufficient masculine and feminine role models for their children without complete separation of work roles and parental tasks? Does a nongender God prescribe that men and women avoid role overlapping in every social arena?

The church must answer questions related to roles connected with extended "parenting" that takes place through the church programs. Does it not need to ensure masculine and feminine sharing among those who lead out in the religious training provided during the nursery and preschool years? The religious rights of children may well demand that they learn that rocking, burping, storytelling about Baby Moses in the bulrushes, bathroom assistance, and group play in church buildings are not exclusively feminine tasks.

**House-care**

Women in the liberation movement maintain that one of the greatest slowdowns in equalizing life responsibilities and privileges comes in the mundane matters of household tasks—cooking, cleaning, laundry, garbage-disposal, yard, and house maintenance. Is this too pragmatic and nonsacred a domain for theology and ethics? If we believe the Gospel account of the activities distribution in the Mary-Martha-Lazarus household, almost every family household has had to deal perennially with the work ethic and the rightness of certain tasks for certain folk!

The movement has been accused of contributing to the dysfunctions of the American household. Indeed, a man *may* be intimidated if he has a macho view of certain roles. Demands of feminists *could* enhance the insecurities of any family member who has not been nurtured to see the worthwhileness of any labor and the maturity of being flexible in task-taking.

## Equity and Responsibility in the Work World

The assessment of one woman scholar and writer in the mid-70s about the impact of the women's movement on women's rights in the business and professional world still obtains. Jessie Bernard maintained that an even greater problem than lobbying to get equal rights legislation is getting enacted rights implemented.[7] No other minority workers have had quite the problem of forcing the implementation of just and moral practices almost entirely on their own behalf. A number of women task forces and professional groups are assuming the task of monitoring the status of women in various work settings.

### The Urgency of the Issue

Between 1960 and the mid 1970s, the number of working women nearly doubled, while the number of working men increased by only one-fourth. Excluding part-time women workers, there are now about half as many women workers as men. These gains notwithstanding, many areas of women's work life need to be improved. Women are still concentrated in clerical, operative, and service positions, and there are still inequities in income according to sex.[8]

Industry has done a better job of affirmative action in both hiring and job promotion than the professions, academic institutions, or even the church. Women in semiskilled and lower white-collar positions have been protected and promoted in fairer proportions than in the managerial and professional positions which carry higher prestige and greater educational expectations. Equal opportunities in hiring, salary, promotion, and corollary benefits become less and less likely as one climbs the occupational ladder.

### Ethics in the Professions

No dramatic accomplishments have appeared since the early 1970s in the legal and medical professions, although the number of women admitted to freshman classes in the professional schools has moved upward toward one-third representation.[9] Motivation and education both lag when women still comprise only 5 percent of the lawyers and no more than 10 percent of the doctors.

Bernard observed that universities are turning out women Ph.D.'s in much larger quantities than they are hiring them.[10] Women may make up about 20 percent of the faculty and administration of higher education but the salary gap between men and women reaches five thousand dollars in larger universities.[11] It is somewhat noteworthy that the smaller private and church-related colleges are dealing more equitably with women faculty than large and prominent universities. The integrity of higher education becomes suspect when one considers the conclusions of a recent survey of the American Association of University Women in six hundred institutions.[12] Despite affirmative action programs, the situation on campus is "change without progress" since there have been no significant gains for women in the last five years with respect to tenured faculty, administration, presidents, or trustees. A fairly common practice is the hiring of great numbers of women in the part-time and untenured faculty ranks, which represent assured minimal salaries. Short-term contracts negate the possibility of upward mobility and consideration for professorial and administrative ranks.

Over eight years there was a drop in the number of institutions without women trustees from 21 percent to 12 percent, but 79 percent of all trustees are still men.[13] The only thing approaching a dramatic increase in any area for women was in the number of institutions providing child-care facilities—from 5 percent in 1970 to 33 percent now.[14]

Belonging in a category to themselves are churches and seminaries. Since this writer first appraised the situation of church, denominational, and seminary placement of women in key leadership roles earlier in the decade, there have been no overwhelming signs of reconsideration of the ethical position concerning their proportion in top-level and policy-making positions. There are still no college or seminary women presidents, minimal increases in the number of women trustees, and proportionately low percentages of female professionals on church staffs.

**Personal Rights—Group Responsibility**

A final ethical consideration basic to women in the work world concerns the tension between the drive to become all for which one has the gifts and training and the responsibility one has to promote the cause for women's equality in general. Some in the women's movement have bitterly accused the women who have achieved "in a man's world" and forsaken their less fortunate sisters. This is not unique to the women's rights group, for Negro groups have branded some of their own as "white man's nigger" and Red Power Crusaders have pointed out the "Paleface Indians." Is it morally defensible for one who has succeeded through hard work and much determination to say to others, "If I can do it the hard way, so can you"? Does one have to be a radical or a joiner to assist in the cause for equality of personhood? Are there direct and indirect ways to promote the cause in one's own "territory" of influence and is one, whether black or red or female, ethically bound to do so?

Sometimes a less-discussed issue is the obligation of women to take "promotions" for the sake of the cause of women's advancement. Does one not have the right to determine which are promotions and which are simply steps up the ladder, according to someone else's value system? Homemakers who are gifted and trained particularly for work in the outside business and professional world have been labeled slackers and accused of hiding their talents behind the draperies when the world and the women's movement need their efforts. Others who refuse to initiate civil suits for equal treatment in hiring, pay, and benefits are accused of being voluntary second-class workers and/or being traitors to their own kind. More questionable are the ethics of those individuals who pat them on the back and give them strokes for not rocking the boat or not giving in to the Peter Principle as many men have, implying in the first instance that anyone who sues for equal treatment is a troublemaker and in the second instance that women would probably be inadequate in any higher position.

The writer knows personally of many of these moral dilemmas. If one believes that the classroom provides one ultimate in satisfaction, challenge, and gift-giving, even if a hierarchy in power and salary exists that would say differently, why is this not the "highest calling" at any point during life or even for one's entire professional career? Should an individual not be free to determine to stay or to opt for a change in "calling" so long as she is honest in appraisal of gifts, experience, challenge, and clarity of call? The Christian must not let the world conform her to arbitrary definitions of promotion for either lateral or vertical moves in a life vocation.

### In Worship and in Service

Dr. T. B. Maston, emeritus professor of Christian ethics, recently placed women and society as the third major concern on his list of current ethical issues. Along with his statements concerning the responsibility of the churches and the denomination to be informed about the women's movement in general, the ERA in particular, and the need to speak out for equity and equality, he observes, "There is a growing feeling that women should have a more effective voice in determining the programs and structuring of local churches." [15] On this matter, he makes these concrete suggestions:

> Churches and church leaders ought to realize that "equal pay for equal work" applies to women employees of local churches and denomination agencies and institutions.
> Christian men and women are equal before God (Galatians 3:28). They should recognize, however, that . . . they have some distinctive functions to perform without either feeling superior or inferior to the other.
> Southern Baptists should study the Scriptures concerning women, giving careful attention not only to the teachings of Jesus and Paul concerning women but also their relations to women.
> The ordination of women as deacons (deaconesses) or ministers is a local church decision. A church . . . should study . . . ordination in the Scriptures.
> Qualified women should be elected to serve on church and denominational staffs without discrimination.
> More qualified women should be selected to serve on the boards of state and Southern Baptist Convention agencies and institutions.[16]

### Local Church Leadership

A number of theological articles, as well as books and program materials, have been written on the role of women in the church. Some of these have been prompted by women's caucuses organized to raise the consciousness of women about their situation and the need to be full persons in the pew and as leaders in the local church. But one must rely on observation and experience, not statistical reports, for the quantitative appraisal of the situation. Such observation would confirm that historically women have figured prominently (predominantly) in the teaching roles for children and youth, in music, and hostessing. They have prepared for the ordinances of communion and baptism, as well as actively promoted the visitation of the unsaved or ill, missionary causes, and crisis intervention.

The ethical question concerning church women, as their secular roles were expanding during this last generation, coincides with the words of a recent popular song, "Is that all there is?" The writer's observation in her own denomination has been that women are slowly but steadily appearing on finance, program, personnel, and pulpit committees in local churches. They are praying, speaking, and leading more in public worship services. They are becoming more visible in the decision-making roles of the church, but equity is far from achieved when one considers that women comprise 51-53 percent of most congregations.

### The Concept of Ordination

Fundamental to the issue of women's leadership in the church, or anyone's leadership for that matter, is the nature of ordination as defined in the Scriptures. What constitutes ordaining, who sanctions it, what body determines which offices require it and which do not? Likewise, where is the authority for determining the relationship of ordination? One churchman suggests, "Ordination is the separation and commissioning of particular persons by the churches for the work of Christian ministry; but the outward calling by the congregation should correspond to and be consequent on the inward calling of the Holy Spirit." [17]

A breakthrough for women in the church appeared in the 1960s when churches which had placed little significance on the ordination of women began to be more open and active in endorsing such "calls to service" on the part of women.

### Women as Ministers

Among the recent and ongoing studies of women in the ministry, two are most notable: SWIM (A Study of Women in Ministry) by various American Baptist groups and *Women Ministers in 1977*[18] published by the National Council of Churches.

About 41 percent of the 211 Christian religious bodies reporting to the *Yearbook of American and Canadian Churches* in 1977 indicated that they were ordaining women ministers. Apart from these 76 denominations, there were 10 in a special category (such as Friends, Latter Day Saints, and Jehovah's Witnesses) on the practice of ordination and 87 others did not ordain women. Among the bodies that did ordain women, there was a combined membership of over 47 million and 10,470 women clergy (4 percent of the total clergy).[19]

Almost one-third of the ordained women are found in 14 Pentecostal bodies (31.8 percent) and 29.9 percent are in paramilitary type religious organizations, such as the Salvation Army, Volunteers of America, and American Rescue Workers. The 10 largest denominations (each above 1 million) account for about 1,830 women ministers. But among these 10 groups, 3—American Baptists (157), the Disciples of Christ (338), and the United Church of Christ (400)—account for 52 percent of the total women clergy.[20] American Baptists recently elected a woman president-elect for 1978-79.

Studies during the 1970s have indicated that there are ethical issues related to the role of the woman minister. She has usually served in small pastorates, been paid substantially less (about four thousand dollars less), or served in junior minister or chaplaincy roles. The National Council of Churches report concluded, "It is expected that the proportion of female clergy ordained to the full ministry in the major denominations will increase slowly, and that the entrance of women into work in local churches probably will not dramatically increase in the forseeable future." [21]

Doubtless, the basic tension to be resolved here is between the personal spiritual response of the woman called into the various types of professional ministry, the admissions policies of the various theological seminaries, and the willingness/openness of local churches to actively consider and seek women candidates for their pastorates.

## Christian Women in the Women's Movement

Finally, Christian women have been active in both secular and religious segments of the movement for women's rights. Recently, FACT (Feminism and the Church Today) noted that a group of religious women, calling themselves "Feminists of Faith," took an active and reconciling role in the National Women's Conference in Houston, 1977.[22] Another nondenominational Christian group encouraging all phases of equality among persons through feminism is the Evangelical Women's Caucus. The spirit of these movements might rightly be that of all Christian bodies, as stated in the FACT brochure: "It is because the goals of the secular Women's Movement are so pervasive, and because it is fundamentally in the spirit of the Gospel, that we are convinced that the church must come to understand it better and interpret it from a consciously Christian perspective."

## Notes

1. Harvey Cox, "Eight Theses of Female Liberation," *Christianity and Crisis* (October 4, 1971), p. 199.

2. "What Next for U. S. Women," *Time* (December 5, 1977), p. 19.

3. "Sex, Society, and the Female Dilemma (A Dialogue)," *Saturday Review* (June 14, 1975), pp. 19 ff.

4. For a provocative critique of Lessing's four novels, including *The Four-Gated City,* see Carol Christ's "Explorations with Doris Lessing in Quest of the Four-Gated City," *Women and Religion* (Missoula, Mont.: Scholars Press, 1974), rev. ed., pp. 41-61.

5. John Scanzoni, "Assertiveness for Christian Women," *Christianity Today* 20 (June 4, 1976), pp. 16-18.

6. For further information, headquarters for this group is 1011 Arlington Blvd., Suite 305, Arlington, Va., 22209.

7. Jessie Bernard, quoted in "You Can't Destroy This Movement," *U. S. News and World Report* 79 (December 8, 1975), pp. 71-74.

8. U. S. Department of Commerce, Bureau of the Census, *A Statistical Portrait of Women in the U. S.,* Current Population Reports, Special Studies, Series P-23, No. 58, Washington, D. C. (April, 1976), p. 1.

9. For detailed data on the professions, see: U. S. National Commission

for UNESCO, *Report on Women in America,* Department of State Publication 8923, Washington, D. C. (November, 1977), p. 2.

10. Bernard.

11. See table, *Higher Education and National Affairs,* XXVII No. 16 (April 21, 1978), p. 6.

12. "Women's Task Force to Monitor Colleges," *Higher Education and National Affairs,* XXVII No. 14 (April 7, 1978), p. 3.

13. Ibid.

14. See chapter 2 in Harry Hollis, ed., *Christian Freedom for Women and Other Human Beings* (Nashville: Broadman, 1975), pp. 19-32.

15. T. B. Maston, "Ethical Issues: 1978 and Beyond," a resource paper prepared for the Christian Life Commission of the Southern Baptist Convention, p. 3.

16. Ibid.

17. J. D. Douglas, *The New International Dictionary of the Christian Church* (Exeter: The Paternoster Press, 1974), p. 732.

18. Constant H. Jacquet, Jr., *Women Ministers in 1977,* Office of Research, Evaluation and Planning, National Council of Churches, 475 Riverside Drive, New York, New York 10027 (March, 1978).

19. Ibid., p. 6.

20. Ibid., p. 8.

21. Ibid.

22. A publication of the Office of Program Operators, National Ministries, American Baptist Churches, U. S. A. (Winter, 1978).

# 8

## Bioethics: Frontiers of the Future

Paul D. Simmons

Science invites, urged by the voice divine,
"Exert thyself, 'till every Art be thine"
(Inscription on mural, U. S. post office, Princeton, N. J.).

"This is only the beginning of what they will do; and nothing that they propose to do will now be impossible for them" (Gen. 11:6, RSV).

A giant leap forward has been taken by science in the last half century that has far-reaching significance for the future of mankind. Major breakthroughs in biological knowledge and scientific techniques have given science vast new powers to govern human history and developments in ways never before possible. The future may now be shaped by planned design and the frontiers of that future can be found in the laboratories of science. This is why the primary question for the future is the way in which scientific possibilities will be influenced by moral values.

### The Nature and Scope of Bioethics

Bioethics is a neologism coined for the discipline which deals with the entire range of moral issues related to the life sciences. Ethics is the study of human values, involving an analysis of moral rules and principles and setting forth the norms and goals by which moral actions are measured.

Bioethics is concerned with establishing ethical guidelines for decision making in the various fields of the life sciences and for the specific problems confronted by scientists. This involves at least three tasks: defining the issues, exploring methodological strategies, and developing procedures for decision making.[1]

The importance of this task can hardly be overstated, for the scientific revolution has direct bearing on human well-being and the future of the world. Science has created a crisis in values. What is at stake is no less than the future of humanity itself. For Potter, the future can be assured only by governing the powers of science with genuinely moral understandings.[2]

This can be illustrated in the two primary areas of concern to human beings: the natural environment and human nature itself. During the past two decades the world has been made aware that technology seems to be making the environment unhealthy if not unfit for human habitation. *Ecology* is the study of living organisms in their relationship to their environment and to one another. However, the ethical issues involve considerations related to inorganic as well as organic substances. The pollution of air and water resources have focused the moral issues involved in the way nature is treated. In addition, the exploitation of natural resources to pander to the desires of a consumption-oriented people is creating a crisis for the future. What resources will be available for future generations when the depletion of presently-known resources can be anticipated within a century? A finite planet has limited resources so that industrial growth cannot be sustained indefinitely.[3]

The most alarming symbol of the nature crisis, however, is that of the nuclear bomb. The atomic energy formula ($E = mc^2$) opened up the secrets of nature so dramatically that the survival of earth itself is now in jeopardy. Unlocking the secrets of the atom unleashed a power that, uncontrolled, can destroy the planet earth and all its inhabitants.

Plainly, scientific technology and research cannot be regarded as a value-free enterprise. The human and survival issues at stake make it imperative that moral considerations be integrated into decision-making processes.

The second major area of concern to bioethics is that of the impact of science on humanity itself. Mankind has become both the subject and the object of scientific inquiry. Medical science poses numerous moral issues. These include behavior control, noncoital reproductive techniques, abortion, euthanasia, genetic engineering, organ transplantation, experimental medicine, psychosurgery, health care systems and distribution, scientific research, and physician-patient relationships.

The powers of science to intervene into the nature and functions of human activity are truly amazing. The birth of children from *in vitro fertilization* has been reported in both England and India. In these cases, doctors fertilized the mother's ovum with the father's sperm in the laboratory. After several days of cell division in the testtube, the fertilized ovum was then placed in the woman's womb where it implanted and developed. Both "test-tube" babies are reported normal and doing well.[4] *Cloning* is another method by which children may be developed in the future. Already performed with simple life forms, scientists now anticipate being able to remove the nucleus from a fertilized ovum, replace it with the material from a spliced body cell and develop a child with the same genetic endowments as the one from whom the body cell was taken. Other exotic possibilities are being discussed as well. Fletcher mentions eight methods of parenting only one of which is nontechnical. That is the coital-gestational method. The other seven are biotechnical, ranging from artifical insemination to cloning. Further, all seven have been attempted, most with success.[5] The day in which coitus may be removed entirely from conception is being forecast by some futurists.

Science is also on the verge of being able to alter genetic features of people. Genes are the major building blocks of a person's biological endowments from intelligence to color of eyes and hair, height, body form, and chemical functions. Of major concern to scientists is the pollution of the gene pool or the spread of deleterious genes throughout the population. The problem is that as science succeeds in correcting the symptoms of illness or limitation more genetic defects are passed into the gene pool. Diabetes, for instance, is an illness which can be controlled but not cured. Thus, many diabetics are kept alive or bear offspring who are also afflicted with diabetes or carry the deleterious gene. In this way, the incidence of genetically based illness such as hemophilia, gout, Down's syndrome, and others is increased. Some geneticists are apocalyptic about the future unless this process can be corrected. Both the parents of children born with genetic problems and the patients themselves would very much desire that such problems be corrected.

Eugenic studies are proceeding along two broad fronts to deal with this matter. *Negative eugenics* is the attempt to alter genetic endowment by removing or correcting the harmful genes themselves. For instance, should doctors discover, using the process of amniocentesis, that a fetus has a genetic deformity, the defective genes might be removed by gene surgery or a specific factor might be inserted into genetic material to correct the problem (gene insertion).

Of even more far-reaching significance is the enterprise of *positive eugenics,* or the attempt to create new human beings altogether. With the discovery of the basic coding material for all genetic structures and the advanced technology of the computer, it is at least conceptually possible that an entirely different creature could be created.

Experiments with recombinant DNA seem to indicate that possibilities from both negative and positive eugenics may be nearer than might have been anticipated a decade ago. Already scientists at the University of California at San Francisco have succeeded in transplanting into bacteria the genes from rat cells that carry genetic instructions for making insulin. There now seems to be no scientific obstacles to doing the same with the genes for human insulin.[6] Even more sophisticated and dramatic breakthroughs can be expected in the near future. Scientists are now "reading" the genetic coding of DNA (deoxyribonucleic acid) with greater rapidity. Such breakthroughs hold the potential of permitting scientists to manipulate genetic material to such an extent that human genetic deformities may be cured, not simply corrected.

Science, then, is moving toward the possibility of fundamentally altering the human species. The problem will not be technical but moral and social. The issue is whether science is adequate to determine what alterations should desirably be made in human behavior or constitution. While it may have the technical knowledge, does science have sufficient moral insight to make these decisions?

## The Moral Issue: Dangerous Knowledge

The awesome power to create totally new life forms now possessed by science portends both promise and threat. The promise is that life and health will be enhanced for the improvement of the human race. The threat is that those powers will turn upon the human race with mass destruction. The threat factor is increased by the realization that technological prowess tends to become an autonomous force, creating the need to be used simply because the technique is available. Moral questions have little effect when brought against the enormous momentum created by developing technology.[7]

Research into the secrets of the atom is a case in point. Having formulated the basic theorem, all that remained was to develop the technology for splitting the atom and unleashing a power never known or experienced. The devastation unleashed on Hiroshima and Nagasaki became a sign of the grave capabilities of science. Mankind now lives under the shadow of the mushroom cloud, ever conscious of the fact that the secrets unleashed by science may destroy the entire human race. Those who speak comforting words regarding the beneficent uses of medical technology speak against this background. The public does well to be suspicious of a jaunty heedlessness that invites disaster. A cartoon recently depicted a scientist giving consoling words to John Q. Citizen by saying "Relax! We keep a tight rein on these things from the very beginning!" By one hand, the scientist was holding a flask marked genetic engineering, about which Citizen was concerned. By the other hand the scientist was tied to a giant who symbolized nuclear knowledge. The size and stupidity of the giant made it clear that he was no longer under the control of his creator.

Scientific knowledge is plainly dangerous to the human race, both because of its enormous potential for destruction and because it can be exploited and misused. One of the problems is that knowledge has accumulated faster than the wisdom to manage it. Thus, specialists in one field may lack a sufficiently broad background to envisage all the implications of their work. Further, all consequences of new developments may not be anticipated or intended. The tranquilizer thalidomide resulted in extensive fetal deformity when taken by pregnant women, for instance.

The dangerous side of scientific research has led some to suggest the concept of "forbidden knowledge." Morally speaking, it is argued, there are some things that ought not be known. Among theologians, Paul Ramsey has argued this position.[8] He is joined by such eminent scientists as Edwin Chargoff of Columbia University and Robert Sinsheimer of the California Institute of Technology.[9] The ethical question is whether scientists are morally justified in entering into and altering the domain of nature at the special level of humanity's genetic arrangement or unlocking secrets that may lead to widespread destruction. Is there for science a moral equivalent to the legal prohibition against "breaking and entering"? [10]

The fact that the call for restraint comes not only from moralists but from scientists, gives the question special force. Ethicists might be accused of moralistic bias or a metaphysical perspective that is inimical to science as such. When scientists sound the alarm, however, the assumption must be made that grave dangers have been perceived.

Sinsheimer believes that any knowledge that is inimical to human welfare is forbidden.[11] The problem is how to prevent the probing and technology of science from destroying some key element in our ecological niche or set loose an uncontrollable pathogen. As he states it:

Physics and chemistry have given us the power to reshape the physical nature of the planet. We wield forces comparable, even greater than those of, natural catastrophes. And now biology is bringing to us a comparable power over the world of life. The recombinant DNA technology, while significant and potentially a grievous hazard in itself (through the conceivable production, by design or inadvertence, of new human, animal or plant pathogens) is a sign of revolutionary new advances yet to be seen.[12]

The danger of the new knowledge has led some to suggest that science should be carefully regulated.[13] Threats are perceived as harmful to individuals, environmental damage from new technologies, long-term hazards resulting from scientific authority, and the challenge to religious or metaphysical assumptions that science represents.

However, there are those who see the threat in very different terms. While recognizing the dangers in certain types of research and applied technology, the real problem is perceived as too much ignorance, not too much knowledge. As Morison suggests, the greater danger to society is *what it does not know*.[14] A great deal is unknown, for instance, about the stability of ecological systems and the physical chemistry of the stratosphere. Until theories are turned into knowledge, irreparable harm may happen to the protection to persons provided by the atmosphere. Even population growth poses a present threat because of human ignorance.

The same is true regarding genetics. Presently vast numbers of people suffer from biological anomalies because science does not know how to control genetic information. Further research is needed so that people can be assured of being born with good genetic endowments. Already geneticists believe they have isolated a gene that could be a cause of mental depression and perhaps of multiple sclerosis.[15] Further research is needed so that persons are no longer subjected to the random and chance combinations of genetic material that may subject them to a lifetime of suffering and limitation. Failure to obtain the knowledge needed to offset the effects of those problems is to subject the human race to almost certain widespread suffering. To believe that science should not pursue its research is to believe that it is better to be subject to forces beyond human control than it is to control these forces.

## The Religious Response

The pretensions and possibilities of science generate opposing outlooks about the future and toward science in general within the religious community. These attitudes reflect assumptions about the task of science, the dangers of scientific knowledge, the impact of science upon humanity, and the relation of science to religious perceptions of God and his work in the world.

### Opposition to Science

Those who oppose science or scientific intervention into nature or biology relect anxiety and fear at the consequences they foresee, or they believe science violates its proper work before God. Their arguments may emphasize one or more of the following points.

* Science threatens to alter radically human life as we know it through genetic intervention or nuclear destruction. Eugenics is regarded by one professor as "Orwellian medicine." Already, Batt points out, people are subject to experimentation and behavior modification. He is even more suspicious, however, of eugenics, fearing that scientists really have designs to pursue man farming: "They don't want to waste their time modifying the behavior of people created by a pair of patently inferior human beings," he says. "They plan to make their own people. And they are serious!" [16] For Batt, man *as he is* is not to be altered.

* Others fear that science will lead to a loss of the idea of the sacredness of life as a gift from God. Ramsey makes this point when he criticizes the new genetics: "Piece by piece of information may destroy our sense that . . . , God made the world and the human creature and they are good." [17] Ellul sounds the same note when he argues that applied biogenetics is an obvious point at which technique desacralizes.[18]

* The morally sensitive are not always in control of the uses of knowledge. This acknowledges, first, that knowledge is power and that only a few people, relatively speaking, are able to exercise that power. Secondly, it is argued, there is no way to assure that only moral persons will use this power. There is always the possibil-

ity that an unscrupulous scientist will create dangerous biochemical agents, that psychotic military personnel will unleash nuclear fury, that terrorists will use nuclear, biochemical blackmail, or that a dictator such as Hitler will use science for totalitarian purposes. Since no absolute guarantees can be given that such things will not happen, they believe it is better not to have the knowledge itself. Only in that way can we be sure such things will not happen.

* Scientists themselves are alarmed, and some are apocalyptic in their attitude. Some of the earliest warnings of the ominous threats posed by the new sciences came from scientists themselves. As in the case of DNA research, they were the first to sound the alarm, some making the general population aware of the danger by resigning publicly.[19]

* The place of God in nature and the progress of the world is being usurped by scientists. Humanity should not "play God," it is argued, since human freedom and choice may destroy the very world that God has created. God alone should govern the course of creation and the future of humanity. To tamper with atoms or genes is to intrude upon the sacred province of God and assure destruction as the judgment of God.

**Support for Science**

A supportive attitude toward science and an optimistic view of the future are generated by those who see the relation of the new knowledge toward mankind and God in very different ways. Some have a visionary outlook for the future that is unreserved in its praises for science. One writer anticipates that in the twenty-first century people will live almost indefinitely—certainly well beyond one hundred years. This, he says, will be achieved through genetic and biological reconstruction, along with antiaging drugs, replacements of perishable organs, and the continuous telemonitoring of vital body functions. He anticipates that "we will deanimalize our anatomies, creating desirable, modular, imaginative new bodies adaptable to all elements of this planet and suitable for existence in space." [20] He is one among many who believe that mankind is now on an evolutionary path toward a human stage free of pain, suffering, and death.

Such confidence and hope may be supported by one or more of the following arguments.

* Scientists have uncovered new possibilities for human health and well-being and are on the verge of major breakthroughs to eliminate the primary sources of human pain, limitation, and suffering. The combination of computer technology and DNA information promises the elimination of genetic defects, the prolongation of life, and the development of a superior human race.

* The public's fear of the new knowledge has been fueled by irresponsible speculation, premature alarm, and science fiction writers more interested in selling books than in creating realistic scenarios of the future. DNA research, for instance, was first thought to hold grave dangers that a harmful bacteria would be developed that could not be controlled. Further research showed, however, that the E-coli strain which inhabits the human gut is actually very unstable in an uncontrolled environment. Thus, new materials are very unlikely to spread and cause havoc.

* Scientists are humane and moral persons who will use knowledge for enhancing life and human welfare. This is based upon a generally high view of human nature itself—namely, that people in general can be trusted to seek to do what is beneficial and right. Furthermore, a certain view of what it means to be a human being created in the image of God is involved. Biéler argues that scientific endeavor belongs to man's stewardship of the earth under God. Man is a steward precisely because he possesses Godlike knowledge. Far from being off limits to investigation, research, and control, nature is to be "domesticated" so that people are no longer subjected to forces they do not understand. Controlling the forces of nature belongs to the very meaning of humanity: "Man is man only to the extent that he remains the master of his own acts and capable of judging their worth, to the extent that, as the author of his own progress, he programs it according to the master plan assigned by God." [21]

* A providential process is at work through evolution that is moving toward an ultimate goal of salvation and beneficence for all. This process may be seen as the purpose of evolution itself or as the divine purpose of God. Scientists may take this view from certain notions of the way nature works while theologians may use religious arguments drawn from eschatology or the nature of reality. Teilhard de Chardin, for instance, believed that all of history is moving toward an omega point where God would bring all things to fulfillment.[22] Teilhard's vision blended his scientific knowledge with his faith in God. His argument ran something like this: (1) evolution is the way God has brought the world through history to the present time; (2) man is the only creature to know he is a product of evolution; (3) through scientific know-how, man is able to direct the course of evolution; therefore, (4) man has a responsibility to use his knowledge to control evolutionary history and guide it toward omega point. For him, what is needed is a knowledge that will replace the crude forces of natural selection with medical and moral factors. He regarded as indispensable "a nobly human form of eugenics" for the future.[23]

### Guidelines for Bioethical Decision Making

The path toward the future will undoubtedly be dominated by science and technology. However, if that future is to bless and not curse, if better societies and healthier people are to be developed, care must be taken to use scientific knowledge wisely and erect safeguards against its abuse and exploitation. The constructive benefits of science can be realized more fully if its destructive capacities are taken seriously. Human values can best be preserved and pursued by consciously and consistently following certain moral guidelines in decision making related to bioethical issues. The following elements seem mandated by a Christian understanding of bioethical decision making.

#### Organic Wholeness and the Sacredness of Life

All of life is a gift of God to be celebrated, cherished, and respected. Human beings are stewards, not creators. Only God is Creator and

Sustainer of all that is. The task of science is to so treat life as to recognize that it has its origins and destiny beyond the ultimate control of human knowledge. This will mean that life will never be casually regarded or irresponsibly destroyed.

Furthermore, this will involve an ethic of quadratic relationships. Traditionally, only triadic dimensions have been recognized: the moral relationships one has to self, to the neighbor (or society), and to God. The ecological crisis has demonstrated, however, that there is a vital fourth relationship—to nature. No form of life or element of creation, nature, persons, or animals, can be treated with disdain or exploited for selfish purposes.

All of life is interdependent and exists with an inner cohesion. No radical division can be drawn between the world of spirit and the world of matter. The relation-in-unity of mass and energy for the scientist is symbolized in the atomic formula. The clue for the Christian is found in the incarnation. There—in Christ—spirit and matter, soul and body, divinity and humanity were seen, not as antithetical but as complementary realities. The world with all its life processes become signs of the working of God for the Christian. The task of working with God the Creator and Redeemer is accepted with gratitude as the responsibility to mold and nourish those processes themselves.

## Stewardship as Choice, Not Chance

Another element is the ethical principle that medical science has an obligation to use knowledge to reduce human suffering. This involves both ameliorating faults and constructing better, healthier bodies. This means that choice and not chance should dominate in human biology. Christians recognize that all of life is a stewardship under God and that mankind is a co-worker or cooperator with God who is bringing about his redemptive purpose for all of creation. Stewards are not passive spectators of the drama in history and nature but active participants in the process toward the future.

Scientific knowledge or technical expertise facilitates human stewardship in the world. Technology and science are not opponents of human, spiritual interests or of the religious enterprise. Rather, such knowledge is an extension of personhood into the world of technique and controlled energy. Thus, it becomes a part of what it means to be human and vital to the tasks of stewardship.

This is important for considerations related to medical intervention into reproductive or genetic processes. Christians cannot accept the notions that whatever is "artificial" is ungodly and whatever is "natural" is godly. Whatever technique serves human need and enhances human well-being is a God-given wisdom that makes possible a more perfect stewardship.

What is needed seems to be an ethic that includes a deliberate, planned, and rational approach to prevent or reduce human suffering, limitation, and early death. Reason and choice, not randomness and chance, seem the way to achieve and preserve the higher human values. This will require, not less, but more knowledge on the part of science. Ignorance or lack of knowledge limits the ability to correct problems. Knowledge becomes power to correct and prevent problems. Not to use that knowledge for patient well-being and the welfare of society would be immoral.

**Freedom and Responsibility**

If science is to enjoy the freedom of research and experimentation, it must also accept the responsibility of restraint in the use and application of its knowledge. There are some things that should not be done even though they could be done. Moral judgments may and will set limits around the use of dangerous knowledge. The moral question is not whether a thing *can* be done but whether it *ought* to be done. Ramsey states this point strongly:

> The sine qua non of any morality at all, of any future for humanism, must be the premise that there may be a number of things that we *can* do that ought not to be done . . . Any other premise amounts to a total abdication of human moral reasoning and the total abasement of man before the relentless advancement of biological and medical technology.[24]

Granted that technology might make cloning a tyrant possible, that would not mean that it should be done. Even though the develop-

ment of chimeras may be possible, making such man-animal creatures seems to pose insurmountable moral problems related to personal capacities and self-identity. By DNA technology, the creation
of deleterious pathogens for use in biological warfare is certainly
*possible*. Both political and scientific personnel involved in such
an enterprise would be judged immoral by standards of human and
social well-being and integrity, however. The freedom of science
is not to destroy but to bless.

## Community Involvement and Shared Responsibility

The issues at stake in bioethics are too important to be left to
scientists alone. Further, the responsibilities for making the decisions
for the future are too far-reaching to be borne by scientists alone.
Any adequate bioethic will involve shared responsibility by the
larger community of which science is a part. How nuclear technology
is to be developed is a matter of public concern, not simply of scientific curiosity. How eugenic knowledge is to be applied toward the
development of *homo superior* is a matter of public interest. The
standards or criteria that count for "superior" should not be left
to the preferences or notions of a particular scientist or even a group
of scientists engaged in such research.

The principle of shared responsibility will involve limiting individual decision making in several important ways. The first level of
control will be within the community of science itself. A second
level is that of public policy and governmental regulation. These
will range from general guidelines for research involving minimal
risk to people to the more complex and strict standards that rule
out practices or experiments that involve clear risks to society.[25]

A third level of shared responsibility will be in the establishment
of public commissions to monitor or assess the activities of science.
These may operate at both the national and local levels and might
include attorneys, clergymen, business and labor leaders, as well
as scientists. Their task would be to weigh the issues, assess the
risks, calculate the benefits, and perhaps aid public discussion and
facilitate consensus in controversial areas. Such groups have served
well in dealing with community struggles over recombinant DNA

laboratories. They might serve an equally vital role in decisions relating to nuclear power plants and other hazardous establishments.

## Love

The final, but most comprehensive, element of an adequate bioethic is love. Love encompasses all that is done to enhance the well-being of persons, society, or creation. Wholeness, health, integrity, strength, happiness, and harmony all belong to well-being.

For the Christian love involves the essence of human responsibility toward God and to the neighbor (society). It also encompasses a moral relationship to nature for man has the mandate to "have dominion" over the earth (Gen. 1:28), always aware of the fact that "the earth is the Lord's" (Ps. 24:1). Loving the neighbor means respecting the dignity and worth of personhood, recognizing basic human rights, and seeking to facilitate growth toward maturity and health. Loving society involves seeking justice in social relationships and person-centered values in institutional structures. Toward nature, love requires care, nourishing, and replenishing. "Love constrains us," says Barnette, "not only to will the welfare of our neighbor, but also to preserve and promote the kind of environment that maximizes the possibility of full selfhood for each." [26]

From the biblical perspective, the most distinctive mark of being human is the capacity to love. Of all the "knowledge" that a person may acquire, the most important is "knowing" how to love. When persons are loving, they reflect the nature of God who is love and the will of God for those made in his image. All human knowledge must, therefore, be used in the service of love. Otherwise, mankind fails to act on the most uniquely human capacity of all and thus humanity is diminished and finally destroyed.

## Conclusion

Mankind's moral response to the challenges posed in bioethical issues will determine whether humanity will be blessed or cursed by this awesome knowledge. Never before in the history of the world has any creature had such a brave opportunity or such a grave responsibility. The gravity of those moral choices can hardly be exaggerated. Augenstein has aptly issued the challenge to "Come, Let Us Play God"—but with appropriate moral commitments:

> Come, let us work together humbly, prayerfully and above all responsibly as we proceed in this awesome business. For the success or failure with which we "play God" in the next few years will determine whether these are the first few moments in mankind's greatest and most exciting hour or the last few seconds in his ultimate tragedy.[27]

## Notes

1. See Sidney Callahan, "Bioethics as a Discipline," *Hastings Center Studies*, Vol. 1, No. 1 (1973), p. 71 and Barbara Ann Swyhart, *Bioethical Decision-Making* (Philadelphia: Fortress Press, 1975).

2. Van R. Potter, *Bioethics: Bridge to the Future* (Englewood, New Jersey: Prentice-Hall, 1971), p. vii.

3. See H. H. Barnette, *The Church and the Ecological Crisis* (Grand Rapids: Eerdmann's, 1972).

4. *The Louisville* [Kentucky] *Times*, Friday, October 6, 1978, p. A-6.

5. Joseph Fletcher, *The Ethics of Genetic Control* (Manhattan Beach, California: Anchor, 1974), pp. 40-41.

6. *Science Magazine* (May 28, 1977) cited by *New York Times*, Wednesday, May 24, 1977, p. A-1 and 9.

7. See J. Ellul, *The Technological Society*, John Wilkinson, trans. (New York: Vintage, 1964), pp. 135 ff. and *To Will and to Do*, C. Edward Hopkin, trans. (Philadelphia: Pilgrim, 1969), esp. ch. 11.

8. In a symposium on recombinant DNA research at Princeton University, Spring, 1977. See also his *Fabricated Man* (New Haven: Yale University Press, 1970), p. 134.

9. See his personal statement in *Daedalus*, 107:2 (Spring, 1978), pp. 23-25.

10. Samuel Enoch Stumpf, "Genetics and the Control of Human Development," in *A Matter of Life and Death*, Harry N. Hollis, Jr., ed. (Nashville: Broadman, 1977), p. 115.

11. Sinsheimer, p. 23. See also David H. Smith, "Scientific Knowledge and Forbidden Truths," *Hastings Center Report*, December, 1978, pp. 30-35, who argues that knowledge (1) gained without free and informed consent, (2) gained only by violations of the right to privacy, or (3) which destroys

cultural institutions or practices, and (4) that erodes character, is forbidden.

12. Sinsheimer, p. 26.

13. See Robert S. Morison, "Introduction," *Daedalus* 107:2 (Spring, 1978), p. xv and David S. Greenberg, "Barriers Against Rogue Science," *Courier-Journal* (Louisville, Kentucky) Friday, August 12, 1977, p. A-11.

14. Ibid., p. xvi. See also Potter, p. 70.

15. *Courier-Journal*, Friday, January 5, 1979, p. B-4.

16. John R. Batt, "Hippocrates as 'Big Brother': An Essay on Orwellian Medicine," in *Should Doctors Play God?* Claude Frazier, ed. (Nashville: Broadman, 1971), p. 133.

17. Paul Ramsey, "Genetic Therapy: A Theologian's Response," in *The New Genetics and the Future of Man*, Michael Hamilton, ed. (Grand Rapids: Eerdmans, 1972), p. 175.

18. Ellul, *The Technological Society*, p. 143.

19. Sinsheimer, *Daedalus*, p. 23-25.

20. F. M. Esfondiary, "Future Tribute," in *New Times*, January 7, 1977, p. 100.

21. André Biéler, *Politics of Hope* (Grand Rapids: Eerdmans, 1974), p. 42.

22. See Joseph A. Grau, *Morality and the Human Future in the Thought of Teilhard de Chardin* (Cranbury, N. J.: Associated University Press, 1976), p. 54.

23. Ibid., p. 299. See also Karl Rahner, "Experiment: Man," in *Theology Digest*, February, 1968, p. 58, who argues that "human self-creation means quite simply that today man is changing himself. To be more precise: Man is consciously and deliberately changing himself . . . . Man today finds that he is manipulable. A radically new age is coming—new in every dimension."

24. Ramsey, *Fabricated Man*, p. 151.

25. See Sissela Bok, "Freedom and Risk," *Daedalus*, pp. 124-126 for an excellent discussion of three strategies necessary to set limits for scientific inquiry.

26. Barnette, *The Church and the Ecological Crisis*, p. 36.

27. Leroy Augenstein, *Come, Let Us Play God* (New York: Harper & Row, 1969), pp. 145-146.

# 9

## The Christian Understanding of
## and Attitude to Nature

### E. C. Rust

Historically the West has been concerned with nature chiefly at the level of exploitation. Nature's value has been associated with its usefulness in human survival. Only artists and poets have concerned themselves with the more spiritual dimension of the natural order, with a consideration of nature's value for its own sake, and with the aesthetic aspect of man's relationship to nature. As Albert Schweitzer pointed out, Western civilization has rarely considered any moral responsibility to the nature realm. Rather the uppermost consideration has been its utility.

### Roots of the Ecological Crisis

Yet, deeply embedded in our cultural heritage there is a Hebrew tradition which sees man as responsibly involved with the natural environment. The biblical text indicates that God was regarded as giving man dominion over the lower orders of nature and placing all things under his feet (Gen. 1:26-30; Ps. 8:3-8). Yet this does not mean that man has absolute power, for his dominion is given him by God and his authority is a delegated authority. This is not to suggest that the so-called Christian civilization of the West has regarded its scientific and technological skills in this way. For man, in his arrogance, has regarded his control over nature as absolute and his use of his skills as solely at his own discretion.

Lynn White has argued that the roots of our contemporary ecological crisis lie in the biblical view of man's relation to nature. He argues that these biblical ideas have created the attitude in which man has become "superior to nature, contemptuous of it, willing to use it for our slightest whim." [1] There is a part truth in this conten-

tion. It is true that the Christian concern with man and his redemption
has often failed to emphasize man's relatedness to his natural environment. In emphasizing man's unique place in the created order,
as made in the divine image, this position has tended to accentuate
man's difference from all the other creatures and to forget that man
himself shares with them in their creatureliness. It has spoken of
man as under God, but it has also forgotten that nature's subordination under man must be seen always in the light of man's responsible
subordination to his Creator.

Science has only increased the problem. Science is God's gift to
his creatures. It provides the means whereby they may exercise
that dominion which he has granted to them. It is significant that
modern natural science came to birth within the Hebrew-Christian
traditions of Western culture and that the early scientists were themselves generally Christian men. But the success of science has, during
the three centuries since it came to full recognition, slowly erased
from men's minds thoughts of the supernatural and transcendent.
Areas of human need, such as sickness, famine, mental and physical
sickness have been taken over by scientific knowledge and its technological accompaniments, where, in earlier centuries, religion and
its prayers had often been man's only resort. Furthermore, the success of science in these areas has made men increasingly convinced
that science and its methodology hold the key to most of their human
needs and ills. It is true that science cannot unveil the ultimate
mysteries or eliminate man's deep-seated feeling for the transcendent
mystery of the universe. But it can and does cover it up and bury
it beneath over concern with immediate sense experience and the
material aspects of life.

This is not to decry science but to indicate the roots of our present
dilemma. What could, under God, have become a blessing to the
human race has been so misused and misdirected that it has brought
judgment and destruction in its train. For, when we do not accept
our scientific knowledge and achievement as stewards and face its
use as those who are responsible to their Creator and their fellow
creatures, it is easy to slip down the inclined plane to the level of

colossal selfishness and irresponsible exploitation. The divine injunction and the Creator's gift to his creatures have become the root of their self-destruction. The God-given ability to have dominion over the lower orders of nature has brought man into a state of ecological crisis because he has ignored his Creator and used his ability irresponsibly.

The account of the Garden in Genesis 3 has ecological dimensions. As Paul Tillich pointed out, the man was tempted to creaturely arrogance (to be like God) by a snake, and the snake is a part of the lower order of creation. It is man's control over nature which tempts him to ignore God and determine his own destiny without any reference to his Creator. The result, too, is significant, for the story symbolizes in the desert man's own judgment. Man's exploitation of nature and of his fellows destroys the idyllic Garden. He finds himself in the desert, bereft of fellowship with God, isolated in selfishness and pride from his fellows, alienated from and opposed by his natural environment, with his life deprived of ultimate meaning.

This biblical theme of judgment is repeated again and again in the Old Testament. Nature turns against man, and the possibility of cooperative unity is replaced by antagonism. Man finds himself in a hostile and alienated environment. The fruitful land becomes a salt desert because of the wickedness of its inhabitants (Ps. 107:33 f.). The animals are related to man by fear and not by trust (Gen. 9:2-3). Even the wild animals, roving at will, are a sign of man's weakness, and God used their existence to reduce Job to silence and to an overwhelming sense of creatureliness (Job 38:39; 39:26). Because of its people's sin, Edom's pastures would be made desolate (Jer. 49:20), and Hazor would become a dwelling place of jackals, a desolation forever (Jer. 49:33). Indeed, the result of man's sin is, in biblical thought, a return of that primordial chaos out of which God called forth the whole cosmic order from nature to man.

This reference to the primordial chaos is a reminder that the unfinished nature of the universe and the evil and frustration in nature are other sources of the ecological dilemma. Not everything in this crisis can be accounted for by man's sinful rebellion against his Creator. These two issues will be considered in turn.

## The Unfinished Aspect of the Universe

The biblical accounts of creation in both Genesis 1 and 2 picture the Creator as beginning with a chaotic, unformed stuff out of which he brought forth cosmos by his creative activity. In Genesis 1 it is a formless void, darkness, a deep; in Genesis 2 it is an arid desert. That God created the formless void is unstated but later developments of biblical thought make such an unformulated assumption explicit.

Science has increasingly made us aware of the developing aspect of the universe and emphasized the presence of random and contingent elements in the cosmic process. The biblical writers pictured creation as a historical process, and modern biology and astronomy alike are bringing this truth home to modern man. The universe is a process, a vast movement in time. Creative process has become a key concept for the understanding not only of the emergence of life and man upon this planet but also of the development of the myriads of galaxies with their constituent stars, including our own galactic universe and the planetary system in which the planet Earth has its place. At the physical level, radioactivity has a contingent dimension, for such atomic disintegration is not predictable except within a certain range of probability. Furthermore, there is an acausal aspect at the basis of energy, as Heisenberg's principle of indeterminacy makes clear. Accuracy on a causal basis has been replaced by probability. Even our scientific laws are now descriptive rather than regulative and grounded in statistical averages. At the biological level, we have grown use to hearing about the evolutionary model of neo-Darwinism with its random mutations, so that contingency enters into the structure of living things and a random aspect appears in the multiplicity of organisms at every level of the tree of life.

All this should not surprise us at the theological levels, and it should certainly not cause us to doubt the affirmations of faith. Even the most naturalistic of evolutionists would have to confess with

Julian Huxley that the primacy of human personality is a *fact* of developmental processes and that "by whatever objective standards we choose to take, properly developed human personalities are the highest products.[2] Many evolutionists would say that there is a directiveness in the evolutionary process and say that there is a longtime orderly progress in evolution and that some coordination of mutations, some mutual reinforcement, would appear to be a necessity at major points of development. Supporters of the neo-Darwinian model and advocates of the view that there is some as yet undiscovered mechanism are at one in supporting some teleological movement and the presence of something more than the mere accumulation of small random mutations. Polanyi contends that a long-range evolutionary progress, such as the development of the human consciousness, requires more than random mutations with adaptive and reproductive advantages. Consecutive steps with a special type of adaptive advantage would be necessary, and so he sees a persistent creative trend under the operation of an orderly transforming principle.[3] However we look at the process, teleological interpretation keeps lifting its head, whether we look for large scale "miracles" or a large number of small wonders that mutually reinforce one another.

Hence we must see a progressive movement from chaos to increasing cosmos, and science points to the presence of the chaotic element as well as suggesting a teleological movement. Theologically the contingent and random aspect need raise no questions, for it is consonant with the ultimate emergence of man with his capacity as a free and self-transcendent being to be creative in relation to his environment. If the Creator is concerned to produce beings who shall be made in his image, then men are intended to be free cocreators with their Maker. But a wholly determined and finished universe would provide no possibility of such freedom and creativity. A completed causal structure could not, indeed, allow for the emergence of free beings. A contingent, acausal aspect would seem necessary in a process which is both to produce free human beings and to provide an area in which they could be creatively free. Thus an unfinished universe should raise no questions for a Christian theologian. Rather he would expect it.

Furthermore, creative change requires warring systems. Challenge and response are of the very essence of a process in which novelty is to emerge. The very structure of such a process would require that unfinished and opposing elements should be ingredient in it. Thus the whole evolutionary process, with its mutations and selective adaptations, requires such a structure if the emergence of the new is possible and ultimately the coming of free and creative spirits. Chaos and cosmos would be intermingled. Teleological directiveness operates accompanied by the random and contingent.

## The Unfinished Universe and Natural Evil

Alongside the evil resulting from man's misuse of his freedom and his consequent irresponsible exploitation of nature, we must place the evil ingredient in the process itself because of the presence of the chaotic and contingent elements. It is, of course, true that we human beings tend to oversentimentalize the surd aspects of nature and read our human feelings into the lower orders of creation. Yet the apostle Paul offers a deep insight into the natural process when he sees the whole creation groaning and travailing in pain together until now, waiting for the unveiling of the sons of God (Rom. 8:18 ff). The frustration of nature is within the divine plan, but it *is* frustration, and nature *is* fraught with suffering. However much we humans may exaggerate the surd aspect of nature, it is present, and the pattern of the cross is discernible in the natural order.

Our Victorian forebears were aware of this pattern to such an extent that it vitiated their belief in a merciful providence and a benign Creator. The Darwinian model of evolution, as developed and elaborated by T. H. Huxley, made much of the negative and destructive aspect of natural selection. Many were repelled by its picture of a nature which seemed, to use Tennyson's phrase, "red in tooth and claw with ravin'." Indeed, that famous poet laureate voiced his theistic doubts in the verses of "In Memoriam."

> Are God and Nature then at strife
> That Nature lends such evil dreams?
> So careful of the type she seems,
> So careless of the single life;
> That, I considering everywhere
> Her secret meaning in her deeds,
> And finding that of fifty seeds,
> She often brings but one to bear,
> I falter where I firmly trod
> And falling with my weight of cares
> Upon the great world's altar-stairs
> That slope thro' darkness up to God,
> I stretch lame hands of faith, and grope,
> . . . . . . . . . . . . . . . . . . . . . . . .
> And faintly trust the larger hope.

Cancer did not begin with the emergence of man, and earthquakes occurred once the earth's crust began to cool around its molten core. Misformed embryos and genetic malstructures are not peculiar to the human race and the havoc wrought by hurricanes and tornadoes did not originate when man went wrong. Suffering and pain, disease and death are wrought into the structure of nature, for this is a world in the making and the making of men is its object. We men are one with nature, for we have come out of its long creative process. So we, too, are subject to the ills which are the birth pangs of an unfinished universe, the consequences of that process of challenge and response without which there is no growth.

We may overexaggerate not only by oversentimentality but also by ignoring the large presence of cooperation in nature. Imperfect and unfinished though the natural process is, the various chemical cycles which sustain life and the ecological pyramid with its cooperative food chains point to something more significant than a nature "red in tooth and claw with ravin'." There is a balance in nature. Oxygen and carbon dioxide, water and nitrogen are kept in balance by the cooperative structure of living things. The picture of carnivores living on herbivores seems to sensitive spirits to offer a blood-be-sprinkled portrayal of nature, yet there is balance even in this. Each group of creatures fills its niche in the whole. The predators serve to keep the balance so that the creatures on which they prey are kept in check from overabundant proliferation. Marston Bates has pointed out that the biotic community "is a functioning unit, *and* the various component populations serve to build up the unit as a whole." [4]

Again, we need to remember that individuation only slowly develops until with man the individual is more significant than the group. But this unique characteristic of man should not blind us to the fact that, at the animal level, the group is significant and the individual is merged in it. Thus natural selection applies to populations and not to isolated individuals. Survival must be understood in terms of the group, and there is no merciless struggle for life within a species. Indeed, Kropotkin has shown in extensive field studies that living organisms constitute a cooperative society in which the best is achieved for all in a given environment.[5] Kropotkin showed that to preserve the weaker members of a group, the whole group will migrate to an area where conditions of survival are more favorable. There is considerable evidence that human altruism has its roots lower down among the higher mammals where long-lasting personal friendships seem to be formed. Thorpe cites field studies of chimpanzees and porpoises. A chimpanzee will deliberately put itself in danger of attack in order to protect a more foolhardy companion.[6] This serves to remind us that moral and personal attitudes must not be necessarily confined to the level of human personal relationships.

## A Universe of Responsible and Responsive Interrelationships

The biblical writers were still influenced by that animism which provided a primitive philosophical base for early man's understanding of his world. It is, therefore, not surprising to find the men of the Old Testament picturing their world as alive and responsive. Everything from heavenly bodies like the stars, the sun, and the moon to the field with its grain harvest, and the fruit trees with their edible bounty, had a life of its own and was capable of response both to its Creator and to man, made in his Creator's image. Such life must be respected by man and not exploited. The field must be left fallow one year in seven to enjoy its own life; the fruit trees must have their fruit unpicked in their first year; a corner of the cornfield must be left unreaped; a righteous man must respect the life of his beast (Lev. 25:1-7; Lev. 19:9-10; Prov. 12:10).

The covenant structure which related man to man and man to God was extended to nature. Nature as a totality was bound to man and to God in the Noachic covenant in which God promised to preserve the regularity of nature, despite the waywardness of man (Gen. 9:8-17). Nature had its own life and thus was quasi-independent, but it was ultimately dependent upon its Creator. The Hebrew pictured the natural entities as endowed with their own peculiar energies by God. They had their characteristic regularities and capacities for response. But the decrees or statutes expressed in such inherent regularities were within God's covenant and in no way limited his activity. Hence, Hosea saw God sending the food to Jezreel by a chain of psychic responses stretching from the heavens (rain); to the earth (fertility); to the corn, wine, and oil (food); and so to Jezreel (Hos. 2:21-22).

Man, too, was bound in covenant to nature. He must respect its life. Israel's land was bound responsively to Israel and was "Beulah" land, married to God (Isa. 62:4). Man had a covenant with the domestic animals, and they were a part of his psychic totality (Job 41:4). This covenant involved him in responsibilities which he must respect. He had no covenant, however, with the wild animals, and they were free to go their own way in God's world, subject only to their dependence on the Creator. Man's respect for nature, for the land and its harvests, for his domestic animals—all these pointed to his covenant responsibilities and implied a moral relationship to nature and its inhabitants.

It is in the light of this that man's place as God's vicegerent must be understood. The Wisdom tradition makes much of this. Man is king over nature by divinely given right. All things are under his feet, and he has been given dominion over God's creation. This biblical viewpoint is reinforced and confirmed by what we have just indicated at the level of modern science. Thus, it is not surprising to find contemporary philosophical thinking attempting to express this cooperative interrelatedness in nature and man's moral responsibility in subhuman relationships.

The traditional dichotomy between mind and matter is being resolved these days by an increasing emphasis on the subjective and the objective, the inner and the outer. The physical is identified with the objective appearance of what is fundamentally subjective and is of the same order as spirit. Great emphasis is placed on the mysterious nature of energy, so fundamental to the universe, the basic stuff of all that exists in the cosmos. Yet stuff difficult to define except as something that does something, stuff that is known in what it does and that takes so many differing forms. It is not surprising, therefore, to find an increasing tendency to regard life, mind, and self-conscious mind or spirit as potential or latent constituents of energy, ready to emerge into actuality when a certain complexity of pattern is attained. In varying ways, this characterizes the philosophical approach of thinkers like William Temple and Teilhard de Chardin. Energy may then take a physical form, but it is fundamentally akin to mind or spirit.

From a specific point of view, the thought of Martin Buber and his disciples Karl Heim and H. H. Farmer has importance. Buber, like the philosophers cited above, emphasizes the dynamic and personal and attacks the static and substantial approach to man and his world.

Human beings fall into two dimensions of relationship—I-Thou and I-It. The first is the primary and immediate level, and in it there is direct encounter and confrontation of wills. Two persons become directly involved with one another and decisions have to be made. Out of the clash of wills, a new situation emerges; personal existence is determined. But when such an encounter ceases and reflection supervenes, the "Thou" becomes objectified into an "It," and the agent becomes the thinker. "I" am no longer the agent who acts and is acted upon. My world becomes an object of thought, crystal-lized and frozen into a realm of substantial concepts, manipulated by my logic, and fitting into my reflective structures. "I" become monarchical, perched upon the balcony, and other persons and the world pass by beneath my ordering glance. The world becomes my world. Its "Thous" become "Its." This applies not only to my relation to persons but also to my relation to the subhuman and physical levels of my world. Thus Buber says that I may have an I-Thou relationship with a tree. Heim sees the world, at all levels, as immedi-ately confronting me with the nonobjectifiable presence and activity of energy, life, and mind. They are nonobjectifiable in themselves just as the core of human subjectivity, self-conscious spirit, is nonob-jectifiable. We move from direct confrontation to the level of the I-It relation. We can only objectify what such actualities do. Their essential being eludes the objectifying process of the human mind, so that the I-It approach does not grasp the ultimately real.

Now it is precisely the I-It attitude which characterizes the scien-tific approach to reality. Its dominance means that the sense of en-counter and its accompanying aspect of responsibility and decision are driven into the background and that the tendency to exploitation and monarchical domination moves into the foreground.

A. N. Whitehead, Charles Hartshorne, and the process thinkers make the same emphasis. In this philosophy reality is characterized by mind and organism, and the objective world is the frozen world of the already-become. The latter point is also made by Buber, Heim, and Farmer—the "It" world is a frozen world because it is past and not in process as is the immediate realm of the "Thou." It is objective because it is fixed in the past, even though the time interval for such objectification be miniscule.

For Whitehead and his followers, the world consists of actual entities in a process of becoming, entities atomic in both space and time. Such entities are intimately interrelated by feeling or prehen-sion, and each is striving to attain satisfaction. This "feeling" may be very rudimentary. It ranges from such an elementary unconscious level to that of the human soul at the self-conscious level. It includes feeling for all other actual entities, including the past actual entities which constitute its own particular process. But it also includes a feeling for the possible goals or subjective aims from which it may select its own immediate objective. When the latter is attained, as a result of the complex structure of feelings which are focalized in the "actual entity," this entity attains objective immortality or satisfaction and becomes an object which other actual entities in process may feel or prehend.

In this way, process thinkers paint a picture of the universe as a process in which the constituent elements are knit together by feeling and, out of such cooperative relationship with its general reinforcement, are moving toward goals which they have selected. The process is thus organic. It is prevented from being chaotic by the persuasive activity of a divine being who, by loving persuasion, guides the process forward and also presents the possible aims or goals which the constituent entities may select.

Whitehead criticizes the scientific approach as subject to the "fallacy of misplaced concreteness." Science freezes the process into a structure of lumps of matter, located in and separated from one another in space and moving in time. By removing the continuity and feelingful interrelatedness, science moves into an abstract realm and relates the substances so created by a structure of causality. In the same way, science falls into the false dichotomy of mind and matter. Thus, science creates a world which man can insensitively and irresponsibly dominate and exploit.

The virtue of this dynamic way of thinking is that it presents a picture much more in keeping with the biblical approach of a cooperative relationship between nature, man, and God. Its weakness lies in its failure to give full play to the personal nature of man as a self-transcendent being, its tendency to emphasize the divine immanence and downplay the divine transcendence, its general preoccupation with an organic rather than a personal model with reality, and its failure to see the world as created out of nothing and other than God's body. It does, however, remind us that God is involved with, suffers with, travels with his world, and that man is bound up in intimate relationship with the lower order of nature. In this sense, it helps to draw out the ethical implications present in the Christian approach to the world. In Christ, we find a God who suffers with all his creatures and bears our human sinfulness in redeeming love.

## The Redemption of Man and Nature

Man's failure to cooperate with his Creator has only magnified the unfinishedness of the universe and its attendant natural evil. Instead of using freedom to become a cocreator with God, man has taken the "It" attitude and exploited the world, with disastrous results for himself and his natural environment. Imprisoned in selfishness and arrogance, proud of scientific achievement, glorying in technological ability, impelled by economic greed and with a demonic hunger for power, man needs to be liberated. He needs to find the way of love instead of selfishness and to practice the way of service in the place of the way of greed. But he finds himself in a prison house from which he cannot free himself. Only a saving word from beyond his own level of being can liberate him. Without such a liberating power, no amount of ethical idealism will suffice. It is not a question of knowing what one ought to do so much as one of possessing the dynamic to carry such idealism into action. Even political machinery with its coercive legalism cannot lumber into effective activity or even be constructed because sinful man in his greed and arrogance obstructs any movement to actualize ethical concern.

The Christian faith speaks of such liberation and finds the motivation and dynamic for ethical concern in the historicity of God in Jesus the Christ. In Jesus' life, death, and resurrection, God lifted human history into the depths of his own life and poured into the world a love strong enough to set all people free from selfishness and sinful pride and to enable them to achieve their destiny as sons of God. In one human life, people have seen, in the midst of history, the kind of person they ought to be. And in and through that same human life, there has been disclosed a reconciling and liberating love which sets them on the high road that God intended for all his children. So there has come into being a new people of God, a fellowship of men and women in whose lives and relationships the life and spirit of the Christ has been perpetuated within human history—the church.

What the Christian faith offers primarily is not an ethical system, a new moral code, but the gift of a new dynamic for living, a motivating love by which sinful people are set free to be the children of God. Hence the center of Christianity is this believing community which, in its life and relationships, as well as in its confessions and creeds, manifests that way of living which fulfills the creative intention of God. The Christian ethic is a new ethic because its motivation lies deeper than mere duty. It is grounded in love for God, a love which flows down through the self-giving of the God-man on Calvary into our lives and so out to our world. And, let it be noted, a love which moves in our self-giving not only to our fellow human beings but also to that natural order which also rejoices its Creator's heart.

Albert Schweitzer was a great Christian humanist, although a far from orthodox theologian. Indeed, at times there is almost a pantheistic note in his approach to reality. But no one can doubt his devotion to the Christ. Nor can the haunting paragraph at the close of *The Quest for the Historical Jesus* be forgotten. There Schweitzer speaks of the Christ still challenging people to follow him and declares that "to those who obey Him, whether they be wise or simple, He will reveal Himself in the toils, the conflicts, the sufferings which they shall pass through in His fellowship, and, as an ineffable mystery, they shall learn in their own experience who He is." [7] Our Lord manifested a reverence for nature and a love for natural things throughout his teaching, and so it is not surprising that Schweitzer made the main premise of his ethical stance, a "reverence for life," often coloring it, however, with a mystical pantheism. He showed an attitude toward nature often seriously lacking in orthodox Christian circles. Indeed he noted the tendency of Western and Oriental philosophers alike to limit ethical concern to the human level. His final comment on traditional Christianity is significant: "Even when sympathy with the animal creation was felt to be right, it could not be brought within the scope of ethics, because ethics were really focused only on the behavior of man to man." [8]

Schweitzer believed that all things were activated by a will to live and thus that there must be a reverence for even cells and crystals. This ethical attitude of reverence means that "so far as he is a free man he (man) uses every opportunity of tasting the blessedness of being able to assist life and avert from it suffering and destruction." [9] Schweitzer carried his position to excess when he came up against problems raised by the functioning of the ecological pyramid. But he did emphasize a dimension of Christian responsibility which until recently has been strangely neglected.

Furthermore, Schweitzer's viewpoint is reinforced by thinkers like Buber, Heim, Teilhard, Temple, and the process philosophers and theologians, and the whole viewpoint stretches back to the near animism of the Old Testament writers. A rational and understandable foundation for an ethical approach to the natural order must lie in the capacity of nature itself to respond at its various levels to man. We must see natural entities as "Thous" if we are to experience moral responsibility in our relationship to them. It is not our intention here to develop this thought philosophically, but merely to emphasize an attitude which critical idealism and panpsychism have sought to express in their own way and which has considerable currency in contemporary thinking. One root of an ethical attitude toward nature must be the recovery of the "I-Thou" relationship. Theologically we need not be ashamed of treating nature as an interrelated whole in which the parts are responsively related to one another and to man himself.

There is another and deeper theological root for an attitude of ethical responsibility to and reverence for nature. This lies in the Christian disclosure itself. If Christ be the historicity of God, then the personal presence of God in this historical life not only affirms our humanity but also affirms the natural order out of which we have emerged by God's creative act. Furthermore, the self-giving love of God, which is there disclosed in the midst of history, embraces not only our broken and sinful humanity but also the natural environment which is the setting for our life as children of God. If the life of our Lord is an affirmation of our humanity, it is an affirmation of our responsible relationship to nature. The love which is evoked in our lives by the outpouring of God's love in this event must find expression not only in our love for our fellows but also in our responsible love for the natural order.

Concomitant with such a love for nature is the note of joy and celebration. We need the spirit of Francis of Assisi, who, in his great "Canticle of the Sun," celebrated his kinship with all living things. He could sing of brother sun and sister moon, of brother wind and sister water, of brother fire and mother earth, praising the Creator for the role they played in his own life. There is a sense of rejoicing and wonder at these creatures which play their part in the divine economy. And does not this echo the cry of the Creator himself when he sees that his creation is good and echo also the celebration of the sons of God on the first morning of creation (Gen. 1:31; Job 38:4-7)? Even a naturalistic writer like Julian Huxley can write: "Enjoyment as well as material resources are being threatened [by our rape of nature]; as my brother Aldous said after reading Rachel Carson's book [*Silver Springs*] we are exterminating half the basis of English poetry." [10]

Again, we need to stimulate our reverence for nature by recognizing its sacramental dimension. In and through the wonder of nature, the Christian is confronted by his Creator and Redeemer. His "Thou" relation with nature merges into a "Thou" relation to the personal Presence who journeys with his creatures and sustains their lives. The whole universe can be sacramental in the sense that it mediates the presence of and points to its Creator. In the sacraments of the church, this sacramental aspect of nature is brought to a focus. For we take bread and wine and water, elements symbolic of nature, and we make them bearers of spiritual meaning. Nature participates in the process of redemption and witnesses to God's redeeming grace. The creatures are drawn up into the Christ's risen humanity and prefigure that ultimate consummation when men and nature alike shall be gathered up in him. Nature attains its true and ultimate meaning in the sacramental aspect of the church's worship. We are reminded that we are co-workers with the Christ in the redemption of all things, nature as well as persons. Bonhoeffer suggests that, in the sacraments, the creatures "are freed from their dumbness and proclaim directly to the believer the new creative Word of God. They no longer need man's interpretation. Enslaved nature does not utter the Word of creation directly to us. But the sacraments speak." 11 We look for a new heaven and new earth wherein a new humanity dwells.

This eschatological note emphasizes the dimension of hope in the Christian attitude to nature. We might, like Tennyson, fall protesting on the world's great altar stairs were it not for this dimension in the Christian faith. Death and resurrection are ingredients in the pattern of the divine historicity. The resurrection carries with it the belief that *all* things will ultimately be summed up in Christ, things in heaven and things on earth (1 Cor. 15:27 f.; Col. 1:15-20; Eph. 1:9-10). Ecological concern is a part of our task as witnesses to the Christ and cocreators with God because we dare to believe that ultimately the whole universe will be drawn up into the life of God and transfigured. What God began in Jesus, his life, death, and resurrection, will be completed when the incarnate presence of the Christ becomes all-pervasive. The God who drew history into himself in Jesus wills ultimately to incarnate himself in the whole process. Through death and resurrection there will come, not just a new humanity, but a new universe. As men find their true freedom in God's will, so nature will find its perfection, the fulfillment of the Creator's vision, in God's full presence. To this end we too must labor in creative discipleship seeking to fulfill that vision in our world.

**Notes**

1. Lynn White, "The Historical Roots of Our Ecological Crisis" in *The Subversive Science,* Paul Shepard and Daniel McKinley, ed. (Boston: Houghton-Mifflin, 1969), p. 349.

2. Julian Huxley, *Evolution in Action* (New York: Harper and Brothers, 1953).

3. M. Polanyi, *Personal Knowledge* (Chicago: University of Chicago Press, 1958), pp. 384 ff.

4. Marston Bates, *The Nature of Natural History* (New York: Scribner's Sons, 1950), p. 122.

5. P. Kropotkin, *Mutual Aid* (London: Penguin Books, 1939).

6. W. H. Thorpe, *Biology and the Nature of Man* (London: Oxford University Press, 1962), p. 64.

7. Albert Schweitzer, *The Quest for the Historical Jesus,* W. Montgomery, trans. (London: A. & C. Black, 1945), p. 401.

8. Albert Schweitzer, *Out of My Life and Thought* (London: George Allen and Unwin, 1933), p. 272.

9. Ibid.

10. Julian Huxley, "The Future of Man—Evolutionary Aspects" in *Man and His Future,* Gordon Wolstenholme, ed. (Boston: Little, Brown and Co., 1963), p. 10.

11. D. Bonhoeffer, *Christ the Center,* J. Bowden, trans. (New York: Harper & Row, 1960), p. 67.

# 10

## Liberation Ethics and Theology

### Bob Adams

The theology of liberation is committed to a certain understanding of the Christian faith and its relationship to the world. It could as well have been called an ethics of liberation if it were not that the word *ethics*, in some contexts, means the social graces, etiquette, or how to live harmoniously with people of the same general station in life. The theology or ethics of liberation rejects contemporary "stations in life" as being manifestations of social injustice and intends to abolish the injustices themselves.

Liberation ethics began among Third World thinkers as a way of understanding life among these people who are politically oppressed, economically deprived, and technologically underdeveloped. Although it has adherents and proponents in Africa and the Far East, its most reasoned and experienced articulations thus far have emerged in Central and South America. Liberation theologians insist that human endeavors, and even divine-human endeavors, can perhaps best be understood within the context of their beginning and growth. A study of Latin American liberation movements is a good illustration of this truth and for that reason will be examined first and will serve as the framework for analyzing other liberation movements.

Liberation theology insists that theology can be done most legitimately when all the relational contexts of those doing the theologizing are given full weight. Thus, theology and anthropology/sociology are inseparably linked.[1] Liberation ethics insists that the human context include social, political, and economic factors and the relationships between the sexes.[2] Whenever such human group interrelationships are critically analyzed, some particular societal model must necessarily be employed. The model accepted by liberation ethicists is Marxist: human groupings confront one another in a way which is basically alienative.[3] Both historical and dialectical materialism claim that societal groupings function in this manner.[4] As Christians, liberation theologians do not accept a thoroughgoing materialism which negates the being of God. However, they do understand that human interrelationships are influenced by materialistic factors and believe that God works in a redemptive way in and through the material.[5]

Liberation theologians share a common perspective and concern with many other Latin American scholars, particularly those who are engaged in the social sciences. They understand their peoples to be the objects of colonialistic oppression, first by the European powers, then by the United States, and now by both the superblocks of East and West.[6] Latin American history is seen as an adjunct to the history of either Europe or North America. Latin American theology, likewise, has largely been little more than an adjunct to the theology of either Europe or North America. The Christian mission in Latin America has also been an extension of the mission of churches in Europe or North America. In any case, Latin America and Latin Americans have not been approached or understood directly but always understood as extensions or objects of some other primary entity.[7]

In summary, liberation theology and ethics represents the efforts of Third World theologians and ethicists to understand their real, human situation as it relates to God and fellow human beings. Both theological and anthropological/sociological perspectives are necessary for this understanding. The latter perspectives are taken from a Marxist viewpoint, which is essentially alienative. Third World history is one of colonialized peoples who have thus been denied a true self-understanding. With these perspectives as a set of given factors (although they have developed historically), the question emerges as to what *liberation* means as a Christian term in this context.

## Salvation as "Liberation"

The basic premise of liberation theology and ethics is that God designs, desires, and purposes that his creation be free from alienation, dependence, exploitation, and oppression. A basic observation of liberation ethics is that God's purposes have been and are being thwarted continually: Man and his condition are the prime focus and example of such frustration. Individual man is understood as a unity and as one who exists in necessary relationships to others. *Man* in the abstract has no reality, and isolated, individual man represents the worst kind of alienated self-understanding. True liberation is salvation, according to liberation theology and ethics, and includes every aspect of social and individual relationships.u0

Such broad understanding of salvation as liberation was already widely shared prior to the specific formation of a "theology of liberation," in what was referred to as "theology of revolution." [8] Revolution, in the sense used here, was considered to be an integral and perhaps historically necessary dimension of salvation.[9] Partially because revolution is usually associated with violence, "theology of revolution" was gradually replaced with "theology of liberation." [10] It may also be true that European-originated "theology of hope" strongly influenced the semantic shift from "revolution" to "liberation," [11] although at least one Latin American theologian rejects this view.[12] Theologians and ethicists of liberation generally do not reject out of hand the possibility of violence.[13]

Liberation theology, given its basic understanding and observation, moves dialectically from praxis (action) to critical reflection, and so on successively. Perhaps the best concrete example of the dialectical movement is to be found in "education for critical consciousness," [14] which has been defined as an attempt "to explore the actuality of a situation in all its relationships until the participants in the exploratory process are conscious of its true meaning, with the permanent result that the conscience is sensitized to the level of action." [15]

Since all human beings are part of life situations, they are equipped already by experience to begin the exploring process which will ultimately result in action. The action changes the former situation in dynamic movement to a new situation which again becomes the subject for further reflection by critical consciousness. This dynamic movement has as its goal a constantly liberating action. Humanly speaking, there is no fixed, final goal because historical experience itself is ongoing. Theologically, however, the *eschaton* or *Parousia* is the final goal.

## Liberation and the Bible

Liberation theologians interpret both Scriptures and history in this dialectic. Certain historical movements are understood as paradigmatic for the ways in which God is related to liberation. The principal paradigm in the Old Testament is the experience of the Hebrew people, first in Egypt and then in the entire Exodus episode. This experience was at once human and divine: divine in that God was active in liberating his people, but human in that the Hebrew experience was primarily political as they dealt with the Egyptian oppressors. The paradigm in the New Testament, except for the unique and unrepeatable experience of the incarnation, is that of the church itself.

Critical reflection on the biblical paradigms teaches Christians today the way in which they should reflect critically on their own situations. Just as people then were oppressed, so today there are people who are oppressed. Just as the possibility for liberation existed then, so too the possibility exists today. Just as oppression and oppressors then were real as historical conditions and persons, the same is true today. Just as liberation then involved whole human beings, so also it does today. Just as people, under God's intiative and leadership, were active in their liberation then, the same is true today. Just as attempts to repress those seeking liberation were real, bloody, and cruel then, so the same is true today.[16]

Liberation ethicists, upon critical reflection about historical experiences, arrive at certain conclusions. Their conclusions are, for them, of deep spiritual and human as well as theological significance. However, they must not be spiritualized or dehistoricized. For, upon reflection, they must be responded to and acted on in the here and now. Following a Marxist analytical process, liberationists see oppressed people as alienated from their own being, dispossessed by those from within and without their geographic environs, cheated of the fruits of their labor, and prevented from achieving what it means to be truly human. Just as the historical process that resulted in these inhuman conditions was primarily political, so must the action be primarily political that leads through a liberating process.[17] The new sphere of obedience for the Christian is politics, that is, the comprehensive situation of power relationships among human beings and between people and nature. Liberationists insist that this political hermeneutic is basic to viable Christian action in the world. For them, the messianic-missionary traditions of the Bible are both understandable and practicable when approached by persons who stand in the one direction of righteousness and hold the same intention of being liberative to the captive.

The essential questions to be asked are, What interests are served by theology? What people or power structures are aided or supported by theological understanding—the wealthy and powerful or the poor and powerless? What difference does it make politically and socially to speak of God? This means that the Bible is to be approached not with the formal questions of demythologizing and form or source criticism but with a criticism of the social context. The ethical question is prior to all formal questions.

### Liberation: Variations on a Theme

These themes are basic to a variety of liberation movements. Each emphasizes the circumstances and perspectives which are unique or germane to its own concern. They vary in the particular way in which liberation is interpreted or in their perception of the oppressor force. These can be indicated briefly.

*The liberation from colonialist imperialism* is sought by those seeking deliverance from political bondage. This may be from foreign powers that have conquered and now rule the native land or from oppressive dictatorial or totalitarian regimes. In either case, the focus is on the governing mechanism of a given geopolitical entity. Political systems that are not based upon justice and deny basic human rights are seen as dehumanizing and depersonalizing. Liberationist theology sounds the Mosaic theme, "Let my people go!" Self-determination, interdependence, and participation in the political process are sought for the masses of people who have been politically disenfranchised. Until people are free from governmental bondage, there can be no true liberation. The task of bringing about political participation by the masses is complicated in Third World countries by the pressure, coercion, and manipulation of the world superpowers.[18]

*The liberation from imperialist colonialism* stresses powerful economic forces that contribute to human bondage. Third World countries are frequently dominated by foreign countries that have extensive economic interests. Through technology and industry, multinational corporations frequently exploit underdeveloped countries for their cheap materials and labor. Too often the economic cycle has favored the wealthy and powerful, not those whose lives produce the goods. For years, Third World countires have furnished raw or semirefined materials which were shipped to industrialized countries for manufacturing. The finished products have then been sold on Third World markets at profit levels considered exorbitant.[19] Furthermore, the powerful wealthy dominate the economy of the underdeveloped country. The gap between the have's and have-not's is radical. In some countries 90 percent of the people live on 10 percent of the wealth while 10 percent of the people control 90 percent of the wealth.

Liberation theology asks, Who produces what and for whom? The economic deprivation of the masses is contrary to the will of God who seeks the well-being of all his people. Thus, liberationists stress a participationist economic model. Until economic justice is attained, the humanizing activity of God is still unrealized.

*The liberation from racist oppression* is the central motif of black liberation theology.[20] Here the problem is not so much deprivation as it is deidentification, the denial of a personal and social identity to a racial group.

A variation on this theme can be noted with regard to the Amerindians. The settlement by whites in North America was done so at the expense of the native Indian. They saw the wholesale destruction of their cities, libraries, families, political systems, and were forcibly removed from their ancestral lands.

Blacks have interpreted their experience in the United States as one of systemic oppression. Their experience began in slavery and continues as a form of covert suppression by discrimination. Thus, Cone calls for a theology based upon the black experience that will result in liberation for both the oppressor and the oppressed. Only in this way can full humanity be recognized and restored.

*Liberation from sexism* is stressed by women theologians of liberation.[21] For them, theology has served the interests of men and has been used to perpetrate male domination and to suppress women in both society and church. Inequity and unjust treatment economically, politically, ecclesiastically, and personally has been the result. For them sexual stereotypes and male-dominated theology are major targets for criticism and revision.

A common theme in each of these liberation movements is the role of religion. The Christian church (in its institutional expression) is seen both as source of oppression and as a possible ally in the struggle for liberation. The Roman Catholic Church has been sharply criticized for its role in the oppression of people in Latin America.[22] Similar accusations are leveled against Evangelical churches.[23] Cone charges that theology has been "white" in North America while Mary Daly believes that the male symbolism of the Christian church must be entirely removed before women can be liberated. Liberationists stress that until God can be understood as brown or red or black or yellow and can be responded to as a loving Creator-Redeemer rather than as a figure of male dominance, true liberation-salvation is impossible. Institutional powers will continue to be oppressive until theology itself is liberated from its narrow interests.

## Christ and Church as Liberator

It is important to note that the central affirmation for liberation theology and ethics is that the God of Jesus Christ is the ultimate liberator. Jesus is the liberated and liberating Lord whose mission was "to proclaim release to the captives and recovering of sight to the blind, to set at liberty those who are oppressed, to proclaim the acceptable year of the Lord" (Luke 4:18-19, RSV). This is central to understanding the mission of the church to the world and its relation to oppressed people.

Other perspectives important to liberation theologians and ethicists follow from this initial understanding, which is one of faith. These are based on empirical observation, either of history or of contemporary working in society. History is understood to move, to progress. Progress is not seen to be automatic or inevitable, except perhaps from a futuristic or eschatological perspective.[24] This dynamic notion of history may be based either upon a process or a dialectical mode or model as over against a static or substantive mode.[25] This mind-set is basic to the hermeneutic with which liberation theologians approach the Scriptures.

There will be no liberation in any case until the level of critical consciousness is raised to the point of action. Knowledge is linked to transformation. Human initiative must be activated. The movement of the dialectic depends on it. The critical level of consciousness is reached when the oppressed group realizes its objectively true state of alienation: from self, from others, and from the fruits of their own labors. History becomes the object of change and transformation as well as an agent for self-transformation. Thus, the societal model of alienation is one of the fundamental understandings which liberation ethicists hold.

However paradoxical it may seem to one who does not share this understanding of alienation on the group level, it does not necessarily apply to individual relationships. That is to say, two people, each belonging to different groups which are alienated from one another, are not necessarily alienated from one another as individuals. They may be attracted to one another; they might even both be followers of the same Lord.

In summary, the theologian or ethicist of liberation will, in addition to his basic trust in God in Christ, also hold as true other perspectives which are understood as given and empirically verifiable. These are history which moves (progresses?) dialectically and societal relationships which are always ultimately alienative.

## Questions for Liberationists

Several questions need to be raised concerning the perspective of the ethics and theology of liberation. The first has to do with hermeneutics and paradigm cases. On what grounds are particular paradigm cases chosen as first-class, primary paradigms? Why, for example, is the Exodus-liberation case chosen over the Canaan-conquering case? Why is not the Suffering-Servant Messiah chosen in place of the conquering, militant Messiah?

Again, given current sociological understandings of societal models as either consensual, manipulative, or alienative—could not a case be made for the church as a fourth model, perhaps understood as reconciliatory? It would seem to be easier for Roman Catholicism, with its longer history of involvement in various roles, to attempt another model than for Protestants to do so. But could not the people of God in both Old and New Testaments possibly serve as a fourth model?

The question of the Christian's relationship to violence is posed by liberation ethics in acute form. Given definitions, such as Freire's, of institutionalized violence, how should Christians respond? The question is not *only* for the complete and thoroughgoing pacifist. Can an ethic of calculated response to institutionalized violence be enunciated and justified?

However, liberation theology and ethics pose crucial questions for those Christians who do not identify themselves as liberationists.

First, how shall we talk meaningfully of justice from our positions of power, control, and relative ease? This deals first with our role as church people who are active in the missionary enterprise. It also addresses us in our political and economic life. How can we respond as equals, as part of God's family, and as members of the human family?

Second, how shall we dialogue concerning our understanding of and acceptance of certain societal models? Is it not true that in theory we think of "the world" in terms of an alienative model, until it becomes a case of "our world" and "their world," in which case we call (from positions of strength) for a consensus? Once the crisis has passed, do we not return to manipulating (oppressing) the underprivileged or powerless? What is needed is repentance. Maneuvers to protect vested interests are no substitute for the altered life-style required of Christian disciples when confronting the oppressed of the world. Only the truly liberated can be genuinely liberative.

Third, how can we respond critically to our own particular perspectives? This is certainly needed for those who do not understand ethics and theology from a radical liberation perspective. The critical task is necessary, however, if theology is to be saved from self-serving perspectives and stultifying, oppressive provincialism. The challenge from the oppressed of the earth must be taken seriously.[26] No casual dismissal of these concerns is possible if the church is seriously to maintain a viable mission to the world in the name of the Christ who delivers all people from the bondages of sin and demonic systems.

## Notes

1. See Gustavo Gutierrez, *A Theology of Liberation: History, Politics, and Salvation,* Caridad Inda and John Eagleson, trans. and ed. (Maryknoll, New York: Orbis Books, 1973), p. 7.

2. See Gustavo Gutierrez and Richard Shaull, *Liberation and Change* (Atlanta: John Knox Press, 1977), p. 1; and Fals-Borda, *Subversion y Desarrollo: El Caso de America Latina* (Ginebra: Foyer John Knox, 1970), pp. 6-8.

3. Those who specifically treat this *vorverstandnis* generally claim a Marxist view. See Jose Miguez Bonino, *Christians and Marxists: The Mutual Chal-*

*lenge to Revolution* (Grand Rapids: Eerdmans, 1976), p. 80. See also Juan Luis Segundo, *Liberation of Theology*, trans. John Drury (Maryknoll, New York: Orbis Books, 1976), p. 57-61.

4. See my *El Mundo Unido—Bajo la Hoz o la Cruz* (Santiago, Chile: Junta Bautista de Publicaciones, 1964), pp. 23-24. See also my article "Theology and Ethics of Liberation," *Collage*, January, 1976, pp. 32-34.

5. See Jose Miguez Bonino, *Doing Theology in a Revolutionary Situation* (Philadelphia: Fortress Press, 1975), pp. XXV-XXVII and Julio de Santa Ana, *"Reflexiones sobre el Sentido de la Accion Christiana en America Latina," Christianismo y Sociedad*, Vol. 1, *enero-abril de* 1963, pp. 36-48. Also see Rubem A. Alves, *A Theology of Human Hope* (Saint Meinrad, Indiana: Abbey Press, 1974), pp. 1-6.

6. For an example from the social sciences, see Manuel Seaone, *Las Seis Dimensiones de la Revolucion Mundial* (Santiago de Chile: Zig Zag, 1960); Luis Quintanilla, *A Latin American Speaks* (N. Y.: Macmillan, 1943); John Reese Stevenson, *The Chilean Popular Front* (Philadelphia: University of Pennsylvania Press, 1942); Claudio Velez ed., *Obstacles to Change in Latin America* (New York: Oxford University Press, 1965) which both predate the commonly recognized beginning (about 1968) for the Liberation Theology movement, and furnish historical background and understanding for the movement itself.

7. A thorough and scholarly treatment of this is found in Orlando Costas, *The Church and Its Mission: A Shattering Critique from the Third World* (Wheaton, Illinois: Tyndale House, 1974).

8. See Richard Shaull, *Encounter with Revolution* (New York: Association Press, 1955), and Francois Houtart and Emile Pin, *The Church and the Latin American Revolution*, Gilbert Barth, trans. (New York: Sheed and Ward, 1965). See also Paul Lehmann, *Transfiguration of Politics* (New York: Harper & Row, 1975), chapter 9.

9. Silverio Ivan Ramirez, "Dimensiones de la Redencion," *LaVoz Bautista* (Concepcion, Chile: Mayo, 1964), pp. 8-9.

10. The word *revolution*, when used in the context of liberation ethics, is often dissociated in some way from a necessary relationship to violence. For example, see Dom Heldera Camara, *Revolution through Peace*, trans. Amparo McLean (New York: Harper & Row, 1971).

11. For a succinct statement of European antecedents, I am indebted to an unpublished paper by Alan Neely entitled, "Liberation Theology in Latin America: Antecedents and Autochthony," given at a Third World Conference in Omaha, Nebraska, October 28, 1977. See also his Ph. D. dissertation, "Protestant Antecedents of the Latin American Theology of Liberation," The American University, 1977.

12. See Hugo Assman, *Theology for a Nomad Church*, trans. Paul Burnes (Maryknoll, New York: Orbis Books, 1975), p. 86, and *Opresion-Liberacion:*

*Desafio a los Christianos* (Montevideo: Tierra Nueva, 1971), p. 106

13. Camara (fn. 10) seems to reject all forms of violence as unacceptable to Christians. Many, however, maintain that violence has been chosen already by the oppressors, and may perhaps successfully be countered by violence. See Assman, *Opresion-Liberacion*, p. 113.

14. Paulo Freire, *Education for Critical Consciousness* (New York: Seabury Press, 1973); and *Pedagogy of the Oppressed*, trans. Myra Bergman Ramos (New York: Seabury Press, 1973).

15. Adams, "Theology and Ethics of Liberation," p. 33.

16. Among brief treatments along this line are Assman's *Theology for a Nomad Church;* Gutierrez, *A Theology of Liberation* (especially ch. 9). See also particularly *Social Justice and the Latin Churches*, Jorge Lara-Braud, trans. (Richmond: John Knox Press, 1969), chapters 3 and 4.

17. See Juan Luis Segundo, *Masas y Minorias en la dialectica divina de la liberacion* (Buenos Aires: Editorial La Aurora, 1973), for a general analysis. Also see Orlando Fals-Borda, *Las Revoluciones Inconclusas en America Latina (1809-1968)* (Mexico: Siglo Veintiuno Editores, 1968).

18. See notes 2, 6 above. See also my unpublished paper, *Revolution in Latin America: A View from The Historical Perspective* (Vanderbilt University Graduate School, 1966). Twenty-two instances of this phenomenon are plentiful in the extreme. Hardly anyone denies their veracity. Some defend the process as just, others explain it as simply an accident of history. See Adolf Berle, *Latin America: Diplomacy and Reality* (New York: Harper & Row, 1962); *Investment in Chile: Basic Information for United States Businessmen* (Washington: Department of Commerce, various editions). Others judge the phenomenon as unjust and immoral. See particularly notes 2, 6, and 7.

19. For a detailing of this charge, see Gutierrez, *A Theology of Liberation*, chapter 6; Fals-Borda, *Subversion y Desarrollo;* and Freire, *Pedagogy of the Oppressed*.

20. See James Cone, *Black Theology and Liberation* also J. DeOtis Roberts, *Liberation and Reconciliation* (Philadelphia: Westminster, 1971).

21. See Rosemary Reuther, *Liberation Theology* (New York: Paulist Press, 1972); Mary Daly, *Beyond God The Father* (Boston: Beacon, 1973), and *The Church and the Second Sex* (New York: Harper & Row, 1975).

22. See Juan A. Mackay, *El Otro Cristo Espanol* (Buenos Aires: La Aurora, 1952); Jorge P. Howard, *Liberated Religiosa en America Latina?* (Buenos Aires: La Aurora, 1946); Robert Cecil Moore, *Piety and Poverty in Chile: A Study of the Economic and Social Effects of Roman Catholicism on Chile* (Nashville: Broadman, 1946). Most treatments of this subject are highly polemical and border on the scurrilous.

23. See J. P. Gillen, "Possible Cultural Maladjustments in Modern Latin America." *Journal of Inter-American Studies* (April, 1963); Ignacio Vergara,

# Liberation Ethics and Theology

# Liberation Ethics and Theology

# Liberation Ethics and Theology

# Liberation Ethics and Theology

# Liberation Ethics and Theology

# Liberation Ethics and Theology

*El Protestantismo en Chile* (Santiago de Chile: Editorial del Pacifico, 1962); Costas, *The Church and its Mission;* Dennis E. Clark, *The Third World and Mission* (Waco, Texas: Word, 1971); Gutierrez in *Liberation and Change,* chapter 3.

24. See for instance, the thought of Pierre Teilhard de Chardin, *The Phenomenon of Man,* trans. Bernard Wall (New York: Harper & Row, 1959).

25. For a more detailed description of this differentiation, see George Eaton Simpson and John Milton Yinger, *Racial and Cultural Minorities: And Analysis of Prejudice and Discrimination,* fourth ed. (New York: Harper & Row, 1972), p. 160.

26. See Charles R. Strain, "Ideology and Alienation: Theses on the Interpretation and Evaluation of Theologies of Liberation," *Journal of the Academy of Religion,* XLV/4 (1977), pp. 473-490.

# 11

## The Black Church and Social Justice

Emmanuel McCall

From about 1964 to 1972 it was popular for young blacks to casti-gate the black church.[1] They were influenced by such men as Stokley Carmichael, H. Rap Brown, and Eldridge Cleaver. Black Muslim and Black Panther spokesmen joined in trying to put the black church out of existence. Black pastors were called "ecclesiastical pimps," "Uncle Toms," and "Oreos." The Yippies, Weathermen, and other underground movements influenced black radicals to believe that the church was an instrument of oppression that should be destroyed. While extremist white groups (KKK and Citizens Councils) burned black church houses because they were the meeting place for civil rights activists, radical black groups burned black church houses believing them to be "instruments of oppression."

"Liberating the offerings," seizing church properties, and intimidat-ing worshipers were only some of the rash of harassments. It was fashionable to cite the religious preferences of political demagogues and their forms of "Christianity" as one of the "white man's ways of keeping the nigger down." As Otis Moss asserts, however, had these people done their homework they would have discovered that the black church neither birthed nor nurtured the Maddoxes, Wal-laces, Bull Conners, Agnews, or Nixons.[2] Rather, the black church birthed the Denmark Vesseys, Nat Turners, Gabriel Prossers, Martin Kings, Andrew Youngs, Leon Sullivans, Jesse Jacksons, J. Alfred Smiths. These men were first of all "men of God" and were deter-mined to change an unjust system by the most viable means consist-ent with Christian understandings.

While recognizing that there is validity in some of these accusa-tions, most blacks know that were it not for the black church the

197

struggles for social justice would have remained infantile. However, for the benefit of whites, it is still necessary to detail the pilgrimage of the black church in its quest for social justice. Therefore, this chapter addresses the following questions: 1) Why has the black church expressed such an intense interest in social justice? 2) What theological, philosophical, social, humanistic, or political ideologies undergird that quest? 3) What forms did the quest take? 4) Who were the shapers of those forms? 5) How did the church relate to the nonchurch, parachurch, or non-Christian oriented movements also interested in social justice? 6) Where are the movements today? What is their substance, nature, and character?

## The Character of the Black Church

A beginning point for answers to these questions is to look at the black church. Since the mid-1960s the word *black* has become adjectival for much surrounding the experiences of Americans of African descent. There are those, even among black Americans, who would deny the reality of a "black church." Ideally, such adjectives should not be needed to describe an expression of *the church.* Historical circumstances make it necessary however. *There is a black church*, not because of the color of its adherents but the character of its substance. Its expressions are different both because of its antecedents in African religions and because of the circumstances which it was forced to address. Gayraud Wilmore has observed that

> Black Christianity . . . was from the beginning, a fusion between a highly developed and pervasive feeling about the hierophantic nature of historical experience, flowing from the African religious past and a radical and programatic secularity, related to the experience of slavery and oppression, which constituted the essential and most significant characteristic of black religion.[3]

This gave unique emphases and particular perspectives not found in the religious expressions of white Americans, says Wilmore:

Blacks have used Christianity not as it was delivered to them by segregated white churches, but as its truth was authenticated to them in the experience of suffering, to reinforce an ingrained religious temperament and to produce an indigenous religion oriented to freedom and human welfare.[4]

Such developments are both understandable and predictable since social and historical experiences serve to modify any traditions received from other groups. Wilmore points out that:

> Most sociologists of religion will agree that religion does much of the same thing for all sorts and conditions of men. But it is a matter of serious debate whether a specific religion of a specific people can be transmitted "in toto" to another people— even in the same geographical area—without certain differences arising on account of ethnicity, nationality, social structure and among their factors.[5]

This is especially true when there is a significant difference in the life-style of the groups in question. The world and reality are perceived in very different ways by slaves than by free whites. As Wilmore says:

> The questions that existence presents to the religious intelligence and imagination of a person who is relatively free to determine his own style of life and vocation are existentially different questions from those which the religious introspection of a slave predicates and seeks to answer.[6]

Out of the African religious past, blacks brought several important perspectives: [7]

1. *A concept of the wholeness of life.* Religion and life were not separate realities, rather, religion permeated the whole life. The distinctions between secular and sacred were not drawn in those ways familiar to the Western mind.

An illustration of how this expresses itself in America's black churches is in the absence of the evangelism *vs.* social action dichotomy that has been a problem for white churches. The black church has not been concerned with this as a problem, not even to call it a problem. Whenever needs have arisen of a personal, social, business, or political nature, black churches have responded. The receiving of special or freewill offerings for other than "religious" causes continue. When black churches talk of "missions" or "mission giving," they do so with reference to specific community or personal needs worthy of concerted support.

Such a notion of wholeness finds parallels in other experiences such as music which may be borderline between "blues" or "gospel," nightclub or church; or in support of educational and vocational activities that benefit the community or in public announcements that are regular features in worship services. It is not accidental that the black church continues to be the one place which can gather an audience at a moment's notice; nor is it accidental that political, social, fraternal, or business gatherings met in black church houses.

This wholeness is now undergoing certain modifications. Public buildings are now available to black organizations; thus, the substance and character of some gatherings are different than when held in church houses. "Town-Gown" conflicts have separated the academic elite and the average person in black churches. Professional expertise is now being shared in other forums apart from the black church. Government assistance has lessened the calls to churches for welfare assistance.

Despite the transformations, the basic concept of wholeness remains. It is most visible in times of crisis.

2. *Religion was intended for the here and now.* John Mbiti notes that African traditional religions do not place great emphases on concepts of the afterlife. The significant role of religion is to permeate this present existence. The dimensions of hope are not other-worldly but earth-oriented. Ghanians have a symbol called a Gy Nyame. The figure has a central core with one appendage from the bottom forming a semicircle pointing toward heaven while the top appendage points towards Mother Earth. The oneness between God and nature is emphasized with this symbol. This is a world-oriented

oneness. As an earth orientation, it is also a this-world symbol.

Black religion in America has emphasized the here and now. Permeating black religious expressions has been the notion of hope. Contrary to popular opinion, it was *here and now* hope rather than *after death* hope. To be sure the after-death concepts which blacks learned from whites was evident. For many heaven was the only place they could expect compensation for enduring life's drudgeries. The sermonic materials aimed at slaves by white preachers reinforced this notion. Dorough provides ample illustrations of this activity.[8]

During the last fifteen years there have developed certain interpretations of black religious music which suggest apocalyptic overtones and double meanings in the lyrics. The theories suggest that slaves would pass coded messages through songs so that while singing in the presence of the master or overseer they communicated a rebellious message to their fellow slaves. The substance of that communication related to hope for the here and now.

J. Garfield Owens has analyzed twenty-seven Negro spirituals.[9] While his published work is devotional in nature, the apocalyptic language theory appears frequently. James Cone also speaks of these double meanings.[10] Dearing King illustrates the theory:

> For instance when black slaves were not allowed to congregate or to communicate in groups, the Negro preacher, who had to keep his identity as a preacher concealed, devised ways of preaching to the slaves. He would tell the water boy to announce the service at given time by singing through the fields: "Steal Away." All of the slaves knew to go to the swampy forest that night for worship. Another slave would be stationed at the big house to ascertain whether or not the acts of worship could be heard. The next morning he went through the fields singing: "O, I couldn't hear nobody pray." [11]

Other illustrations of the double meaning conveyed by Negro spirituals can also be cited. For instance, when slaves were trying to escape to the North, other knowledgeable slaves might sing "Wade in the Water." This was an instruction on how to throw bloodhounds off their trail by wading upstream. Or, since there were few road signs and slaves could not read or see at night, runaways were pointed North by "Follow the Drinking Gourd," the North Star pointer on the Big Dipper. According to these interpretations, "Swing Low, Sweet Chariot" was a hope that the underground railroad system would transport them over the Ohio River (River Jordan).

Slave preaching was also concrete and earthbound. Moses, Joshua, and the judges of Israel were favorite sermonic personalities. Their activities of deliverance were celebrated in black worship. The *acts of God* in delivering "his people" were celebrated by song, sermon, and prayer. The theme of deliverance and freedom ran throughout the black psyche. The black church, whether in formal setting or in the daily routine, was the one and only safe vehicle through which these themes could be expressed. Hope was for the here and now.

It is obvious then, why social justice has remained a major emphasis of the black church. There were no other forums available to black people in search of human dignity, either through the courts, laws, governments, or the persons employed by them. Of necessity the black church had to become "all things" to black people. It birthed, supported, and sustained education, business enterprises, benevolent societies, provided a community forum for the dissemination of ideas, and even gave now popular artists their first starts. Tony Heilbut catalogs some of the popular entertainers whose beginnings are traceable to the black church.[12]

Even now the black church offers the substances of both resources and personnel to the struggle for social justice. A recent illustration is the NAACP's struggle for survival when threatened with extinction because of the bond required by a Mississippi judge handling a lawsuit on behalf of Port Gibson's boycotted businessmen. Black churches, judicatories, associations, ministers conferences, state, and national denominational agencies, individually and collectively rallied to the cause.

## Parachurch Movements for Social Justice

There are three organizations dedicated to seeking social justice which are sponsored by black churches. These may be regarded as parachurch movements. They are not churches but they are extensions of the life of the black church. Such groups have existed in various forms and in various locales throughout the history of the black church. Of concern at this point are those contemporary movements which grew out of the civil rights struggle of the sixties.

Support for these movements has crossed denominational lines. At times they displaced the denominational agendas. This is illustrated by the effect of the civil rights movement upon black Baptist associations. Prior to 1954 (the year of the Supreme Court decision on public schools) many black associations served as collecting agencies for monies supporting elementary and secondary education. As government monies became available and educational institutions took advantage of their resources, many associations were left without a reason for being. Then in 1955 the Montgomery bus boycott began. As the momentum for this thrust in social justice expanded nationally, civil rights became the consuming passion for most blacks regardless of denominational affiliation. Other agenda items were set aside. New alliances were formed and new organizations designed to pursue various strategies for social justice received church monies and priority in church schedules. Sunday evening worship services were cancelled for participation in mass meetings needed to formulate strategy or engender support. Pastors and denominational leaders who refused to support "The Movement" soon found themselves in the precarious predicament of a dog caught in the median of a four-lane expressway. They were assailed from all sides.

When the major emphases of the civil rights movement were realized (about 1965), black Baptist associations found themselves in a vacuum. Without a developed structure or model for other mission activity, the perplexing question was, What do we do now? A few resolved this question. Others are still struggling for purpose, identity, structure, and survival. Three are of special importance because of their special emphases, their continuing role in the struggle for social justice and their relationship to the black church.

1. *The Southern Christian Leadership Conference* (SCLC) is best remembered for Martin Luther King, Jr. Originally called the Montgomery Improvement Association (MIA), its origins may be traced to Thursday evening, December 1, 1955, when Mrs. Rosa Lee Parks refused to give up her seat to a white man according to the "transportation segregation" law of Montgomery, Alabama. Following her trial on December 5, 1955, blacks in Montgomery launched a 381 day bus boycott that: 1) gave impetus to blacks nationwide to challenge segregated practices and laws of all public accommodations, 2) provided a viable *tool* (boycott) for challenging questionable practices, 3) refocused the attention of the black church on social justice, 4) created conscience stirring among white Christians in support of social justice, and 5) initiated a movement that kept social justice as the top agenda item for the next ten years.

The success of the MIA encouraged others to duplicate these tactics in such cities as Baton Rouge and New Orleans, Louisiana; Tallahassee, Florida; Birmingham, Alabama; Atlanta, Georgia; and Columbia, South Carolina.

Blacks in these cities had also been caught up in the desire to bring an end to public segregation. The bus boycott of Baton Rouge, Louisiana, in 1953 had failed. The Supreme Court ruled against Columbia, South Carolina, on April 23, 1956, in the case involving Mrs. Sarah Mae Fleming. While the verdict was "that segregated seating was unconstitutional on intra- as well as interstate vehicles of public transportation" no means of enforcing the decision were advanced.[13] The success of the MIA provided a method of challenge to segregation practices and impotent court decisions.

Because of MIA's success, its leader, Martin Luther King, Jr., was called upon to share these effective strategies with other black leaders. On January 10-11, 1957, the first conference for what developed as SCLC was held in Atlanta. Sixty persons from twenty-nine communities in ten states attended.[14] The significant factor here is that the initial call was extended by black clergymen—King of Montgomery, the Reverend Fred Shuttlesworth of Birmingham, the Reverend C. K. Steele of Tallahassee, and the Reverend T. J. Jemison of Baton Rouge.[15]

Throughout its history SCLC has been dominated by churchmen, both on the officers list, board of directors, regional or state affiliates, (chapters) and by the people participating in supporting its activities.

The dominance by churchmen and the disagreement over nonviolent philosophy led to the formation of splinter groups. One such splinter was the Student Nonviolent Coordinating Committee (SNCC). SNCC was student-led and controlled, although organized by seminarians John Lewis and Charles Sherrod. Their leadership was displaced by those who saw violence as the only viable response to social injustice. SNCC is best remembered for Stokley Carmichael who popularized the term *Black Power* and accompanied it with the raised clinched fist.

"Black Power" as a slogan had several connotations. To some it meant the coalescence of black people for social, political, and economic mobility. The idea was to unite black people as a force either for or against stated objectives. The slogan soon was identified with black revolutionary military militancy. As blacks united in pursuit of certain goals, they were met with stiff resistance from some whites opposing those goals. The visible symbols of the Afro hairstyle, raised clenched fist, the military beret, and an ammunition sling with the adopted colors of red, green, and black, raised negative emotions in whites and those blacks who were either passive or committed to nonviolence as a strategy.

"Black power" as a military strategy was regarded as absolute folly by most black leaders. The ambiguity between the concept as military strategy and as a social, political, or economic force was a divisive factor. Again, the black church through its various denominational expressions, from its pulpits, from its influence in various sectors made itself felt in condemning the military model which appeared to be counter-productive, while still pressing the claim for social justice. As a result, such groups as the Black Panthers, SNCC, and CORE (Congress of Racial Equality), soon branded the black church as "an enemy of the people." Black church houses were assaulted, some were burned, black preachers were considered "Uncle Toms" and were insulted, assaulted, threatened, and some were killed. Worship services were disrupted from internal dissidents (some youth and young adult choirs used their vantage point for disruption), and from external groups who intimidated those entering church houses, "liberated" offerings and/or church properties. Because of the sacred respect which blacks have maintained for spiritual things, those lacking that respect were disfavored. They found neither sympathy nor support.

Among the several positive aspects of "black power" was one development that has had necessary and lasting effects—the "Black Is Beautiful" movement. America's value system has until very recently extolled only the virtues of "whiteness." Beauty, culture, and class were determined *only* by caucasian standards and models. Those aspiring higher values were enjoined to "think white," "become white," or as close to it as one could come. Madame C. J. Walker became extraordinarily rich by marketing "skin lighteners" and "hair straighteners" designed to help blacks approximate whiteness. Lighter skinned persons were given preferential treatment at every sector because of such notions.

The "Black Is Beautiful" movement became a practical way for the black church to maximize the concept of human dignity and individual worth. No longer was the prime emphasis on becoming what one could not become but in affirming God's creative acts. Blacks, especially women, were encouraged to deeper levels of self-awareness and acceptance. Instead of seeing themselves *only* as fat maids and domestics, *only* working in household attire, the emphasis was on becoming attractive in all aspects. One of the ways in which black churches reinforce these ideals is through fashion shows. It is not uncommon, especially in or near urban centers, for black churches to sponsor three or four such events annually. The desired goals are not the sale of merchandise but demonstrations of how physical beauty can be enhanced. The additional by-product is the enhancement of self-acceptance, self-awareness, and self-improvement.

The demise of SNCC is further evidence of the power of the black church in social justice. The black church, while insisting on social justice, has refused to support unchristian ideologies and methodologies. Organizations espousing those views have been short-lived as illustrated also in the demise of CORE and the redirection of what is left of the Black Panthers. They are now committed to community improvement through service organizations. It is worth noting that two former Panther leaders are now professed Christians. Bobby Seale was influenced by the ministry of Dr. J. A. Smith at Allen Temple Baptist Church, Oakland, California. Eldridge Cleaver, upon his return to the United States in 1976, has freely told of his conversion and has even been used in television spots sponsored by the Baptist General Convention of Texas (SBC). This writer vividly recalls being in worship services where the Panthers or other imitators of their style attempted to "liberate the offering" by armed intrusion. In each city where this occurred, the strength of the black community consolidated against such groups and tactics, and gave full support to the churches.

SCLC is a much diminished organization. It is not dead, only diminished. A variety of reasons have been offered for its current status: 1) the absence of the charisma of a Martin King, Jr., 2) the departure of very competent men such as Andrew Young (former U.N. Ambassador), Wyatt Walker (pastor in New York), Jesse Jackson (PUSH), 3) the failure to adopt strategies other than marching and boycotts, 4) the diminished resources from churches, foundations, and philanthropic organizations, and 5) the "redirection" of resources to the multimillion dollar memorials honoring M. L. King, Jr.

The successor to King, Ralph David Abernathy, resigned as president of SCLC in March, 1977, in order to run for the Fifth District congressional seat (Georgia) vacated by the appointment of Andrew Young to the United Nations. He lost in this bid. He continues as pastor of the large and historic West Hunter Street Baptist Church,

Atlanta, Georgia. SCLC still sees validity in its existence and is committed to being a viable arm for social justice undergirded by Christian principles.

The uniqueness of SCLC is in the methods used—nonviolent protests, boycotts, marches, sit-ins, kneel-ins, and pray-ins. These methods were duplicated across the nation wherever black people mobilized for social justice. The success of these methods depended upon mass participation, enthusiasm, and commitment to a philosophy of nonviolence. Pastoral emphasis in worship services helped stimulate people to participate. Black church houses were the preparation sites for the marches. The influence of the buildings and all they symbolized, the worship experience preceding the marches, and the use of religious music sustained the enthusiasm. The discipline was nurtured mostly by the influence of the preacher. Without the presence of Christian leaders chaos might have resulted.

Black boycotts did not begin with the MIA or SCLC. When most states passed segregation laws (1891-1906), boycotts were one of the methods of protest. Successful ones were conducted in three Georgia cities, Atlanta (1892-1893), Augusta (1898), and Savannah (1899). Other less successful boycotts were held in Jacksonville and Pensacola, Florida (1901 and 1905); Montgomery and Mobile, Alabama (1902). Between 1900 and 1906 other boycotts were held in Atlanta and Rome, Georgia; New Orleans and Shreveport, Louisiana; Little Rock, Arkansas; Houston and San Antonio, Texas; Vicksburg and Natchez, Mississippi; Richmond and Norfolk, Virginia; Chattanooga, Knoxville, and Memphis, Tennessee. Where they were effective, this form of protest resulted in concessions or the removal of offensive restraints. The role of the black church in all of these struggles has been unmistakable.

2. *PUSH.* The second strategy used by the black church in achieving social justice is symbolized in *People United to Save Humanity* (PUSH). The forerunner for PUSH was Operation Breadbasket, a program of SCLC designed to negotiate a percentage of jobs for blacks with those businesses supported by blacks, such as food stores, manufacturers and industries. Breadbasket was effective due to the charismatic leadership of Jesse Louis Jackson who used Chi-

cago as his base of operation. When Ralph Abernathy and SCLC demanded that the Breadbasket's office move to Atlanta, a conflict arose resulting in Jackson's forming his own organization and continuing to use the same methodology.

The PUSH program includes: 1) black expositions that promote industries and goods made by blacks as well as white businesses favorable to blacks, 2) seminars, conferences, and workshops on issues of crucial concerns to the black community, such as drugs, unemployment, job skill training, education, community organization, black-exploitation films, youth problems, geriatrics, immoral influences, 3) negotiations with businesses in an attempt to increase job participation for blacks, and 4) continued awareness of the dynamics of political options.

The basic appeal of PUSH's support is to black church leadership. The September 19, 1974, issue of *Jet* contained a photo gallery like a "Who's Who Among Black Churchmen" in support of PUSH. This organization's success is not only based on the charisma of Jesse Jackson, but also on the identification of social and moral issues of concern to the black church. In local communities where there are PUSH affiliates, black churches have found an ally in assisting their quest for social justice.

One other aspect of PUSH (since 1975) is its insistence on excellence among blacks. This note has been sounded in public schools, assemblies, youth rallies, youth social gatherings, and concerts. This note has been sounded in response to the activity of the dope pusher, peddler, addict, prostitute, numbers-runner, pimp, and hustler. This is not the first time this emphasis has been heard, but it is a different note for recent times. The social activism of the 60s tended to make excuses, rationalization, and justifications for inabilities or weaknesses among blacks. Few dared attack those repressive forces from within the black community. PUSH did. The initiative by PUSH found resonant support from black churches needing someone to lead the way. To its credit, PUSH is helping to internalize other issues that must be addressed from within, while it also addresses those outside the black community.

3. *Opportunities Industrialization Center, Inc.* (OIC). The statement

"For the people I want ham and eggs on earth instead of milk and honey in heaven," [16] is descriptive of the attitude embodied in OIC. Created in 1964, OIC exists to provide job training for the disadvantaged, unskilled, and previously unemployable.

Having come from a West Virginia background of extreme poverty the Reverend Leon Sullivan, OIC's founder, knew the drudgery that inner-city blacks faced: "The benefits of the free enterprise system weren't filtering to my people. We were getting crumbs. I decided we should get some bread instead." [17] To get the "bread" OIC launched a program of searching out the underdeveloped, providing options in training, a place for training with resources and teachers, and job placement and referral services.

The initial center was organized and financed from black church resources, namely, the Zion Baptist Church of Philadelphia, Pennsylvania, of which Sullivan is pastor. Sullivan launched a 10-36 Plan among his parishioners. Fifty members were asked to put up $10.00 each a month for thirty-six months. Instead of fifty he got more than two hundred. These funds were invested in those projects designed for self-improvement. After the quality of the graduates from these training programs validated the investment, foundations, businesses, and government took an interest in OIC. Today more than ninety centers are operating around the nation.

OIC is important because many of the nationwide centers are modeled after the Philadelphia operation. Undergirded with a constructive philosophy, "Build, brother, build; not burn, baby, burn," OIC provides a positive response to joblessness, unemployment, idleness, underemployment, wasted potential, welfarism, survival crime (stealing), and a multitude of other ills inflicted by urban settings.

OIC represents the black church's response to the practical aims of social justice. It is more than protest. It is action. It is action that produces self-respect and contributes to the good of the whole community. One unique feature about OIC is its broad racial appeal. Programs include people—black, Indian, Oriental, Hispanic, or white. Depending upon its locale, it ministers social justice to people in need. It uniquely attempts social ministries,

"To proclaim liberty to the captives
and recovery of sight to the blind,
to set free the oppressed
and announce the time has come when the Lord will save his
    people"

(Luke 4:18-19).[18]

## Conclusion

The concern for social justice is woven deeply into the fabric of the black church. The experience of slavery and the continued oppression of society give special meaning to the stories of deliverance in the Scripture. In turn, the biblical imagery provides symbolic expressions among blacks that have often eluded their slavemaster or racist hearers. Religious services in the black church have provided humanizing power in the midst of dehumanizing forces in society. Furthermore, those groups which have been most effective in working for social justice have strong roots of support and direction in the black church. Far from simple acquiescence to injustices or a retreat into otherworldly hopes, the black church has been and continues to be deeply involved in the struggle for social justice.

### Notes

1. Throughout this paper the term *black Church* is used to include black Christians of all denominations.

2. Emmanuel L. McCall, *The Black Christian Experience* (Nashville: Broadman, 1972), p. 110.

3. Gayraud Wilmore, *Black Religion and Black Radicalism* (New York: Doubleday and Co., 1972), p. 4.

4. Ibid., p. 5.

5. Ibid.

6. Ibid.

7. For these perspectives I am indebted to Osadolor Imasogie, "African Traditional Religion and Christian Faith," *Review and Expositor,* Vol. LXX,

No. 3 (Summer, 1973) and John Mbiti, *African Religions and Philosophy* (Garden City: Anchor Books, 1970).

8. Dwight Dorough, *The Bible Belt Mystique* (Philadelphia: Westminster Press), 1974. See chapter 4.

9. J. Garfield Owens, *All God's Children* (Nashville: Abingdon Press), 1971.

10. James Cone, *The Spirituals and the Blues* (New York: Seabury Press), 1972. See chapter 2.

11. Cited in McCall, p. 38.

12. Tony Heilbut, *The Gospel Sound: Good News and Bad Times* (New York: Simon and Schuster), 1972.

13. Ed Clayton, ed., *The SCLC Story* (Atlanta: SCLC), 1954, p. 12.

14. Ibid.

15. Ibid.

16. *Nation's Business*, "Opening Doors to Opportunity," April 1970, p. 48.

17. Ibid.

18. This quotation is from the *Good News Bible* in Today's English Version. Old Testament: Copyright © American Bible Society 1976; New Testament: Copyright © American Bible Society 1966, 1971, 1976. Used by permission.

# 12

## The Church and Political Action

### C. Welton Gaddy

Back in the late 1960s Henlee Barnett wrote, "Significant decisions which are determining our destiny are being made not so much in the realm of religion as in political action at the local, national, and international levels."[1] That explicit observation was followed by an implicit admonition, "If we are realists, we will see that the decisive action in regard to justice and human welfare is taking place at the polls, in the courts, and in other theatres of political action."[2]

Barnette's words were published just after the assassination of Martin Luther King, Jr. Prior to that event all such remarks were considered avant-garde statements of the contemporary task of God's people. In the wake of that tragedy, however, with the charismatic voice of the nation's foremost civil rights dreamer silenced and the hopes of minorities laying lifeless in the streets, these words seemed[3] more "establishment" than "prophetic." While some communions in Christendom cumbersomely continued the timeworn debate regarding the appropriateness of the church's involvement in political action even for purposes of good, others, who had already been actively involved in various political systems, began to question the viability of the political process as a means by which change could even be facilitated or freedom and justice established for all.

During the late 1960s and the early 1970s the churches of the nation flexed their political muscles in a previously unparalleled manner. Lingering debates on the propriety of political involvement were overshadowed by the emerging primacy of political action. Numerous church groups began to work on national issues with a political vigor up until this time evidenced only in local option elections regarding the sale of alcohol and the legalization of gambling. One observant reporter wrote, "Church officials practice the ancient art of lobbying with fervor peculiar to the dedicated . . . . Political pressure peaks under the Capitol dome in the halls of Congress." [4]

Significant successes on civil rights issues encouraged Christian activists engagement in a lengthy debate with governmental leaders regarding the United States' military involvement in Vietnam. That campaign moved slowly and frequently with frustration, but its conclusion was decisive and fraught with satisfaction. Most students of the American political process agree that the cessation of the United States' participation in the war of Southeast Asia, as well as the enactment of major civil rights legislation at home, was hastened considerably as a result of political pressures exerted and encouraged by church people.

Theorists complemented the work of activists. Positive accomplishments in the civic arena were matched with political publications in the academic arena. A spate of new books emerged to discuss the old questions of church-state-political action relations in a novel manner. Armchair theologians as well as scholarly treatises bandied about terms such as *political evangelism* and *political theology*.[5] Denominational publishing houses made available primers for political action and briefs on legislative issues.[6] Confidence in "the system" was generally affirmed and the possibilities of the political process roundly applauded. Apparently a new day had dawned.

Then came Watergate. A surge of negativism swept across the nation.[7] Spirits among the citizenry were low. Good leadership models were desperately needed. Pessimists seemed to prevail.

Tody the recurring debate regarding the church and political action is on again, but with much less excitement than was present a decade ago. Gone is the us-against-them certainty of the pre-Watergate era.[8] Questions of whether the church *should* influence political action almost have been buried under an avalanche of evidence that the church *does* influence political action—whether in a manner that is subtle or overt, active or passive, positive or negative.

Emphasis at the present moment is not upon the *if* of ecclesiastical involvement in political spheres but upon the *how*. How best can the church serve as a beneficial participant in the political process? Can the church act in a politically effective manner as an institution of society and retain its unique religious identity as the people of God? Below is the beginning of a response to such questions. No effort has been made to be comprehensive. The aim is to be provocative.

The church of Jesus Christ has a moral responsibility to be involved in the political process. That responsibility is evidenced in the message which the church proclaims, the ministry which the church performs, and the model which the church exhibits.

### The Message: "to Caesar . . . and to God"

The word of the Lord has always been received, delivered, heard, discussed, and obeyed in specific political settings. Old Testament prophets proclaimed God's truth in the courts of kings and from the podiums of the marketplace as faithfully as they did within the cultic centers of Judaism. New Testament evangels spoke the words of Christian peace in a context of cultural diversity and political hostility, as well as in more stable situations of acceptance and fellowship. Each expression of God's word embraces a dialogue between divine truth and the human situation. Every authentic proclamation of the message of the church is born out of the perpetual intercourse which takes place between the content of the divine will and the needs of the contemporary situation.

Entrusted to the church is a message called *gospel*. Jesus Christ is the content of that *good news*. Thus, the priority proclamation of the church is a positive word—a divine gift can be accepted, grace can be received, redemption can be experienced, faith can be exercised, hope can be realized. No sooner is this promise of blessings spoken, however, than statements of responsibility are sounded. The Christ to be trusted in redemption is to be followed redemptively.

Jesus Christ is Lord!—that is both the confession and the challenge of the church. All of life is to be subsumed under Christ's lordship.

Thus, the gospel is neither totally political nor totally nonpolitical. The message of the church may legitimately be labeled a personal gospel, a social gospel, an individual gospel, or a political gospel.[9] All of these dimensions of reality are present. The message of the church is gospel.

Though little or no opportunity existed for first-century Christians to take part in political action, principles of responsible Christian citizenship did emerge from within this primitive community of faith. A basic component of the church's continuing message related to political action was informed by Jesus' crucial comment regarding his followers' posture toward the state—"Render unto Caesar the things that are Caesar's, and to God the things that are God's" (Mark 12:17). In today's idiom, the meaning of that message is: take politics seriously but not too seriously.

## Take Politics Seriously

Both the church's faithful obedience to Jesus' message and faithful proclamation of Jesus' message mandate a serious grappling with the political process. In fact, in an open, citizenry-centered government, the guaranteed civil rights of the church intensify the imperatives of the church's religious responsibility. Speaking forcefully about and effectively to various systems of government is a matter of giving to God what is God's and to the state what is the state's. Thus, a politically-oriented message is not just an ecclesiastical communications technique for social relevance but an ethical trait of religious fidelity. Responsible citizenship, individually and institutionally expressed, is a characteristic of loyal discipleship.

At the point where the truths of Scripture intersect the concerns of society the church is to stand and speak its politically-oriented message. Seldom, if ever, will the declaration of an authentic word from God by the church not have pertinence to the politics of this world.

*Exploding myths.* Culture rather than Scripture has too often served as the source of the church's message. Consequently, the straightforward imperatives of the New Testament sometimes have been elevated to an idealistic status intended to reduce their applicability to the contemporary community. Basic ethical principles have been categorized as lofty moral axioms irrelevant to the present social situation and impractical amid tough political realities. Under the guise of a respectable piety, the Christian message has been divorced from social-political concerns after a pattern predictable in radical secularity. The unfortunate result has been the propagation of culturally-based myths as biblically-based truth.

Truth is the essence of the church's message. Biblical fidelity and theological integrity create an impatience with deception. The message of the church thus explodes myths and concentrates on truth.

Proclamation of the incarnation eradicates the mythological barrier between the sacred and the profane in life. The church can no more be relegated to only one realm of existence than can the church's Lord. All of life is within the purview of the church's concern even as all of life was within the scope of Christ's compassion.

The church gives no credibility to polarizations of humble servanthood and political leadership. Calls to exhibit personal humility and invitations to exercise political power are sounded simultaneously.

Heresy is the church's charge against efforts to emphasize a salvation so personal as to exclude any social responsibility. Assurances of the blessings of redemption are consistently associated with assignments of duties in society.

Politics and religion are wedded within the message of the church rather than divorced as one popular myth mandates. A Christian's faith commitment to the ultimate concerns of life (religion) results in efforts to influence the process by which life is organized, governed, and directed (politics).

*Exegeting reality.* The church makes an invaluable contribution to the political process through its honest assessments of reality. Because the perspective of the church transcends the dynamics of any one event or the hours of a particular period of time, the church speaks with profound insight and meaning. Careful distinctions are made between the sources and the symptoms of problems, as well as between the criticisms and the solutions of problems. While in one instance, the words of the church may be prophetic; in another instance, the words may be pastoral.[10]

Persistent problems of a serious nature within an open political process point more to a weakness among the citizenry than to a flaw in the system.[11] Old adages, such as "politics is inevitably dirty," are challenged as irresponsible cop-outs. The reality is that politicians, people, have a propensity for evil. In question is not the validity of the system—it may be used morally or immorally—but the nature of the personnel within the system. For example, a deficit budget in which human welfare programs are cut while military spending is increased represents not so much economic inefficiency in the government as misordered priorities among the public.

When the church speaks pastorally and prophetically, its message exegetes reality—political reality and religious reality—and makes possible an honest assessment of what must be done—persons must be changed and/or systems must be altered. Because of the nation's critical need for this kind of confrontation with reality, the message of the church must be considered no small element in the church's involvement with the political process.[12]

*Encouraging dialogue.* Hard realities of human experience, perplexing problems in the political process, and lofty concepts of theological thought are brought into dialogue by the message of the church. Issues such as freedom, justice, war, ecology, and the like are moral as well as social-political concerns. No dimension of these matters must be overlooked; all must be discussed.

Could it be that abuses of power in the political realm are related to the statements about "principalities and powers" in biblical texts? Is it possible that the demonic elements of another day may have emerged today in the forces of grinding poverty, unchecked militarism, and depersonalizing crime? Do foreign aid programs and policies on agricultural subsidies have anything to do with religious convictions about world hunger? Within the message of the church the content of historic faith interacts with the concerns of political action. The result is a better informed Christian citizenry acting with greater wisdom in the political process.

Not only does the church encourage an interchange between ideas but it also invites a dialogue between all persons and mandates a dialogical mission for members. Recognition of a diversity of gifts within the fellowship of the church results in a "calling out" of those believers most capable of ministry in the political arena. Initial encouragement and sustained support are offered to these folks who by their conscientious presence in government assure a continued dialogue between the kingdoms of this world and the kingdom of God.

Because of a passion for truth, a concern for reality and an interest in dialogue, the church heeds and heralds the same message—take politics seriously! Yet, there is another dimension of meaning in Jesus' words regarding Christians and government.

**But Not Too Seriously**

Care must be taken lest allegiance to finite patterns of authority usurp a recognition of the preeminence of the infinite power of God. Life is more than politics. The church is more than a political institution. Thus, political action is neither the singular nor the primary emphasis in the church's message. Politics is important, but not ultimately important.

*Distinctive direction.* The message of the church in and to the political process is of the greatest benefit when it is most distinctive. If the church has no more to contribute to considerations of a particular issue than that which can be read in the newspaper or heard via the electronic media, it will do well not to speak. The church is not just another political pressure group and its message no mere proposition within some lobbyist's plan. Distinction is the church's justification for participation in politics.

In most instances the church will do well to advocate a direction in political action rather than issue a directive regarding political action. Concern for the political minutiae of methodological strategies is not nearly so important within the church as are affirmation and support for general legislative goals. Desire for a better program of welfare or a more effective health care delivery system does not have to be tied to one particular means of implementation. In a helpful discussion of the ambiguity of political issues, James Wall made this same point. After stating the invariable ambiguity of politics, approving the church's support of general political purposes, and warning against the church's unconditional approval of specific solutions, Wall remarked that, "while an ideology that is political is appropriate for the political arena, an ideology grounded in the Christian faith is not actually an ideology at all, but rather an openness to ambiguity and a trust in God, who sanctifies no single political solution." [13]

*Penultimate provision.* Politics is penultimate. The church must never allow the impressive possibilities of the political process to blot out a recognition of the limitations of that process. There are some things that politics cannot do. Government is incapable of inculcating a genuine faith among the citizenry. A majority of supporters in a ballot cannot assure the victory of morality in an election. In truth Christian morality is not up for a vote, cannot be decided by a vote.[14] The kingdom of God will not come as the result of a presidential or congressional proclamation. Politics is important—extremely important—but only as a means to a greater end. As that truth is recognized, so is it acclaimed.

Christianity brings to the political arena a helpful word about what is essential. In a sphere where law is sovereign, the church speaks of the primary authority of the divine will and the absolute necessity of obedience to God. Amid assemblies where winning seems to be everything, the church holds up some phenomena which are more important than winning—personal integrity for example. Senator Mark Hatfield, in a very personal manner, put the matter in proper perspective, "Remaining in politics at all costs could never be the purpose of my life . . . . politics was simply one avenue for trying, as best I could, to be a faithful follower of my Lord and his Kingdom." [15] The church affirms that political action should be so viewed by everyone.

Amid the proliferation of political rhetoric, the message of the church must continue with distinction. Let there be no mistake, the church's message is good news even though to some it may convey undertones of judgment as well as overtones of hope. This message penetrates life with truth—challenging evil and supporting good, moving faith into action, involving people with God, affirming piety and politics, and ushering the church into the world.

### The Ministry: "Your way of life (politeusthe, 'politics') should be as the gospel of Christ requires"

The church has political responsibility beyond its proclamation. Because issues about which the church cares and needs to which the church ministers become politicized, "the church is 'up to the steeple' in politics whether it likes it or not." [16] Ministry in Christ's name sometimes mandates action in the political arena.

### Love and Power

A major challenge confronting the contemporary church is the need to find specific ways of expressing personal love in a generally impersonal society. One-to-one relationships retain importance and must not be replaced. However, amid explosive growth in population size and the dominance of corporate enterprises, not all love can take this form. Numerous groupings of people evoke a compassion from the church which can never know the satisfaction of intimacy through associations of neighbor love. Care for these faceless individuals in particular may find its greatest expression through involvements in a political process.

Most of the major issues which currently create human need and require Christian ministry are subjects of political debate. Pivotal decisions regarding the future disposition of these concerns are being made by governmental bodies. Thus, the church's involvement in political discussions on how to help hurting people is as much an act of compassion as is participation in a local family crisis.

Love for people who are hungry will work to alleviate hunger. Love for persons abused by society will not rest until law facilitates justice for all. Actually, whether the object of love is a group or an individual in need, spontaneous emotional commitments of concern require long-term comprehensive methods of care. Political action may be the servant as well as the evidence of ecclesiastical compassion.

Beneficial involvement in politics requires an effective exercise of power—an ability to influence the decisions and actions of other people. Though sometimes thought to be the antithesis of love, power is actually an instrument of love which is consistent with the nature of God and compatible with the politics of the world.[17] Love provides the initial motivation for an exertion of power and criteria for determining the ethical utilization of people. Thus, power is a precious commodity among the possessions of compassionate people.[18] Like all other trusts from God, power must be used responsibly.

The church in the United States has power. In the past it has been used both to encourage and to repress, to promote and to retard various social-political developments. For some reason, churches have seemed ready to reveal their power in relation to issues which could be categorized as personal moral concerns (sales of alcohol, practice of gambling, availability of pornography) but hesitant to influence decisions on ethical issues of a more social nature (energy conservation policies, ecological regulations, governmental budgetary allocations).

Today questions persist regarding when and how the church will use its power. Will the church ever again be characterized by the power of thundersome silence and obstinate abstention in relation to pressing matters of morality which practically cry out for help? Or, will the church be known for the consistency of its effective influence on behalf of good even as for its persistence in the faithful proclamation of the gospel? Silence or absence as an expression of power may sometimes be in order when the product of careful deliberate planning on how to stymie evil. However, neither is ever justifiable when the result of moral cowardice or political apathy. Jürgen Moltmann has correctly pointed out that "when pious circles declare themselves 'unpolitical,' they must be reminded that whoever is silent in the face of injustice cooperates with it." [19] Needed now are positive expressions of power rooted in the church's nature and addressed to the needs of humanity in such a manner as to be unmistakably recognized as "ministry."

## Instruction and Involvement

Some people would relegate the church's role in political action entirely to the task of instruction—providing information on issues of importance, education on what to do about these, and direction on how to begin work. Such a position implies that the church must work only through the actions of individual members. As various Christians become politically involved in different places, the church may be said to be involved.

By its very nature, the role of the church in politics is unique. Though it is not just another political pressure group, the church is not without political responsibility. Seldom should the church become institutionally involved in politics. However, times do arise when issues are of such importance, basic moral principles are so jeopardized, and opposition is of such a nature that institutional involvement is required. The civil rights struggle certainly surfaced such a moment. A crucial word from Gayroud Wilmore has continuing validity, "Unless the church can be responsible enough to the reality of an organized society, and faithful enough to use the economic and cultural power of its own to change the situation, it cannot be indignant if most laymen, much less people outside the church, find it impossible to do what they feel morally obligated to do." [20]

Direct political involvement of an institutional nature is a viable option for the church. However, when this course of action is chosen, the church places itself in a precarious position. The church must operate by the same political ground rules that govern other organizations. Yet the church must retain its distinctiveness from other groups. In addition to acting in a politically-sociologically effective manner, it must also be biblically based, theologically sound, and ethically consistent. Though the church never relinquishes its moral commitments to maintain any activity, it may sometimes have to settle for less-than-desired conclusions to maintain some form of ministry—fragmented justice and minimal morality rather than complete justice and maximal morality. However, in such situations the real issue is the church's faithfulness—not the establishment of a Christian government (a theological misnomer) but the establishment of a Christian influence within government (a moral imperative).

**Forgiveness and Reconciliation**

Reconciliation may well be the ultimate political act. The best of both politics and religion seeks an orderly form of corporate existence characterized by freedom and justice. Thus, the church extends its ministry of healing to divided communities politically just as it does to fragmented individuals personally.

In a context of civil pluralism efforts at reconciliation often require acts of political power. Pressure is exerted to bring together dissenting sectors of society whether within a coalition formed to accomplish a particular purpose of common concern or within a civil forum structured for dialogue on community stability. Wholeness is the intent—persons living together with peace, order, and equality. Such cooperation—communion—between radically different segments of the citizenry is the first realistic step toward genuine community— the goal held in common by conscientious politicians and committed Christians.

Whatever the goal or the means of political action, some people are likely to be hurt by it.qConfrontations between good and evil, legislative battles between various pressure groups, and campaigns between political opponents usually produce winners and losers. Such facts are continuous matters of concern for the church. Among the people of God there can be no demonstrations of power for power's sake, no haughty victories, and no absolute enemies. When one has suffered because of the exercise of power on behalf of good or one has been broken by necessary revelations of wrongdoing, the church is present to offer forgiveness and support. When individuals have been tried and found wanting by a court of law, they are confronted by the church with an offer of grace. The spirit of love which inspires the church's attempts at political action is sufficiently strong to sustain the church's efforts in living with the consequences of that action.

Perhaps ambivalence best characterizes the church's political struggles with opposing groups. Dislike for societal evils which seek community sanction and governmental approval is complemented by concern for the persons who work toward these ends. Lengthy labor to defeat a particular proposal is never a justification for attempts to destroy a person. Stringent statements of resistance against some principle do not negate sensitive statements of concern for that principle's proponents.

Love stands at the beginning of the church's attempts at political action as motivation. Love seeks political involvement and embraces the utilization of power. Similarly, love appears at the ending of all such political action as conclusion. Love seeks reconciliation and offers forgiveness.

### The Model: "You are like . . . a city built on a hill"

The authority of the church's message and the power of the church's ministry in relation to political action are directly related to the credibility of the church's constituency as a political model. What is encouraged must be exemplified. What is commended to others must become incarnate within the church.

As defined by James Gustafson, "the political structure of the church . . . is the patterns of relationship and action through which policy is determined and social power exercised." [21] The church *is* a political community. It recognizes positions of authority, adopts some form of government, provides methods for member participation, establishes patterns of decision making, and accepts requirements for accountability. Thus, unless the church can point to its own corporate existence as a model of political integrity—diversity transcended by communal harmony—it has little to contribute to other organizations.

Problems arise at this very point. More than one observer feels that church politics may be less honest in many instances than secular politics. Frequently persons within the church even deny the presence of politics. Others camouflage the ecclesiastical political system with a barrage of pious terminology. Obviously, in such a situation opportunities for reform and novelty are minimal. Needed are a studied recognition of how decisions are made within the church and a guarantee of openness by and accessibility to that system.[22]

Essential is institutional integrity. A church which cannot accept diversity within its membership cannot function effectively within the political system of a pluralistic society. A church incapable of listening to honest controversy will be repulsed by political dialogue. A church unwilling to reveal the contents of its budget and the provisions of its policies cannot command the respect required of a participant in an open political process. A church afraid of sunset laws in relation to its programs cannot demand such regulations from others.

The community of believers must demonstrate within its life trust, openness, mutual service, and hope. Only then can the church be true to its nature as "a model, even a revelation, of God's will for corporate existence." [23]

No question remains regarding the fact of the contemporary church's involvement in political action. A democratic form of government invites such participation. Christian theology demands it. Political-sociological data document it. Only to be resolved now is the determination of what kind of political action will characterize the church. That matter gets settled on a daily basis by local churches in their home communities, as well as by the larger fellowship of churches which impinges upon the total life of the nation. In both contexts the issues at stake are big ones. The moral principles involved are critical. The people of God can make a difference for good.

Obviously the church is not just like every other, or any other, political group. But one distinctive is most prominent. Though enmeshed in the world as moral salt and light and involved in politics as spiritual-ethical leaven in a civil loaf, the church is related to a kingdom which both penetrates and transcends these realms. Herein is the confidence which enables Christians to take political risks unthinkable by others, the assurance which gives to believers a sense of victory even in defeat. Accountability for the church lies far beyond the civil forums of this world and resides within the compassionate judgments of God. For this reason, being right is more important than winning, faithfulness is more crucial than recognition, and integrity is a concern greater than position.

To the Christian church in every age has been given the promise propagated through the pastorally oriented, politically relevant book of Revelation (Rev. 11:15). The words of the Apocalypse encourage political action but keep it in proper perspective. The message, ministry, and example of the church in relation to the political arena cannot be fully understood apart from some acquaintance with this conviction—"The power to rule over the world belongs now to our Lord and his Messiah, and he will rule forever and ever!" [24]

**Notes**

1. Henlee Hulix Barnette, "Protestants and Political Responsibility," *Review and Expositor,* Summer, 1968, p. 299.

2. Ibid.

3. Note my use of the word *seemed.* Henlee Barnette has seldom written, spoken, or acted in a less than prophetic manner. In this particular instance, the context in which his words were read blunted the sharpness by which they were characterized when written.

4. James Luther Adams, *The Growing Church Lobby in Washington* (Grand Rapids: Eerdmans, 1970), p. xi.

5. For example, see Richard J. Mouw's two books *Politics and the Biblical Drama* (Grand Rapids: Eerdmans, 1976) and *Political Evangelism* (Grand Rapids: Eerdmans, 1973). Dorothy Soelle describes political theology as "a theological hermeneutic, which, in distinction from a theology that interprets reality from an ontological or existential point of view, holds open a horizon of interpretation in which politics is understood as the comprehensive and decisive sphere in which Christian truth should become praxis," *Political Theology,* John Shelley, trans. (Philadelphia: Fortress Press, 1974), p. 59.

6. Some examples are Dieter T. Hessell, *A Social Action Primer* (Philadelphia: Westminster, 1972) and James M. Dunn, ed., *Politics: A Guidebook for Christians* (Dallas: The Christian Life Commission of the Baptist General Convention of Texas, 1970).

7. Patrick Caddell found that in 1974, 61 percent of Americans thought their opinions did not matter. In fact, 68 percent of the public believed that its leaders lie to them. John B. Anderson, *Vision and Betrayal in America* (Waco: Word Books, 1975), p. 19, citing *The National Observer*, June 1, 1974, p. 22.

8. James M. Wall, "Living in the Political Briar Patch," *The Christian Century*, November 1, 1978, p. 1027.

9. Karl Barth said, "It is not a good sign if the community is in fear and trembling when a homily becomes political: as if it could be apolitical . . . the community will understand it politically even if the word 'political' remains unspoken." Jurgen Moltmann, "The Cross and Civil Religion," Thomas Hughson and Paul Rigby, trans., *Religion and Political Society* (New York: Harper & Row, 1974), p. 15.

10. Implications of the individual's pastor-prophet relationship to politics are spelled out in C. Welton Gaddy, *A Profile of a Christian Citizen* (Nashville: Broadman, 1974), pp. 59-67, 99-100.

11. The noted sociologist Robert Bellah recently spoke regarding the context of the church's message. His remarks were addressed to a "corrupt" society. At stake, from his point of view, is a rabid self-interest which he described as corruption. Thus, the church must speak to this civic consciousness which currently finds expression in luxury, dependence, and ignorance and which ultimately can destroy the republic. "The Role of Preaching in a Corrupt Republic," an address to the Fosdick Ecumenical Convocation on Preaching, The Riverside Church, New York, October 18, 1978.

12. "Attempts to resolve the great policy debates of the Republic in the next generation will rest ultimately upon our ability first to solve the fundamental causes of our discontent. The nation needs a new moral vision," Anderson, p. 29.

13. Wall, p. 1028.

14. Congressman John Anderson observed, "It is beyond the ability of the government to answer the great moral questions which face a people," p. 15.

15. Mark Hatfield, *Between a Rock and a Hard Place* (Waco: Word Books, 1976), p. 29. Bishop Lesslie Newbigin offered a similar and supportive word: "Christians will be able to play their proper role in a secular society precisely in the measure in which they are rooted in a religious reality, in the knowledge of satisfactions which go beyond the aims of that society," Edward Huges Pruden, "The Pastor's Role in Politics," *Review and Expositor*, Summer, 1968, p. 313, citing Lesslie Newbigin, *Honest Religion for Secular Man* (Philadelphia: Westminster, 1966), p. 129.

16. Wallace E. Fisher, *Politics, Poker, and Piety: A Perspective on Cultural Religion in America* (Nashville: Abingdon, 1972), p. 21. James E. Wood, Jr., has recorded a beneficial insight, "The plea 'let us not drag the church

into the political arena' simply fails to recognize that, for good or ill, the churches are already in the political arena, and have been since our earliest history," "The Church and American Politics," *Review and Expositor*, Summer, 1968, p. 281.

17. "Love is the foundation, not the negation of power," Paul Tillich, *Love, Power, and Justice: Ontological Analysis and Ethical Applications* (New York: Oxford University Press, 1960), p. 49.

18. "Blessed are the powerful who acknowledge that their power is a gift that imposes ever new responsibilities and offers ever new though costing joys," James Luther Adams, "Blessed Are the Powerful," *The Christian Century*, June 18, 1969, p. 841, cited in James E. Wood, Jr., "A Theology of Power," *Search*, Fall, 1973, p. 49.

19. Jurgen Moltmann, *The Passion for Life: A Messianic Lifestyle*, M. Douglas Meeks, trans. (Philadelphia: Fortress Press, 1977), p. 47.

20. Gayroud S. Wilmore, *The Secular Relevance of the Church* (Philadelphia: Westminster, 1962), p. 50.

21. Mouw, *Political Evangelism*, p. 42, citing James Gustafson, *Treasure in Earthen Vessels* (New York: Harper & Row, 1961), p. 31.

22. Keith R. Bridston is one who has called for a reform in church politics. From his perspective "what is required for healthy church politics is an assimilation in its piety of the reality of its politics," *Church Politics* (New York: The World Publishing Company, 1969), p. 87.

23. Mouw, *Politics and the Biblical Drama*, p. 56.

24. This quotation is from the *Good News Bible*, the Bible in Today's English Version. Old Testament: Copyright © American Bible Society 1976; New Testament: Copyright © American Bible Society, 1966, 1971, 1976. Used by permission.

# 13

## The Church and the Search for Peace

E. Earl Joiner

The question of war and peace poses a problem which all the Christian wisdom of the ages has failed to solve. Even the church has developed no clear consensus on the solution to the problem. The various perspectives toward war represented in the history of Christianity point to a divided mind if not to fragmented loyalties. Even so, the church has demonstrated great concern for peace and, at certain times, has made great contributions to mankind's search for peace. Perhaps never before has the message of the gospel of peace been so desperately needed. The automated battlefield, the proliferation of nuclear weapons, and the balance of terror are all signs of the threat of annihilation under which the world lives. The purpose of this chapter is to explore Christian understandings toward war and peace and indicate ways in which the contemporary church may actively participate in the search for peace.

### War and Peace in the Bible

Part of the church's difficulty in dealing with this question lies in a certain ambivalence in the Bible itself. Both support for and opposition to Christian participation in war has been argued from the Bible. Even this ambivalence is evidence of profound concern for the problem.

The word *war* or one of its cognates is found approximately 215 times in the Old Testament and 21 in the New Testament, a total of 236 times. In the Old Testament the word is used to refer to the Hebrews' violent conflict with their neighbors and sometimes with each other. Most of the references are found in the Deuteronomic and priestly literature. Despite the influence of the prophets on the

Deuteronomic literature, the point of view which prevails in Deuter-onomy is different from that which prevails in the thought of the classical writing prophets. Whereas war is taken for granted in Deu-teronomy and some rules governing its conduct are laid down (Deut. 20), it seems generally disapproved by the classical writing prophets. Isaiah and Jeremiah condemn it specifically (see Isa. 2:4; 3:2; Jer. 49:26; 50:30).

However, comparatively little evaluation of war as a moral issue can be found either in the Old Testament or in the New Testament, except for sections in apocalyptic literature, where it is approved, but not as a final solution to human problems. Apocalpytic writers envisioned the complete absence of war in God's plan for the future. All conflict will cease; the end will bring peace.

The concern for peace is consistently and profoundly presented throughout the Bible. The word *peace* is found approximately 249 times in the Bible. Of these, the Hebrew word *shalom* is found 162 times in the Old Testament, and the Greek word *eirene* is found 87 times in the New Testament. Moreover, one of these terms for peace is found in 55 of the 66 books of the Bible. The largest concen-tration of the term occurs in Isaiah and Jeremiah. In both Testaments, the word is frequently found in the context of a greeting which ap-proaches the form of a prayer, such as "Go in peace."

Paradoxically, the constant prayer for peace in the Old Testament may root in the persistence of war. It is also a curious paradox that, while the Hebrews regarded war as a natural state during their early history, they also longed for the day of peace. However, peace was not regarded simply as the absence of war. It is rather a condi-tion of well-being and security.[1] War may be a hindrance, an obstacle to be removed, but ending war does not bring peace, only its possibil-ity.

Analysis of the various references to war and peace in the Old and New Testaments indicates five categories into which most pas-sages fall. The first category would include those passages which approve war as a crusade to destroy the enemies of God who were evil. In early Israel, especially during the tribal amphictyony, the readiness to fight was regarded as part of a man's service to Yahweh. This notion of the "holy war" is common in the Deuteronomic literature, but appears in the priestly literature as well (see for example Ex. 15:3; Num. 10:35; 31:1-20; 32:20; Deut. 7:1-2; 13:15-16; 20:1-4; Judg. 3:1-2). This is by no means the dominant Old Testament attitude, however, as seen by the fact that it seems never to have been applied after the Conquest. Indeed, Bainton doubts that it was really ever put into practice at all.[2] The idea of the holy war largely disappeared during the period of the writing prophets. However, it enjoyed a partial revival during the time of the Maccabees, and was the basis of the Jewish rebellion against the rulers of Alexander's empire.

A second, closely related viewpoint is reflected in other passages which seem to take war for granted as a necessary fact of life. Sometimes it may be regarded as tragic, but still necessary and normal. Much if not most of the Old Testament seems to imply this view. The passages where this disposition is displayed usually refer to a particular war in which the Hebrews are engaged, or imply that war in general is a normal part of life. These are found throughout the Bible, and compose a majority of passages.

A third category of biblical passages includes those which seek to explain war. These are in the minority especially in the Old Testament. There war is sometimes viewed as the means by which Israel is punished for her disobedience (see Amos 5:1-5). In the New Testament the book of James explicitly states that war results from lust (Jas. 4:1-3).

Fourth, there are those passages which suggest guidelines and regulations for conducting war. Deuteronomy 20 is the classic and comprehensive example. Here some limitations are given which are suggestive of the just war theory. Nothing like this passage is to be found in the New Testament. Luke 14:31, where Jesus refers to preparation for war, cannot be taken as instructions for war, only as a reference to common practice which Jesus used for illustrative purposes.

Finally, there are those passages which condemn war, disapprove it, and/or suggest that the intention of God for humanity is the absence of war, or, more precisely, "peace." Though this attitude is present in Isaiah's picture of the messianic age (Isa. 2:1-4; 9:6-7; 11:1-9), and a few other places in the Old Testament, it is more prominent and explicit in the New Testament. Here, most of the passages which appear to take war for granted are either symbolic comparisons between spiritual and military warfare (2 Tim. 2:3-4) or apocalyptic references to wars fought in heaven where God himself takes charge (Rev. 17:14). Cadoux seems correct in arguing that none of Jesus' specific statements on war and discipleship can be used to defend direct Christian participation in warfare.[3] He concluded that Jesus' attitude was one of disapproval of violence, though he may have recognized the necessity of such in the governments of an imperfect world.[4] Some recent research paints a more revolutionary picture of Jesus. S. G. F. Brandon, for instance, argues that Jesus was a revolutionary militant and that the church simply revised the original picture of Jesus' character.[5] Most scholars dispute such arguments and support a view of Jesus as a revolutionary figure who taught and used only nonviolent tactics.

## War and Peace in the Early Church

Whether the prevailing estimate by New Testament scholars that Jesus encouraged nonviolence is correct, it is clear that the early church interpreted him as doing so.[6] The attitude of pacifism, which is never explicitly stated in the Old Testament but is clearly suggested in the New, became the dominant position in the early church. Though the reasons for the triumph of pacifism are not perfectly clear, the most obvious explanation would appear to be that they generally understood it to be in line with the teaching of Jesus.

For a time in the early church, however, the question of Christian participation in war was not raised for a couple of reasons. For one thing, Christians, like Jews, were not generally required to be soldiers. Also, many early church readers of the Old Testament related the Old Testament stories to another era, as Marcion did. Yet when soldiers came to be included among the ranks of converts, the foundation was laid for a change of viewpoint.[7] Bainton indicates that, in some areas, the church gradually relaxed its pacifist position long before Constantine.[8] Indeed, it may be that the ancient arguments in favor of pacifism represented efforts to save a traditional stance on this significant moral issue when it was in fact in process of eroding. It is also possible that they represented efforts to establish a viewpoint not yet fully decided in the early church. The first argument for pacifism was put forth by Tertullian (A.D. 155-240), who argued that when Jesus told Peter to put up the sword, he placed a ban on the sword for all Christians.[9] Tertullian's view is correctly called legalistic pacifism since he regarded the word of Christ as law for Christians.

The second type of pacifism, representing a combination of the Christian view of love with a non-Christian view of the physical as inherently evil, was put forth by Marcion (A.D. 130-180). His emphasis on the contrast between love and violence led him to repudiate the Old Testament and its God. His type of pacifism is often called holiness pacifism because he said the Christian is called to be holy and to kill is not holy. Although Harnack was sympathetic with Marcion,[10] Bainton does not regard this type of pacifism as Christian.[11]

The third type of pacifism, set forth by Origen, is called pragmatic or redemptive pacifism. In his view, Christians might contribute more to society by their spiritual warfare, their prayers, and their moral example than by fighting.

Despite the defenders of pacifism, by the time of Constantine it was a minority viewpoint. The just war theory as elaborated by Augustine (A.D. 354-430) became the dominant position. Exactly why this happened is not clear, but a combination of several possibilities might be considered. First, the views of Celsus, who suggested that Christians were parasites on society because they enjoyed the benefits of Roman order but were unwilling to share their support, may have had considerable influence. Second, and closely related, the Church may have been influenced by the apologists in their efforts to make Christians appear respectable before the Romans. Third, the rejection of Marcion's otherworldliness may have driven the church closer to accepting participation in the world's institutions. Finally, the Church may have been profoundly influenced by the fact that the empire changed its attitude toward the Church. Whatever explanation is correct, it is clear that gradually Christian writers came to view the Church and the empire as partners rather than as adversaries. Although instances of pacifism persisted, the transition to a different view was symbolized by the fact that, whereas in the first century A.D. Christians were allowed exemption from military service and only pagans were required to fight, by the fifth century only Christians were allowed in the imperial army.[12]

## From the Medieval Church to the Modern Situation

The elaboration of an argument in defense of the new situation was presented first by Ambrose, who had borrowed from the Stoics. He also borrowed freely from the Old Testament and solved the problem of pacifistic references in the New Testament by assigning them to private morality and to the clergy.[13] He stated only two requirements of a just war: just conduct (limiting retaliation and avoiding abuses) and nonparticipation of the clergy.

To these requirements Augustine added several others for a war to be justifiable. First, war must have a just object or intent, such as to vindicate justice and restore peace. Where possible to restore justice without resort to war, violence should be avoided because peace is the ideal. Second, a war must have a proper authority, which meant that only those in public office could sponsor a war. For him, this excluded the individual from moral responsibility for the war. That is, if it is wrong, the ruler, not the individual, is blamed. Finally, for Augustine, the dominant motive for war must be love, which does not preclude cruelty when it is for the good.[14]

The great empire in the context of which Augustine developed the just war theory had largely disintegrated by the end of the fifth century A.D. Although the just war theory was not forgotten, it became more difficult to apply. After the failure of a series of other efforts to take the warlike qualities of new leaders to whom the

Church tried to minister, Pope Urban IV in 1095 called for peace within the Christian world and war against the Moslems who by then had occupied the Holy Land. This began the Crusades, reminiscent of the crusading spirit of the ancient Hebrews in the era of conquest and settlement. The strange combination of zeal for defense of the Christian faith and the lust for blood which resulted, soon brought the crusading century into disrepute. Despite criticism, however, the crusading idea survived well into the Reformation era,[15] and in certain forms, down to the present time.

These three attitudes—pacifism, the crusade, and the just war theory—all came to America with the diversity of colonists who settled the New World. They played significant roles in American thought, with varying degrees of strength, according to the situation and the disposition of the American people at a given time. In the early Colonial wars including the Revolution, mingled elements of the just war theory and the crusade were found. World War I became a crusade to make the world safe for democracy and to end war, so that a new order of society could be brought in. Entered with enthusiasm, it soon lost its glamour, and it is not surprising that after the war many leaders in England and the United States made commitments to pacifism. The churches, moreover, with a degree of enthusiasm and strength without precedent, agreed to work toward outlawing war. Obviously, many thought it was possible.

Such optimism proved to be naive, and the realism of the few critics who warned of the danger was validated by the rise of Hitler and World War II. Reinhold Niebuhr, who earlier had shared with many others the common inclination to pacifism, now argued for the necessity of war as a means of defending or achieving justice. At first the United States was divided on the issue and for a time polls taken among many church leaders indicated that a majority opposed United States involvement. Slowly, however, opinion shifted and with the attack on Pearl Harbor by the Japanese, pacifism lost ground significantly, and a sober restatement of the just war theory emerged.

## Contemporary Alternatives

The Korean War and the Cuban missile crisis raised again the issue of war and peace. Perhaps the war in Vietnam and recent debate over United States involvements there, however, provides the best background for contemporary discussion of the problem of war and peace. All three of these events, together with the cold war between the Communist nations and the United States, have combined to stimulate new discussions of alternative ways to deal with problems of maintaining peace in a divided and insecure world. International economic problems have complicated the discussions, but have not stifled them. On the contrary, the complexities of the modern situation have served to stimulate discussions especially of the alternatives to the just war theory and pacifism.

Since the development and use of the atomic bomb by the United States just before the end of World War II, there appears to be a shift by many from support of a just war theory to a practical theory of pacifism, similar to the utilitarian pacifism of Origen. At the same time, a new and precise defense of the just war theory has emerged in the writings of Paul Ramsey.[16] Out of the debate over recent problems and the relevance of the old views has come an elaboration of several alternatives which have emerged in recent discussions and are posed as live options for the consideration of the church today.

*Pacifism.* It seems appropriate for Christians to ask whether the early Church understanding is required today and whether pacifism should be considered normative. Pacifism is still defended, of course, and all the ancient arguments—legalism, utilitarianism, and holiness—are still used. Modern technology has added additional types. For instance, there are those who do not oppose war in principle, but who argue that the dangers of nuclear war has made all war unthinkable.

John Cogley and Walter Millis, for example, present arguments in favor of pacifism as a practical necessity.[17] Others argue that only nuclear war must be rejected. The problem with adopting this type of relativism is that it does not take account of the fact that modern technology makes it possible for conventional warfare to be extremely devastating.

Therefore, one must ask whether the case for pragmatic pacifism can be convincing. Gordon Zahn finds it so. He argues eloquently for nonviolence as a powerful force which may well be considered a usable alternative to war. The illustrations he gives, however, fail to demonstrate beyond doubt the validity of his argument. For example, he cites the nonviolent actions of the black leaders in the South in the 1960s and connects those movements with the changes that came in the South. While there is little doubt that freedom rides and sit-ins made their impact, there were other factors that influenced social attitudes and legislation, as well. The widespread fear of violence and the legal efforts by the National Association for the Advancement of Colored People and other organizations, which had been active long before the Supreme Court decisions were handed down,[18] were also influential. Zahn's reference to Gandhi's successful nonviolent campaign to gain independence for India is a more appropriate illustration, but it may be debated whether a similar approach would have worked or would work in many other cases. Tolstoy's pacifism did not prevent violence in Russia, for example.[19]

Further, Zahn's assumption that a nation can easily be trained in nonviolence and, once thus trained, could frustrate a mobilized nation and create a new set of rules for dealing with the problem of war is naive. In fact the way he poses the alternatives, as being between the East and West, Red or dead, and the possibility of frustrating both East and West, using aggressive but nonviolent methods of resistance, are not realistic appraisals of the available options. The wisdom of absolute commitment to either position might not be learned until it is too late to benefit from it. Zahn recognizes, of course, that in order for his approach to work, present value systems would have to be changed.[20] Still, the conclusion that his argument assumes a rosier picture of existential human nature than the facts of experience warrant is hard to avoid.[21]

Nevertheless, the witness of the pacifist is needed, for it supplies a quality of moral revulsion to war which is often overlooked in the cool, logical arguments of war's defenders and is desperately needed to ensure the quest for peace.[22]

## The Crusade

Many moralists assume that the credibility of the crusade ethic was effectively eroded following the disillusionment of World War I.[23] This assumption is incorrect, however, for contemporary discussions of war still show hints of the crusade idea. John C. Murray, for instance, discussing "Morality and Modern War," [24] suggests that one attitude is the view that Communism is the great enemy of Christianity. All its values and aims, therefore, are to be opposed whatever cost may be required. Murray does not consider this approach morally acceptable. He includes this view among the alternatives, however, for he sees it as an option to be countered. Moreover, while Christian moralists rarely support the crusade notion, more than a few Christians supported United States involvement in Vietnam as a crusade against Communism. Hopefully, the crusaders are now in a minority, for with the weapons available today, the crusading spirit in modern war is a dangerous and suicidal approach. Still, it seems a live option for many; as T. S. Eliot suggested many years ago, the alternatives have to be simple and these minds tend to move to extreme positions.[25] More recently, Peter Berger argued that people with intense political commitment are often dominated by bad motivation, and therefore, often bring about bad results. He suggests that only those whose political commitments are dominated by compassion for human suffering are to be trusted.[26] This requirement and the realities of modern war require rejection of the crusade idea of war as a viable option for Christians.

## The Just War

At one of the first meetings of the American Society of Christian Ethics, Paul Ramsey sought to bring up to date and defend the just war theory. He later expanded the paper into one of the best treatments of the subject available today.[27] Ramsey contends that the new situation justifies a shift in focus away from war theory to another closely related topic, namely that of foreign policy.

First, however, it seems necessary to restate the just war theory. Ramsey, like many others, has pointed out that all-out war, using the most devastating weapons available today, is unjust, unthinkable. This conclusion itself reflects the use of just war criteria. All-out war is unjust because: (1) the danger of nuclear war may outweigh any strategic advantage to be gained, and (2) such a war would be a violation of God's intention for humanity because it would destroy persons' chances of becoming what God intended them to be. He would go further and say with the pacifists that *all* war is bad. The basic concerns for love and service to the neighbor motivated both the original condemnation of force, and, in the new situation which emerged with Constantine, approval of the use of force.[28] In the current situation, however, this same concern for the neighbor requires condemnation of war. Though saying that this is so does not end the matter, it seems necessary to keep the pacifist revulsion to war in the forefront in order to avoid allowing the just war theory to degenerate into the kind of thinking that departs from practical reality.

At the same time, the condemnation of war cannot be absolute if order is to be maintained and the alternatives are carefully considered. It is instructive in this connection to recall that although he was a committed pacifist, Albert Einstein was responsible, perhaps more than anyone else, for persuading President Roosevelt to project work on an atomic bomb. He did this because he thought the Americans' acquiring of the bomb would be less evil than if Hitler developed one first.[29] Although he and the other scientists, who solved the theoretical problems which made the manufacture of the bomb possible, had no intentions that it would be used, they certainly saw the possibility that it *might* be used as the lesser of two evils. Similarly, it seems conceivable to argue even when one rejects all-out nuclear war that circumstances may arise where limited war may be the lesser of evils. It is in the context of this kind of thought that a number of moralists have argued recently for limited war as the only kind of war that may be justified. However, they vary widely on how the limits of war are to be defined. Several types of limits have been suggested. The first has already been mentioned. It is the limitation of means. Weber is right when he suggests that originally the prime question was the cause and the end. Now the prime question is the means.[30]

This leads to a second limitation, which is that war should be limited to military targets and not civilian targets. Ramsey, for example, justifies the use of nuclear weapons in principle, but only in a limited way where the goal is military and not civilian. He adds that megaton bombs are ruled out, however, because with them the distinction between military and civilian targets cannot be maintained.[31] The problems with both the consideration of alternatives and the effort to define limitations is the difficulty in calculating with reasonable certainty what alternatives one should consider and how the limitations one chooses will affect new alternatives.[32] There is risk in such an approach, so much so that Batchelder argues that events have proved the inadequacy of an ethics of calculation.[33] The ethical realism of Reinhold Niebuhr held that the risk of calculation is necessary because strategists are often caught in a moral trap where all the alternatives are bad, so that there is no clear choice between what is obviously good and what is unequivocally evil.[34]

It seems clear, therefore, that limited war is in principle less evil than all-out war, as Ramsey and others have argued. At any rate, it appears that many nations have come to think so, for the world has avoided all-out war and nuclear war for thirty years, despite the increasing number of nations with nuclear capability. Unfortunately, the limited wars that have occurred during that time, when one considers the total cost of human life, devastation of property, and suffering, might raise doubts about the comparison with all-out war. Harold Taylor points out, for example, that from the end of World War II to 1969, there were ninety-seven wars with an estimated twenty to thirty million deaths and uncounted millions of refugees. Many of these were colonial wars, with overt and covert intervention by outside powers which have supplied most of the weapons. In some cases, Nigeria and Pakistan, for example, no efforts were successful in stopping the killing until it ran its course.[35]

What these facts suggest is the need for some new imagination in dealing with international conflicts. Otherwise, more limited wars may emerge in the future. Nevertheless, the fact that in 18 percent of the cases mentioned by Taylor, some outside agencies were able to settle the conflict and bring a quick end to the war offers some hope. Also, in the past few years, despite some blunders, American foreign policy has shown some promise. The Middle East crisis, for example, while far from solved and still posing a threat to world peace, would have been much worse without the diplomatic efforts and cooperation of many countries.

The proliferation of nuclear power among small nations, however, makes it imperative that such cooperation increase in the future, and that frustrations in communication with the major powers (Russia, China, and others) not allow national diplomatic leadership to give up efforts at negotiation. The danger of the limited war erupting into nuclear war is great enough, but the danger does not make such a war inevitable. Many now agree that the world must avoid such a war.

The meaning of the just war criteria in the current situation, therefore, has changed. Earlier the criteria had to do with military force. Now they have to do with other types of force as well.[36] This does not preclude military preparedness. Stephen Cary argues that in the past a good case could be made that military preparedness prevented war, but not now.[37] While this may be true, military preparedness may do certain things. For example, it may reduce the likelihood of war and may, therefore, buy time to work for justice and peace in other ways. These other ways should receive major attention.

Thus, just war theory, as traditionally considered either in relation to all-out war or limited war, is not the major issue which should engage the attention of moralists, political leaders, and the church. The issue which should have major attention is foreign policy. Of course some of the same uncertainties exist here as those encountered in dealing with the problem of war. George F. Kenan says,

for example, that one can seldom guess the consequences of a particular action in foreign relations. Thus, it is better to depend on sound
principles for determining methods than on calculating predictions.[38]
Perhaps so, but it is necessary to try. Hard work should be done
by our nation's leaders to anticipate the consequences of the principle on which one acts and the method chosen. The greatest hope
for peace lies not in debate over war theory but the development
of a foreign policy that will prevent war.

## Conclusion

Several years ago Harold Stassen said in a convocation at Stetson
University that America must put Christian ethics into practice in
foreign policy. It may be that the church today has the greatest
opportunity in its history to assist in the implementation of this
suggestion. It is probably true, as Hero says, that the churches in
the past and the present have exerted little influence on foreign
policy. But it is also true, as he says, that it still has great potential.[39]
To realize some of its potential, the church needs to give serious
attention to the following suggestions. First, the church should study
domestic policy in economics, social justice, and the environment
and urge its own leaders to give careful attention to domestic problems without neglecting other issues. The reason is that the eyes
of the world are on the United States, and our influence in the outside
world will be affected by what is done at home. Work should be
done through individuals in strategic positions to implement constructive changes.[40]

Second, the church should urge political leaders to work for curbing
the arms race. Support for presidential efforts in the face of criticism
and frustration is needed. This suggestion is not intended to discourage military preparation, but there is room for debate as to whether
we may be over prepared. Arthur Simon argues that we are.[41] To
curb the arms race would perhaps require a reordering of our priorities and might create domestic economic problems, to be sure; [42]
but it would be a good example to the smaller nations, who are
also involved in military spending which some can hardly afford.[43]

Third, the church should urge national leaders to give greater attention to areas of greatest need in determining who shall receive foreign aid. Often in the past, American policy in aid to other countries has been calculated in terms of buying political and military favors, and humanitarian concerns have been secondary. It may be that American motives may be misunderstood, but that risk is not as great as the risk that other countries will see through the kind of motives that have shown through past American mistakes. Simon, for example, points out that the United States cashed in on the food shortage before the Middle East countries cashed in on the oil shortage.[44]

Fourth, the church should encourage those efforts which study the causes of war as well as the processes that promote peace. Such organizations as the Institute for World Order, for example, deserve the interest and study of Christians everywhere, for the building of world community is in line with the purpose of Christ as the author of Ephesians understood it (Eph. 1:9-10). The church may, of course, assume that lasting peace cannot come until the lordship of Christ is recognized by all men, but it should not allow such a belief to discourage cooperative endeavors to achieve peace in working with various nonchurch agencies.[45] While the United Nations may not be able to guarantee peace, it is one of those agencies which deserves support. The building of world community requires the cooperative efforts at mutual understanding by many people. The church and its educational institutions could increase such understanding by including more curriculum materials in its educational efforts which would increase international understanding. The energy given to war would be more productive in seeking peace.

Fifth, the church should support those efforts to extend amnesty or pardon to those who, though not conscientious objectors to all war, do nonetheless object to a particular war whose wisdom and legality is debated by vast numbers, if not the majority, of citizens. In so doing the church would show concern for those who remind us all of the need to end all war.

Finally, the church should criticize the view, popular in conservative Christianity, that war is inevitable. War many be probable, but it is not inevitable. The church must do all it can to reduce that degree of probability. Fidelity in preaching the gospel of peace, persistence in pursuing a just foreign policy, and consistently working for a world community of brotherhood and international cooperation will assuredly reduce the prospects of war.

## Notes

1. Roland H. Bainton, *Christian Attitudes Toward War and Peace* (New York: Abingdon, 1960), p. 17.

2. Ibid., p. 51.

3. C. J. Cadoux, *The Early Church and the World* (Edinburgh: T. and T. Clark, 1925), p. 97. See Oscar Cullman, *The State in the New Testament* (New York: Scribner's Sons, 1956) and J. H. Yoder, *The Politics of Jesus* (Grand Rapids: Eerdmans, 1972).

4. Ibid., p. 41.

5. S. G. F. Brandon, *Jesus and the Zealots* (Manchester: University Press, 1967).

6. See Cadoux, pp. 117 ff. and Bainton, p. 67.

7. Cadoux, pp. 118-120.

8. Bainton, p. 70.

9. Ibid., p. 82.

10. *Encyclopedia Britannica,* Eleventh Edition, Vol. 17, pp. 691-693.

11. Bainton, p. 82.

12. Ibid., p. 88.

13. Ibid.

14. Ibid., pp. 95-99.

15. Ibid., pp. 100-121.

16. Paul Ramsey, *War and the Christian Conscience* (Durham: Duke University, 1961).

17. John Cogley and Walter Millis, *The Moral Dilemma of Nuclear Weapons* (New York: The Council on Religion and International Affairs, 1961), pp. 26, 30.

18. Gordon Zahn, *An Alternative to War* (New York: The Council on Religion and International Affairs, 1963), pp. 9-10.

19. Ibid., pp. 11-13.

20. Ibid., p. 17.

21. Stephen G. Cary, "The Pacifist's Choice," *The Moral Dilemma of Nuclear Weapons,* p. 34.

22. Steven S. Schwarzschild, "Theologians and the Bomb," *The Moral Dilemma of Nuclear Weapons*, p. 22.

23. Winthrop S. Hudson, *Religion in America* (New York: Scribner's Sons, 1965), p. 363.

24. John C. Murray, "Morality and Modern War," *The Moral Dilemma of Nuclear Weapons*, pp. 7 ff.

25. T. S. Eliot, *Essays, Ancient and Modern* (New York: Harcourt, Brace and Co., 1932), p. 33.

26. Peter Berger and Richard Neuhaus, *Movement and Revolution* (New York: Doubleday, 1970), p. 18.

27. Ramsey.

28. Ibid., p. xvii.

29. Robert C. Batchelder, *The Irreversible Decision* (New York: The Macmillan Co., 1961), pp. 26-35.

30. Theodore R. Weber, *Modern War and the Pursuit of Peace* (New York: The Council on Religion and International Affairs, 1968), p. 13.

31. Ramsey, pp. 167-168.

32. See Ernest W. Lefever, "Facts, Calculation and Political Ethics," *The Moral Dilemma of Nuclear Weapons*, p. 38.

33. Batchelder, p. 266.

34. See Paul Ramsey, *The Moral Dilemma of Nuclear Weapons*, p. 48.

35. Harold Taylor, "A Curriculum for Peace," *Saturday Review*, September 3, 1971.

36. Theodore R. Weber, *Modern War and the Pursuit of Peace* (New York: The Council on Religion and International Affairs, 1968), pp. 28-31.

37. Cary in *The Moral Dilemma*, pp. 34-35.

38. George F. Kenan, "Foreign Policy and Christian Conscience," *The Moral Dilemma*, p. 69.

39. Alfred O. Hero, Jr., *American Religious Groups View Foreign Policy* (Durham: Duke University Press, 1973), pp. 197, 236-237.

40. Ibid., pp. 238-246.

41. Arthur Simon, *Bread for the World* (Grand Rapids: Eerdmans, 1975), p. 129.

42. Kenneth E. Boulding does not regard that as an impossible obstacle, however. See his article, "Can We Afford a Warless World," *Saturday Review*, October 6, 1962.

43. Simon, p. 128.

44. Ibid., p. 9. See William J. Barnds, *The Foreign Affairs Kaleidoscope* (New York: The Council on Religion and International Affairs, 1972), p. 67.

45. See Hero, p. 238.

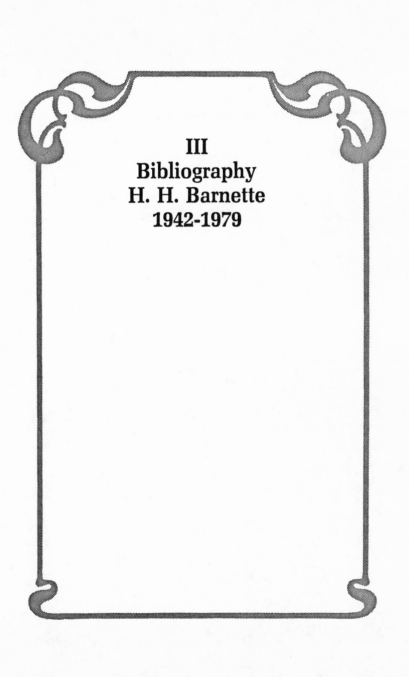

# III
# Bibliography
# H. H. Barnette
# 1942-1979

# Bibliography: Writings and Publications

by Henlee Hulix Barnette

1. *Books*

*Christian Calling and Vocation.* Grand Rapids: Baker Book House, 1965.

*The Church and the Ecological Crisis.* Grand Rapids: Eerdmans Publishing Co., 1972.

*Communism: Who? What? Why?* Nashville: Broadman Press, 1962.

*Crucial Problems in Christian Perspective.* Philadelphia: Westminster Press, 1970.

*The Drug Crisis and the Church.* Philadelphia: Westminster Press, 1971.

*Has God Called You?* Nashville: Broadman Press, 1969.

*The Holy Spirit in Christian Ethics.* Nashville: The Christian Life Commission, 1954. (Reprinted in booklet form from *Review and Expositor,* Fall, 1954.)

*An Introduction to Communism.* Grand Rapids: Baker Book House, 1964.

*Introducing Christian Ethics.* Nashville: Broadman Press, 1961.

*Introducing Christian Ethics.* Translated into Chinese by Wayne Wei-Yuan Siao. Hong Kong: Baptist Press, 1967.

*The New Theology and Morality.* Philadelphia: Westminster Press, 1967.

*Students Study Guide in Christian Ethics.* Nashville: Seminary Extension Department, 1965.

*Teachers Study Guide in Christian Ethics.* Nashville: Seminary Extension Department, 1965.

2. *Dissertation*

"The Ethical Thought of Walter Rauschenbusch: A Critical Interpretation," unpublished Th.D. dissertation. Louisville: Southern Baptist Theological Seminary, 1948.

3. *Contributions to Books*

"Christian Ethics," in Graeme O'Geran, *et. al.*, eds., *An Introduction to the Social Sciences*. Harrisburg, Pa.: Stackpole Company, 1953.

"Christian Ethics and Western Civilization," in *General Education in a Democratic and Christian Society*. The National Protestant Council on Higher Education, 1951.

"The Christian Community in Action," in *Church and Community Action*. Nashville: The Christian Life Commission, 1958.

"Communism," "Juvenile Delinquency," and "Walter Rauschenbusch," in *Encyclopedia of Southern Baptists*. Nashville: Broadman Press, 1958.

"Jesus, the Master Teacher," in Stella O. Barnett, comp., *Better Church Bulletins*. Fleming H. Revell Company, 1955.

"The New Ethics: Love Alone," in Harvey Cox, *The Situation Ethics Debate*. Philadelphia: Westminster Press, 1968.

"The Profile of Prejudice," in Foy Valentine, ed., *Christianity and Race Relations*. Nashville: The Christian Life Commission, 1964.

"Rehabilitation of the Gambler," in Ross Coggins, ed., *The Gambling Menace*. Nashville: Broadman Press, 1966.

"Saints in a Space Age," sermon in Raymond Brown and Morgan Patterson, eds., *Professor in the Pulpit*. Nashville: Broadman Press, 1963.

"Who Is Called?" in David K. Alexander and C. W. Junker, eds., *What Can You Believe?* Nashville: Broadman Press, 1966.

"The Word of God and the Races of Mankind," in Foy Valentine, ed., *Christianity and Race Relations*. Nashville: The Christian Life Commission, 1964.

"The Anatomy of Extremism," in *Extremism: Right and Left,* edited by Elmer West. Grand Rapids: Eerdmans Publishing Co., 1972.

"Alcoholism," "Gambling," "Highway Safety," in *Baker's Dictionary of Christian Ethics,* edited by Carl F. H. Henry. Grand Rapids: Baker Book House, 1973.


4. *Tracts*


"Baptists, Roman Catholics, and Religious Freedom." Nashville: Sunday School Board of the Southern Baptist Convention, 1955.

"Toward a Theological Basis for Social Work." Reprinted from *Western Recorder,* December, 1957.

"Urban Culture Challenges the Churches, Nashville: The Christian Life Commission, ca. 1955.

"Juvenile Delinquency: A Challenge to the Churches." Nashville: The Christian Life Commission, ca. 1955.


5. *Articles* (in chronological order by publication date)


"Jesus on Jefferson Street," *Western Recorder,* June 18, 1942.

"Race Relations," Report to the Florida Baptist Convention, Daytona Beach, November 16, 1949. Published in the *Florida Baptist Convention Annual,* 1949, pp. 31-34.

"The Functions of Departments of Religion in Church-Related Colleges," *Christian Education,* March, 1950, pp. 56-65.

"Racial Segregation and Higher Education," *Window of the Y.W.A.,* March, 1950, pp. 6-8.

"The Role of the Church in the Conservation of Youth," *Review and Expositor,* April, 1950, pp. 173-177.

"Paths to Peace," *Florida Baptist Witness,* December 28, 1950, p. 1.

"The Church as a Force in the Redemption of the City," *Florida Baptist Witness,* May 10, 1951, pp. 1-3.

"The Contemporaneous Christ," *The Expositor*, September-October, 1951, pp. 309-310.

"The Church as a Force in the Redemption of the City," *The Tie*, October, 1951.

"Southern Baptist Churches and Community Problems," *The Quarterly Review*, January-February-March, 1952, pp. 66-69.

"Wonder How Methodists Stack Up?" *The Methodist Layman*, September, 1953, p. 33.

"Baptists and Religious Freedom," *Southern Baptist Home Missions*, April, 1953, p. 7. Also published in *Florida Baptist Witness*, April 6, 1950, pp. 2-3.

"An Analysis of Membership of Rural Pastors on Boards, Committees, Southern Baptist Convention, 1953," *Western Recorder*, June 25, 1953, p. 5.

"Southern Baptists in the Country," *Southern Baptist Home Missions*, October, 1953, p. 14.

"The Holy Spirit in Christian Ethics," *Review and Expositor*, October, 1954.

"Statement of H. H. Barnette, Teacher, Southern Baptist Theological Seminary," *Review of the United Nations Charter*, pp. 473-476. Hearing before a Subcommittee of the Committee on Foreign Relations, United States Senate, 83rd Congress. Second Session on Proposals to Amend or Otherwise Modify Existing International Organizations, Including the United Nations, Part 5, June 7, 1954, Louisville, Kentucky.

"Problems of the Rural Preacher," *Review and Expositor*, July, 1954.

"Whose Is the Blame?" *The Teacher*, November, 1954, pp. 4-5.

"The Rural Missionary: His Milieu, Message, and Mission," *Western Recorder*, February 17, 1955, p. 3.

"Why I Believe in Hell," *Western Recorder*, July 21, 1955, p. 23. Also published in *Baptist and Reflector*, May 5, 1955, p. 14.

"Brotherhood, Our Unfinished Business," *The Pastor*, 1955.

"Negro Students in Southern Baptist Seminaries," *Review and Expositor*, April, 1956.

"Christian Principles of Conduct," *Sunday School Adults*, April-May-June, 1956, pp. 2-3.

"Communist and Christian Ethics," *Review and Expositor*, July, 1956. Reprinted in *O Evangelizador*, (Brazil), 1956.

"How Honest Am I?" *Baptist Young People*, October-November-December, 1956, pp. 15-17.

"Holy Is His Name," *Baptist Young People*, October-November-December, 1956, pp. 18-20.

"Living My Convictions," *Baptist Young People*, October-November-December, 1956, pp. 21-23.

"The Role of the Seminary in the Future of the Country Church," *The Baptist Program*, January, 1957, p. 21.

"Theological Education in a Time of Tension," *The Baptist Program*, April, 1957, pp. 5 ff. Also in *Western Recorder*, June 13, 1957, pp. 15-17.

"Making Christ Real in the Home," *Baptist Married Young People*, April-May-June, 1957, pp. 15-17.

"Answers to Family Tensions," *Baptist Married Young People*, April-May-June, 1957, pp. 18-20.

"The Christian Home a Beacon," *Baptist Married Young People*, April-May-June, 1957, pp. 21-23.

"High Ideals in the Home," *The Young People's Teacher*, May, 1957, pp. 13-15.

"Is Christ the Answer?" *Western Recorder*, May 16, 1957, p. 7.

"What Can Southern Baptists Do?" *Christianity Today*, June 24, 1957, pp. 14-16.

"Pastoral Counseling of Candidates for Church Vocations," *Review and Expositor*, July, 1957.

"Paul's Preaching and Policies for the Present," Series in *Arkansas Baptist* beginning July 18, 1957.

"Baptist Churches Behind the Iron Curtain?" *Tie*, September, 1957, p. 3.

"Baptists in Poland," *Baptist and Reflector*, September 12, 1957, pp. 11-12. Also published in other state papers.

"Toward a Theological Basis for Social Work," *Western Recorder*, December 12, 1957, p. 3.

"The Church in Soviet Russia," *Christianity Today*, December 23, 1957, pp. 3-5.

"Walter Rauschenbusch: Baptist Thinker and Leader," *Baptist Leader*, January, 1958, p. 6.

"The Relevance of the Whole Gospel," *The Baptist Student*, June, 1959, pp. 19-21.

"Love in Interpersonal Relations," *Western Recorder*, August 6, 1959.

"Why a Christian Cannot Be a Communist," Numerous Baptist state papers, 1960.

"A Christian Looks at Communism," *The Window*, July, 1960, pp. 9 ff.

"Grave Injustice," *Biblical Recorder*, October 22, 1960, p. 19.

"Remember the Sabbath," *Sunday School Builder*, September, 1961.

"The Christian Remembers the Sabbath," *Sunday School Builder*, January-February-March, 1962.

"Christian Principles of Conduct," *Sunday School Adults*, January-February-March, 1962.

"The Bible and Communism," *Western Recorder*, February 15, 1962, p. 14.

"The Decision Concerning Honesty," *The Baptist Student*, June, 1962.

"A Bill Wallace Offering," *Religious Herald*, July 26, 1962, p. 5.

"Toward a Theological Doctrine of Vocation," *The Baptist Faculty Paper*, Fall, 1962.

"Baptists Behind the Iron Curtain," *The Baptist Training Union Magazine*, November, 1962, pp. 16-19.

"Consider Your Call," *Baptist and Reflector*, November 1, 1962, pp. 5 ff.

"Communism and Youth," *Western Recorder*, August 15, 1963. Also published in other state papers.

"Christians and Capital Punishment," *The Baptist Program*, October, 1963.

"One Way of Life: Personal and Social," *Review and Expositor*, October, 1963.

"Professors for Proposal," *Biblical Recorder*, November 2, 1963, p. 21.

"Southern Baptist Churches and Segregation," *Baptist Standard*, February 12, 1964, pp. 7 ff.

"The Highest Calling," *The Baptist Student*, March, 1964, pp. 6 ff.

"U. S. Distrust of the Soviet Union," *Western Recorder*, March 5, 1964, p. 3 f.

"Furloughing Missionaries and Finances," *The Baptist Record*, April 2, 1964. p. 4.

"The Pastor and Politics," *Western Recorder*, June 4, 1964, pp. 11 ff.

"Baptists and the Becker Bill," *Baptist Message*, June 4, 1964, pp. 3, 15.

"The Divine Spirit and the Democratic State," *Baptist and Reflector*, July 9, 1964, pp. 3 ff.

"Racism: Facts and Fallacies," *The Baptist Training Union Magazine*, September, 1964, pp. 20 ff.

"Peril and Possibility of Nuclear War," *The Baptist Training Union Magazine*, November, 1964, pp. 18 ff.

"Christian Approaches to Communism," *The Religious Herald*, December 17, 1964, pp. 6-7, 14.

"Southern Baptists and Theological Semantics," *The Watchman-Examiner*, December, 1966, pp. 8 ff.

"Christians and Capital Punishment," *Baptist Men's Journal*, October-November-December, 1966, pp. 8 ff.

"Martin Luther King in Retrospect," *Capital Baptist*, May 23, 1968, pp. 6-7.

"Protestants and Political Responsibility," *Review and Expositor*, July, 1968.

"Vietnam: Proposals for an American Exodus," *Western Recorder*, August 15, 1968, p. 10.

"Seminaries and the National Crisis," *Western Recorder*, August 15, 1968, pp. 10-11.

"Just One Gospel," *Arkansas Baptist News Magazine*, August 22, 1968, p. 4.

"The Cross Is for Real, Man," *Home Missions*, April, 1969.

"War and the Christian Conscience," *Review and Expositor*, May, 1969.

"The Anatomy of Extremism," *The Baptist Program*, November, 1969.

"The Spirit and Search for a Style of Life," *Western Recorder*, February 7, 1970, pp. 10-11.

"The Christian and War," *Training Adults*, January-February-March, 1970.

"Toward a Christian Life Style," *Home Missions*, May, 1970.

"Nation's People Hunger," *The Baptist Courier*, July 2, 1970.

"The New Morality: Reconnaissance and Reply," *Proceedings 1970 Christian Life Seminar*, Published by the Christian Life Commission, Southern Baptist Convention.

"Ethics and Evangelism," *Western Recorder*, June 19, 1971, p. 3.

"Agony and Amnesty," *The Christian Century*, September 29, 1971, pp. 1133-1134.

"Toward an Ecological Ethics," *Review and Expositor*, Vol. LXIL, 1, 1972, pp. 23-25.

"Amnesty: Who Is It We Should Forgive?" *Gadfly*, April 24, 1973, pp. 1, 5.

"World Missions: The Environmental Abuse," *World Missions Journal*, January, 1974.

"Why Bolt the Baptists?" *The Baptist Standard*, August 28, 1974, p. 12.

"Evangelism and Ethics," in Charles L. Wallis, ed., *The Minister's Manual*. New York: Harper and Row, 1974, pp. 64 ff.

"Ecocide! Are We Committing Ecological Suicide?" *World Mission Journal*, January, 1974, pp. 16a-17.

"Ethical Issues: 1975," a resource paper dealing with sixteen issues for the Christian Life Commission of the Southern Baptist Convention and distributed to denominational leaders, 1975.

"Personal Integrity," in *Proceedings, Christian Life Commission Seminar*, Nashville, 1975.

"What Is There to Celebrate?" *Florida Baptist Witness*, November 27, 1975, p. 24.

"Patriotism," *Florida Baptist Witness*, February 19, 1976.

"Civil Religion in America," *Review and Expositor,* Vol. LXXIII, No. 2. Spring, 1976, pp. 151-159.

"On Being Born Again," Associated Press, Religious News Service, National Courier, *Baptist Message,* June 24, 1976, and many state papers.

"The Lustful Look," *Western Recorder,* November 11, 1976.

"The Promise of Pardon," *The Louisville Times,* December 9, 1976, A-23.

"Capital Punishment: Right or Wrong?" *World Mission Journal,* Volume 47, No. 10, 1976.

"The Infallibility of the Bible," *The Florida Baptist Witness,* January 20, 1977, and *Western Recorder,* March 29, 1978.

"Toward an Ecological Ethic," *The Student,* Vol. LVII/8 Feb. 1978, p. 30 ff.

"Genetic Engineering: Custom-Made People," *Florida Baptist Witness,* Mar. 2, 1978, and other Baptist papers and secular press.

"Biomedical Ethics: A 'Now' Christian Concern," *Western Recorder,* Mar. 8, 1978 and other Baptist papers and secular press.

"Behavior Control: Conduct by Chemicals," *The Maryland Baptist,* April 13, 1978, p. 3 and other Baptist papers and secular press.

"Biomedical Reproduction," *Florida Baptist Witness,* Mar. 23, 1978, and other Baptist papers and secular press.

"Euthanasia: Death with Dignity," *Western Recorder,* March 29, 1978.

"Homosexuality: Toward a Christian Response," in *Lifestyle: Christian Perspectives, 1978.* Christian Life Commission Seminar *Proceedings,* pp. 33-38.

"Christian Ethics and Homosexuality," in *Homosexuality in Christian Perspective,* Pub. by Christian Life Commission of the Southern Baptist Convention, Nashville, Tenn., 1978; also in *Illinois Baptist,* July 12, 1978.

"Homosexuality: Some Empirical Perspectives," *Western Recorder,* May 10, 1978.

"Biblical Perspectives on Homosexuality," *Western Recorder,* May 17, 1978.

"Christian Response to Homosexuality," *Western Recorder*, May 24, 1978.

"The Psychiatric Patient as a Person," *Pastoral Psychology*, vol. 27, No. 1, Fall, 1978.

"Euthanasia: Death with Dignity," *The Student*, Jan. 1979, LVII/7.

"Homosexuality: Toward a Christian Response," *The Student*, March, 1979.

"Southern Baptists and Christian Ethics: Present," *Western Recorder*, April 4, 1979.

"Southern Baptists and Christian Ethics: Future," *Western Recorder*, April 11, 1979.

## 6. *Publications Edited*

*Review and Expositor* (New Trends in Theology), July, 1957.

*Review and Expositor* (The American Political Scene and the Church), July, 1968.